CONTEXT, CONTENT, AND COMMUNITY IN ART EDUCATION

Beyond Postmodernism

CONTEXT, CONTENT, AND COMMUNITY IN ART EDUCATION

Beyond Postmodernism

EDITED BY

Ronald W. Neperud

Teachers College, Columbia University
New York and London

Published by Teachers College Press, 1234 Amsterdam Avenue, New York, NY 10027

Library of Congress Cataloging-in-Publication Data

Neperud, Ronald W.
    Context, content, and community in art education : beyond postmodernism / edited by Ronald W. Neperud.
        p.   cm.
    Includes bibliographical references and index.
    ISBN 0-8077-3444-6 (paper : acid-free paper). — ISBN 0-8077-3445-4 (cloth : acid-free paper)
    1. Art — Study and teaching. I. Title.
    N85.N36 1995
    707 — dc20   95-11627

ISBN 0-8077-3444-6 (paper)
ISBN 0-8077-3445-4 (cloth)
Printed on acid-free paper
Manufactured in the United States of America
02 01 00 99 98 97 96 95   8 7 6 5 4 3 2 1

Contents

Foreword

Daily, thousands of teachers of art encounter students, colleagues, and community members seeking to make clear and persuasive the importance of study in art as part of the larger rubric of education. In today's educational surround there are mounting calls for greater clarity and succinctness in setting forth what students should know and be able to do as a result of their schooling. The rhetoric about "the arts as a way of life" or "fundamental human values articulated and realized through the arts" still abounds; but increasingly, there are calls for understandings more closely linked to school operations and more personalized consequences. Gone are the days when the work of schools was "left to professionals" with unquestioned confidence that "they know what they're doing."

More recently (1994), there were two major publications: *National Standards for Arts Education,* developed by The Consortium of National Arts Education Associations (Theatre, Music, Art and Dance), and *Arts Education Assessment Framework,* prepared by The Council of Chief State School Officers and approved by the National Assessment Governing Board. Seen from afar, one might assume that we are now well on our way toward achieving the clarity and understanding being sought. After all, consensus documents describing "what every young American should know and be able to do in the Arts" along with a National Assessment of Educational Progress Framework should take us a long way on the desired pathway toward the confidence and informed support we would wish for. Alas, I fear that such will not be quite the case.

To be sure, the publication of National Standards and an Arts Education Assessment Framework *are* important steps in initiating a much-needed dialogue about the substance of art education and directions for its future. The fact is, however, that art education is a field consisting of many components and cross-currents. This volume represents a much-needed starting point for discussions that need to take place. It contains thoughtful and thought-provoking essays addressing many of the concepts and issues central to an enlarged view of art education. As Ronald Neperud observes, "Art education as inquiry and as practice draws upon many fields and disciplines, some dealing directly with art such as the creation, criticism, history, and aesthetics of visual arts. Other inquiries, sometimes tangential to direct applicability, also are important to our conceptions and practice of art education. The feminist movement, conceptions of aesthetics, multiculturalism, and other social issues, such as class, although often treated separately, usually overlap in the shaping of contemporary art education."

Maxine Greene's essay, "Texts and Margins," makes the case for the centrality of art and artistic processes as creating a challenge to seek new encounters in our experience. Hers is a call to mobilize the community of educators committed to "emancipatory pedagogy." What is important to recognize and emphasize is that we are now in a context in which there is an unprecedented shifting of ideas about previously held assumptions about truth and reality. She makes reference to the writings of Herbert Marcuse, who reminded us of the "qualities of art that allow it to indict established reality and evoke images of liberation." Living at the "margin" requires a kind of strength and openness to experience. Her concluding thought is a "heralding of more shocks of awareness as the time goes on, more explorations, more adventures into meaning, more active and uneasy participation in the human community's unending quest."

What should be the art educator's position in reacting to and giving leadership in our present situation? Clearly, we are not in need of more simplified, singular, linear, sequential mandates as to what should happen in our classrooms. Arthur Efland concludes that "in the current state of affairs an eclectic approach to an art curriculum is mandated, this in spite of the fact that it invites contradiction and inconsistency." After all, he observes, "an art curriculum reflecting the conflicting diversity in the nature of art, would not be eclectic at all; it would simply represent the state of art at the present time." Efland's essay, along with Karen Hamblen's "Art Education Changes and Continuities: Value Orientations of Modernity and Postmodernity," offers a broader perspective within which we can track the evolutionary shifts in thinking about art education. As Hamblen observes, "The new incorporates the old in its details, and, conversely, the traditional contains the seeds that forecast its own demise."

What are the dynamics of change? What are the understandings that would enable our grasping the dynamics of our present situation? Kerry Freedman's essay, "Educational Change Within Structures of History, Culture, and Discourse," suggests that "change in art education, like other social change, must be considered a historical and cultural issue." Her analysis helps us to understand the consequences of efforts to "organize information" while losing sight of the relativity of knowing "what works." Janet Wolff's essay adds to these insights via the sociology of art as it informs our explanations of the origins and operations of the aesthetic domain. Postmodernist thinking calls for another kind of resolution for the ambiguities with which we are dealing. As Wolff concludes, "it remains to be seen whether, in a proper engagement between the sociological and the aesthetic, these questions of value and relativism can be addressed in the postmodern age."

Yet, here we are; poised in a state of transition and flux, reaching for a larger sense of knowing, while seeking to maintain greater awareness and understanding of our traditions. June McFee makes the point: Education should be at the heart of cultural change. Most would agree; however, what McFee then poses are the obvious questions: "What culture's arts should be taught to whom and how?" These are serious difficulties we face with a large portion of our teaching force being ill prepared for teaching in ways that address the ideas and values of cultures other than their own. Patricia Stuhr's essay then offers particular insights as to why the responsibilities for art educators should be understood as an "interdisciplinary, cooperative, and shared endeavor."

Truly, the field of art education is in a state of transition! There are compelling arguments for expanded notions of content, and context. Appropriately, Ronald Neperud's concluding essay addresses the consequences of "changed views of environments and of design education." Increasingly, we are coming to recognize the interconnectedness of elements that contribute to the fabric of our existence. Our expanded visions of art education are bringing us back to an enriched grasp of self-knowledge and creative process. Ideas of a "global village" are bringing us to a deepened sense for community. For art teachers, it is no longer sufficient to dwell upon hand-eye coordination or formal elements of two- and three-dimensional forms as if these are the central concerns for our teaching. Neperud's references to an "interactive view of environment," "the ecological nature of environment," and the "classroom and school as environment" pose the question for us in today's context: In what ways can our actions as teachers of art become socially situated and responsible to the values we hold?

These essays, along with those of Wanda May and Don Krug, help to extend and enrich the needed dialogue regarding the nature of art education: Taken together, we have a volume that informs and challenges the field. Most importantly, this book does not rest upon singular and simplistic assertions. In his Introduction, Ronald Neperud observes that "postmodernism demands that the audience of art become involved in the discursive process of discerning meaning." So too, for community participation in the processes of education in the arts.

Jerome J. Hausman

Acknowledgments

In acknowledging the contributions of others to whatever success one may experience, I always think of those who have had an enduring effect upon me, such as parents and influential teachers. Furthermore, many graduate students have made my teaching and researching an interesting enterprise through their curiosity, imagination, and intellectual stimulation. Additionally, I thank those who have contributed more immediately to realizing this volume, notably Jane Jones, who has typed numerous drafts, well beyond one's expectations, and Al Divine and Allen Goldsmith, whose computer wizardry has been invaluable.

INTRODUCTION

Transitions in Art Education: A Search for Meaning

Ronald W. Neperud

The contemporary era of art education is affected by momentous social and ideological changes that strike at our conceptualizations of art, of teaching and learning, and of curriculum development. Young children still search after meaning through depicting their world, just as graduate art students search for idiosyncratic imagery, hoping to make sense of their world. The traditional imagery and valuing of art no longer provide the universal "truths" that once provided stability in teaching about art. The methods used to help students to create and understand art are being questioned more now than ever before.

In the visual arts, at least until recently, two major orientations of how we come to know and value tradition and change have dominated — modernism and postmodernism. These contrasting ways of knowing in the search for meaning have had such a pervasive effect on art education, as well as the context within which it operates, that to propose new directions for art education without understanding these contexts would be fruitless.

It is important to understand something about postmodernism because it is interwoven into how teachers make decisions about what and how to teach. To Hutcheon (1989), "postmodernism is a phenomenon whose mode is resolutely contradictory as well as unavoidably political" (p. 1). In this sense, teachers' actions toward art education are political, for their decisions about whether to follow a discipline-based, a socio/cultural, or some other approach are ideological choices. To act upon an ideological choice is political. An awareness of differences allows for choices to be made, whereas unquestioning and unreflexive acceptance of a position precludes choices. Teachers can either be aware of the political choice being made or act on unexamined assumptions, in which case choices are limited to an assumed framework.

This volume is designed to assist teachers to understand some of the changes that have taken place in art education in recent years, the context within which the changes have occurred, and possibilities for moving beyond the modern/postmodern debate in art education, particularly toward reconstructionism. The modern/postmodern debate is examined as the background against which art education is changing. The thesis for an alternative post-postmodern paradigm for art education is developed.

THE MODERN/POSTMODERN DEBATE

How art should be taught, ranging from the elementary classroom to the university studio, has always been, and probably always will be, an area of contestation, marked by tensions arising from the dynamic interplay of contrasting views of what constitutes art, its values, and how best to know it. Until recently, modernist views tended to dominate, but now, with the rise of postmodern views, the debate between these orientations has become more heated. These debates have been characterized by contrasting value orientations, such as the degree of focus on objects versus context, and the attention given traditional aesthetics and history versus the development of new approaches, as well as universal versus specific contextual meaning.

Postmodernism involves changes not only in the visual arts but in architecture, film, music, drama, photography, video, dance, and literature as well. In the visual arts, modernism dominated until the early 1960s when changes began to erode accepted truths. The resultant changes in art forms and values associated with these movements have resulted in differing views of art education ranging from discipline-based to socio/cultural art education. Conflicting underlying assumptions and practices add tensions to the continuing debate about the role of art education in contemporary life.

There never has been a clear demarcation of the shift from modernism to postmodernism, and evidence of both intermingles, along with some new directions to make the separation and categorization of events even more difficult.

Postmodernism is best understood in the context of modernism, which it derived from, reacted to, or opposed. There is no one event or set of circumstances that gave birth to postmodernism. Its definition is equally in doubt, with as many definitions as commentators; consequently, it frequently has become a buzzword with little meaning. However, modernism/postmodernism has some currency in art education since these positions, reflecting degrees of ideological orientations, represent continuing conflicts among art educators.

Habermas (1990) sees the debate as arising out of the eighteenth-century

Enlightenment, when modernity developed into three autonomous spheres: science, morality, and art, or "specific aspects of validity: truth, normative rightness, authenticity, and beauty" (p. 60). These spheres developed into structures under the control of special experts.

> As a result, the distance grows between the culture of the experts and that of the larger public. What accrues to culture through specialized treatment and reflection does not immediately and necessarily become the property of everyday praxis. With cultural rationalization of this sort, the threat increases that the life-world, whose traditional substance has already been devalued, will become more and more impoverished. (Habermas, 1990, p. 60)

Habermas believes that art during the mid-nineteenth century became a critical mirror revealing the "irreconcilable nature of the aesthetic and social worlds" (p. 61). Art, representing one of the domains, changed; the others did not, leaving the irreconcilable differences. This meant that the layperson could either educate himself/herself in order to become an expert, or, as a consumer, one could use art and aesthetic experience in one's life. Applied to contemporary life, we find that neither solution has completely dominated, although these are the very goals that art education experts have often advocated and that are sources of tensions and debates among them.

The modernist view of art and architecture that prevailed during post-World War II became a style that exemplified a set of ideas. This style dominated the visual arts as well as the form of contemporary buildings (Jencks, 1986). Galleries and museums promoted and explained modern art to the public. Formalism as a set of values that focused predominantly on visual qualities, became synonymous with the movement through the writings of Clement Greenberg (1990) and others. Several developments eroded the dominance of modernism.

The gap between "highbrow" and "lowbrow" cultures, between the fine art defined by aestheticians, art historians, and critics, and the mass arts preferred by popular culture, broadened and was seen as representing a lack of standards and as an unbridgeable gap between elitism associated with modernism and the growing prominence of mass culture.

In the visual arts, the critic Hilton Kramer took extreme exception to developments just as he continues to do today. In response to Lucy Lippard's comments in the catalogue of the *Art & Ideology* exhibit at the New Museum of Contemporary Art in New York that "all art is ideological and all art is used politically by the right or the left," Kramer (1990) responded, "The governing assumption is a belief that all claims to aesthetic quality are to be regarded as mere subterfuge, masking some malign political purpose. . . . that the politics being served by this effort to discredit all disinterested artistic activity is the politics of the radical Left" (p. 111). Kramer regarded "this movement toward the politicization of art in this country is an attempt to turn back the cultural and political clock" (p. 116). From his perspective, it was a turning back, not to the radical culture of the 1960s, but to the "Stalinist" social consciousness of the 1930s.

What is interesting is that this debate raised a question that still figures prominently among art educators today. Can art be politically or socially disinterested by focusing on art's formal issues, such as predominates in a modernist perspective? An affirmative answer further acerbates the separation of art from the culture that sustains it, and ignores the contextual interactions that surround the production and valuing of art in contemporary society. The modern/postmodern debate has confounded the once clear dominant view of art offered by modernism.

The term *postmodernism* has such a varied history, and is of such an orientation, as to make a definitive definition contradictory to its varied meanings. Confusion over postmodernism has not been helped by differences among major authors. Linda Hutcheon (1989) has deftly negotiated the many meaning nuances of postmodernism in *The Politics of Postmodernism*. She observes that

> Habermas, Lyotard, and Jameson, from their very different perspectives, have all raised the important issue of the socioeconomic and philosophical grounding of postmodernism in postmodernity. But to assume an equation of the culture and its ground, rather than allowing for at least the possibility of a relation of contestation and subversion, is to forget the lesson of postmodern's complex relation to modernism: its retention of modernism's initial oppositional impulses, both ideological and aesthetic, and its equally strong rejection of its founding notion of formalist autonomy. (p. 26)

In addition to the continuing debate between aesthetic interpretations associated with modernism/postmodernism, postmodernist thought has had the effect upon art education literature of raising the issues of race, class, and gender, as well as of the research methodology used to reveal hidden truths. The strong relationship of postmodernism to feminism should be noted, a relationship of particular importance for art education.

The prevalent patriarchal and masculine basis of much art has been criticized by feminist thought; feminism has had profound effects upon postmodernism in terms of the politics of representation. However, feminism and postmodernism, while sharing a certain cultural base, are not interchangeable. Hutcheon (1989) believes, "Few would disagree today that feminisms have transformed art practice: through new forms, new self-consciousness about representation, and new awareness of both contexts and particularities of gendered experience" (p. 143). Photography, video, film, and performance art are seen as having challenged

> the humanist notion of the artist as romantic individual "genius" (and therefore of art as the expression of universal meaning by a transcendent human subject) and the modernist domination of two particular art forms, painting and sculpture . . . . we are always dealing with systems of meaning operating within certain codes and conventions that are socially produced and historically conditioned. This is the postmodern focus that has replaced the modernist/romantic one of individual expression. (Hutcheon, 1989, p. 143)

Modern/postmodern debates serve as a brief introduction to those issues that have particular pertinence to contemporary art education, such as the meaning of art situated in social and historical contexts. Issues of race, class, and gender have entered our dialogue of art (Lippard, 1990) and consequently art education.

Russell (1993) gives a postmodern interpretation of art and aesthetics that helps illuminate a theme of this volume—the relationship of context to content in an era of change and contradictions. For a long time we have recognized art as extensions of recognized patterns of modernist aesthetic development; however, new aesthetic questions, new creations, and interpretations of aesthetic experience arise that may point to the next logical development,

> having, in fact, effected a fundamental transformation of the practices of art or literature. Such is the case with the recently emergent art and literature known under the somewhat provisional name of "postmodern" . . . the postmodern presages a radical alteration of art, of its means of describing the world, its relationship to its audience, and ultimately, its social function. (p. 287)

Russell sees modernism as disintegrating into an extreme form of *defensive individualism,* a direction that Gablik (1991) has corroborated in several accounts of artists' defense of their works when publicly questioned. Individual actions, language, and art were seen as ineffective in altering society; modernism failed to create significant meaning, isolated as it was from society. Alienated from society and self-conscious, modern art became self-reflexive. In opposition to cultural meaning systems, art could end up only referring to itself.

In keeping with Habermas's (1990) contentions, audiences had to constantly learn the aesthetic conventions of artistic styles and how to interpret their messages (Russell, 1993). Feldman (1967) emphasizes critical processes as the means to cope with difficulties in interpreting modern as well as other art. These critical processes, which if effective at one time, no longer adequately serve as an avenue to postmodern meanings. "But what self-reflexive, postmodernist art demands first of all is that the justifying premises and structural bases of that speaking—no matter what the convention or style—be investigated in order to see what permits, shapes, and generates what is said" (Russell, 1993, p. 292). Postmodernism has led, in effect, to an examined questioning of artistic or other discourse, which runs counter to blind acceptance of expert pronouncements.

While postmodernism is linked to the outcomes of modernist practices, it differs fundamentally in its relationship to society; it is that difference that is at the heart of a postmodernist art education. Postmodern art education questions accepted assumptions about the nature of art, children's artistic development, and teaching practices. The social contexts of the creation and valuing of art have been raised as legitimate issues in art education theory and practice. Issues of race, class, gender, sexual orientation, and multiculturalism are now being discussed as essential to postmodern art education discourse. Aesthetic autonomy, normative statements, and judgmental pronouncements are questioned.

The model of art as a self-contained discourse also applies to social discourse; thus, art cannot be considered as separate from cultural languages. The meaning systems that apply to art take their place as part of the semiotic systems that structure society. The meaning of art is dependent on and intertwined with the context of society—the multidimensional network of Marshall (1992). Marshall reaffirms the role of language in postmodernism and relates it to society in ways that art education scholars have drawn upon in their recent inquiries.

> Postmodernism is about language. About how it controls, how it determines meaning, and how we try to exert control through language. About how language restricts, closes down, insists that it stands for some *thing*. Postmodernism is about how "we" are defined within that language, and within specific historical, social, cultural matrices. It's about race, class, gender, erotic identity and practice, nationality, age, ethnicity. It's about difference. It's about power and powerlessness, about empowerment, and about all the stages in between and beyond and unthought of. (p. 4)

Contemporary art, aesthetics, and art education, situated within social discourse, have begun to deal seriously with the social issues as indicated by Marshall.

Considering that art is a function of these social contexts, Russell (1993) asks, "How is the art context contained in, parallel to, or separate from other forms of social discourse: a political campaign, an economic system, the dynamics of 'repressive desublimation' (Marcuse)? And furthermore, what is it about an artwork that makes people want to view it, to experience it and think about it?" (p. 294). Rather than seeking to puzzle out the meaning of art through modernist analysis, interpretation, and evaluation, from the post-modernist perspective one assumes that the work is already connected to the world and that "whatever is perceived, known, described, or presented in art or experience is already charged with meaning by the conceptual patterns governing the artist's orientation and cultural recognition, . . . an expanded vision, a vision of interconnectedness in society, of 'intertextuality' or even 'inter-contextuality'" (Russell, 1993, p. 294). Art in this postmodernist sense is treated not as separate from the world, but as a vital part of human existence.

Postmodernism demands that the audience of art become involved in the discursive process of discerning meaning. This postmodernist view of art means a very different approach to teaching about art than was contained in our previous misconceptions that meaning was given by the high priests — critics, aestheticians, and historians — who were the keepers of *the* truth or meaning. Instead, meaning is inextricably connected to the tangled and changing web of context to be constructed by the audience. This means that there is no single meaning or truth, but one that is constructed by all who seek to understand art. Consequently, context is not simply the addendum surrounding content, but a dimension that cannot be ignored. These post-modern interpretations mark a turning point, a significant shift, in how meaning is sought through art education and within the lives of us all.

The dominance of art and aesthetics associated with modernism has been questioned by both postmodernism and feminism. Additionally, questions relating to the politics of power and representation have been raised. Not as frequently mentioned, but of considerable import, have been the *methodologies* employed by postmodernists and feminists, particularly, deconstruction (Cherryholmes, 1985), critical analyses, semiotics, and poststructuralist approaches that serve art education researchers as tools to critically examine long held assumptions and to avoid normative, essentialist, and nonjudgmental statements. The development of critical literature in educational thought has effectively changed how we perceive schooling, education, ideology, and power (Apple, 1982, 1988).

ART EDUCATION ISSUES

Art education as inquiry and as practice draws upon many fields and disciplines, some dealing directly with art, such as the creation, criticism, history, and aesthetics of visual arts. Other inquiries, sometimes tangential to direct applicability, also are important to our conceptions and practice of art education. The feminist movement, conceptions of aesthetics, multiculturalism, and other social issues, such as class, although often treated separately, usually overlap in the shaping of contemporary art education. Feminist inquiry in art education serves as an example of how art education scholars' inquiries and interpretations have been influenced by several issues raised by postmodernist thought.

Feminism has been a major area of inquiry in the postmodern era, drawing upon deconstructionist, semiotic, poststructuralist, and other critical theories. Most intellectual disciplines have been affected by these theorists; art education inquiries are no exception. Recent feminist interpretations employed by art education scholars are reviewed and examined for their implications for theory and practice. Sandell (1991) finds feminist pedagogy to address the needs for social change and the development of strategies for empowerment and building community. Hagaman (1990), surveying feminist inquiry in art history, art criticism, and aesthetics, finds a

> clear relationship of concerns and criticism across these three disciplines. In each area, feminist scholars have attempted to claim a place for the work of women and to uncover hidden (or not-so-hidden) biases inherent in the roles and representation of women within the discipline in question. Additionally, feminist scholars have taken a deconstructive stance, challenging the very frameworks and processes of these disciplines as traditionally understood. (p. 33)

She urges that artists, art history, and critical criteria be studied in ongoing, examined, and specific contexts.

Garber (1990) also has examined the implications of feminist art criticism for art education: "Drawing on critical methods such as poststructuralism, Marxism, and psychoanalysis, feminist critics in the arts and humanities are at the forefront of practices that work to strategically undermine the status quo" (p. 17). The bases underlying practices are "social analysis, political activism, and self-knowledge" (p. 19), which examine the effects of social systems and institutions on how women are viewed, the political nature of activism, and the validity of subjective experience as related to one's self-worth. This subjectivity is echoed in Korzenik's (1990) contention that the acceptance and use of women's strengths "will direct our attention, our curiosity, our caring, to different features of our history. Permitting our recognizable lives, our feelings, to enter our work is a decision of a higher order of magnitude" (p. 54). Similarly, Garber (1990) concludes that feminist art criticism as fluid and ongoing, set against a consciousness of one's relationship to the world, "can become a student's active response to and intervention into the world" (p. 24).

The language that one chooses in speech or in writing soon provides an indication of sexist bias or lack of equitable treatment of a topic. Obvious gender stereotypes, omissions, and distortions are revealed through one's language. At times, seemingly sympathetic intentions are belied by contradictory sexist language of dominating masculine terms. An editor's role in assuring gender-balanced representation in text materials suggests that one should "incorporate nonbiased gender-sensitive terms; select . . . art images that incorporate a substantial amount of artwork by women; design components that enhance the worth of every artist" (Turner, 1990, p. 62). These are considerations that not only could, but should, be incorporated into every classroom practice.

CONTENT IN ART EDUCATION

Art education content, particularly the staple of fine art of the Western world emphasizing formalistic values and the visual structures of stylistic differences, has been critically analyzed and found wanting in recognizing gender, social, and ethnic issues. The deconstructive feminist analysis of art history and aesthetics has been especially critical of art content as usual. As the title of this book implies, content becomes transformed through art education transitions. The content of art education often has shifted from emphasis on process to product orientations, often in response to changes beyond its boundaries. Today, art education content that is not responsive to social context runs the risk of becoming disconnected from life-sustaining nourishment.

Histories of art education reveal how markedly its purposes and content have changed in relatively short time spans (see Efland, 1990; Logan, 1955; Wygant, 1983, 1993). Also, a survey of art education textbooks of the past 30 years reveals how instructional content designed for elementary and secondary art teachers has changed not only in focus, but also in the very language used to explain concepts. The preparation for art education has changed as attention to disciplines such as sociology and anthropology has provided new insights (McFee, 1961). Postmodern critiques reveal just how dramatically the content of art education has changed.

1. The content of art studies is less likely to be accepted as directly given by experts (artists, critics, aestheticians, art historians, textbook writers, curriculum specialists, and other authoritative sources).
2. Knowledge is more apt to be socially constructed by teachers and students; knowledge is not accepted as given, but is interpreted according to student and teacher needs.
3. Content is historically and culturally situated and does not exist as a universal truth with no connection to life of particular times and places.
4. There is a willingness to accept subjective, personally oriented experiences with art as a legitimate source of information.

5. The singular focus on museum and gallery fine art has been supplemented by culturally diverse creations of "outsiders," folk artists, people with disabilities, the institutionalized, people who make things at home, yard art, and others.
6. The concept of a linear foundational art instruction has been questioned; in particular, traditional basic design and drawing disciplines are no longer regarded as the sole prerequisites for creative development.
7. Studio-dominated art activities have been supplemented by aesthetic, art history, critical, and multicultural studies.
8. A focus on the meaning of art has supplemented, if not replaced, structural, formalist studies.
9. Teachers are increasingly regarded as legitimate interpreters, as well as creators and translators, of art instructional content; they are no longer the medium through which information created by others passes.

The meaning of these content changes is that teacher education, including continuing education, must be constantly updated if art studies are to remain vitally connected to students' daily life. A constant reminder is that *content is intimately linked to context;* information divorced from its functional context, such as the elements and principles of design, is academic rather than functional knowledge. Furthermore, design applicability derives its meaning from historical context or subjective interpretation.

Content cannot be conceived of as just a bit of new information that can be added to the old. Rather, existing concepts as the basis for perception become transformed through experience. Additionally, through analysis and reflection, existing information is related to other ideas through associational processes. What I am suggesting is that there is dynamic tension between old and new concepts. Through the processes of perception, analysis, and reflection we give greater prominence to certain content as opposed to other content. For example, if color theory were taught as an academic universal, content would soon be outmoded relative to new color relationships that artists, such as Rothko, create in their work. At the same time, we do not abandon existing content, serving as it does as a transition to the new.

Content, whether referring to concepts, processes, or bits of relatively discrete information, is always changing, being absorbed and transformed into new experiences. Discussions of content in contextual settings comprise transitions in art education providing access to new experiences. In this manner, content is a vital, although changing, dimension in art education transitions. New emphases are constantly developing as attention turns to recognizing emerging social issues: multiculturalism, gay and lesbian recognition, the poor and voiceless, and the exceptional and disadvantaged.

CONTEXT IN ART EDUCATION

Context is an integral part of transitions. Any information that is acquired exists in some context; the meaning of a proposition or schema is dependent on relationships and associations with other schemata, in effect, as part of an associational network. Brenda Marshall in the introduction to *Teaching the Postmodern* (1992) presents a view of network that pictures the association of elements or nodes. She begins with a random listing of processes, authors, disciplines, and movements that

> shuffle uncomfortably in a shared space. . . . Each is a node within a multi-dimensional network, one of uncountable nodes. From each node project threads which tangle with the threads of other nodes. . . . Sense made here is limited, local, provisional, and always critical. Self-critical. That is sense within the postmodern moment. This is the postmodern. (p. 2)

Marshall's network is an apt view of context in the postmodern sense.

The network of propositions, varied though they may be, constitute context. Context consists of those associated propositions or schemata that one is willing to accept as pertinent to a concept under consideration. A question that is frequently raised is, What context is pertinent to understanding a particular art object? From a sociological perspective, Wolff (1981) sheds some light on the question by recognizing political, social, and other ideas that influence the creation of art. It is not a simple direct relationship "whereby political, social and other ideas are simply transposed into an aesthetic medium. The actual material conditions of artistic production, technological and institutional, mediate this expression and determine its particular form in the cultural product" (p. 63). It is necessary to understand the aesthetic codes and conventions accepted at the time of the work's creation.

Wolff (1983) also discusses the *specificity* of art in the realm of aesthetics, concluding that "art has its own specificity, first, in the relatively autonomous structures, institutions and signifying practices which constitute it, and through which it represents reality and ideology" (pp. 107–108). She warns that one cannot ignore political and social features of aesthetic judgments. One begins to realize that the discussion of art certainly must recognize the contextual complex surrounding the creation and perception of art, serving to illustrate how context impinges on the meaning of any object or event. Just as one cannot ignore political and social features in the discussion of art and aesthetics, so too one cannot ignore them in art education discourse.

Hart (1993) has framed the contextual issue as the formalist/contextualist debate in multicultural aesthetics. On the one hand, there are those who believe that art is art, whether created by Western artists or by indigenous peoples—that art is understood and valued for its formal structure. On the other hand, the argument is that without understanding the context within which the art of "others" is created, used, and valued, we impose a Western interpretation that does injustice to the art of others. Without contextual information we have no basis for understanding the work of various cultures, including that of people who make things in our society.

A somewhat broader view of the cultural context of cognitive activity is seen by Rogoff (1990) as consisting of those societal structures that contribute to human activities—economic, political, medical, religious, and educational systems. Cultural institutions, technologies, and traditions built by previous generations "are influential in setting the problems that need solving, providing technologies and tools for their solution, and channeling problem-solving efforts in ways that are valued by local standards" (p. 43). This means that the institutions of culture at particular times provide the context for the meaning of concepts and objects.

Recently, Kristin Congdon (1994), art educator and chair of the National Art Education Association Research task force on questions of context, lists seven subject areas for study within the broader context category. These include: history, values, culture, environment/ecology, settings, partnerships/collaborations, and policy. Within each area, several research questions are included. For example, within culture she asks, "How does (and should) culture (race, ethnicity, age, occupational identification, economic status, disability, sexual orientation, religion, etc.) influence theory and practice of art education and our notions of what art is, or is not? How should research about varying cultures be approached, given the lack of art educators of color and the growing prevalence of students of color?" (p. 2). This, along with previous literature, points to the increasing importance of context in studying content, as well as serving to illustrate the complexity and interconnectedness of context, depending upon how one cross-sections each area.

From a postmodern perspective, context is that tangled web of relationships among the contents of life that are ever changing and shifting. It would seem that interpretations by individuals at various times and with different purposes always would be important in creating that shifting web of context. This means that in the teaching about art there can be no one context that a teacher weaves for student understanding of art. Different teachers, and students, each with their own background of experiences, will have a somewhat different perspective of what context means and thus what art means depending on the role of interpretations. This also means that art history and aesthetics cannot be distilled into an essence that can be taught in a linear authoritative fashion, rather, the role of context interacting with content must be considered. Furthermore, these views raise important questions about the feasibility of current efforts to establish "standards" in art education; the shifting webs of content and context are antithetical to all but the most general of standards.

TOWARD A POST-POSTMODERN ART EDUCATION

There is no doubt that the postmodern critiques of art, educational thought, gender, social class, and related issues that have employed critical analysis, semiotics, poststructuralism, and other deconstructionist approaches, have played an important role in revealing biases and power structures detrimental to equitable practices. After our biased assumptions and practices have been deconstructed, then what?

What have critical analyses of art education contributed to the field? How can we build upon the insights that have been gained without falling back upon accepted practices? Traditional association of progress with change has been questioned, indicating that progress is not a straight linear construct. In response to the question of what follows deconstruction of long held ideas and practices, I am optimistic that as educators our practices somehow will address some of the inequities revealed by critical educational thought. There is a growing body of voices indicating that either/or antagonistic paradigms will not advance education in general or art education in particular.

Since art is so central to views of art education, whatever one's ideological position, I think that we should consider how it might offer a direction beyond pessimism. Gablik (1991) offers two views of postmodernism, a *deconstructive* and a *reconstructive* version, representing opposing philosophical positions. Probably, most views of postmodern art are of the contradictory deconstructive type. "Reconstructivists are trying to make the transition from Eurocentric, patriarchal thinking and the 'dominator' model of culture toward an aesthetics of interconnectedness, social responsibility and ecological attunement" (p. 22). It seems relatively unimportant whether one labels this view as postmodern or post-postmodern. What is important is that the reconstructivist position as outlined by Gablik recognizes those values that go beyond a prevailing deconstructivist emptiness. This view sets a tone in an extremely important dimension of art education that is in concert with developing views of pedagogy.

Giroux (1983) has recognized that radical theorists have made important contributions to "unraveling the relations between schools and the dominant society," but have "failed to escape from a crushing pessimism or from the inability to link in a dialectical fashion the issue of agency and structure" (p. 235). Giroux raises the "question of how the 'excluded majorities' have and can develop institutions, values, and practices that serve their autonomous interests" (p. 235). This is the kind of question that needs to be raised in view of the significant contributions that art education scholars have made in discussing issues that reveal the hidden agendas, curricula, and practices that have been embedded in our thinking during the past several decades, such as the discussion of feminism in this chapter. Having stripped away the membranes obscuring our vision, how can we proceed to develop views that profit from deconstructed beliefs and practices?

There is an optimism inherent in both Gablik's view of art and Giroux's pedagogical approach that is echoed among a growing number of art educators. Pearse (1992) indicates that we are in a postparadigmatic world, beyond the dualistic modern, postmodern dichotomous categories. He suggests, "The postmodern view has features which evoke both optimistic and pessimistic responses. As we approach the twenty-first century, optimists would envision an art education in which local cultural practices are valued. . . . Pessimists would see an aimless, fragmented, relativist art education, cut off from standards of excellence" (p. 251). Sullivan (1993) also moves beyond pessimism in suggesting, "But if a critical posture is to be empowering it has to be enacted in some way" (p. 14).

The developing sense of interconnectedness, social responsibility, and ecological attunement point to new relationships that can work toward the empowerment and interaction of students, teachers, and community in attaining greater equity in representation and voice (May, 1989). There is a sense of optimism in Michael Apple's *Teachers and Texts* (1986); he cautions that the academic ideological world not be separated from the life about which it professes a concern.

> Those who engage in critical scholarship in education should have constant and close ties to the real world of teachers, students, and parents, and . . . they need to be closely connected to feminist groups, people of color, unions, and to those teachers and curriculum workers who are now struggling so hard in very difficult circumstances to defend from rightist attacks the gains that have been made in democratizing education and to make certain that our schools and the curricular and teaching practices within them are responsive in race, gender, and class terms. (p. 204)

I sense a growing optimism that an art education reawakening to the interconnectedness of art and life will result in changes that matter.

TRANSITIONS

New art education concepts are not created without antecedents, but are founded upon existing practices or ideological precursors in opposition to, or as extensions of, prior circumstances, as, for example, multicultural or discipline-based art education movements. Multicultural art education has among its roots the civil rights movement, concepts and practices in general education, an anthropological awareness of other cultures, and a knowledge and appreciation of the art created by other societies. Also, discipline-based art education evolved from an interpretation of Manual Barkan's, as well as others', ideas presented at the 1965 Penn State art education conference, and the extensive histories of art practices, criticism, art history, and philosophical aesthetics. These art education movements, concepts, and practices are transitional between antecedent and subsequent developments. Furthermore, they are constantly changing and evolving, representing, as Karen Hamblen suggests in Chapter 2 and Kerry Freedman in Chapter 4 of this volume, "continuities and discontinuities."

At any point in time, there exist transitions as ties between the past and the evolving present, some of which serve as important markers of developing concepts and practices. Kubler in *The Shape of Time* (1962) points out how artists are not free agents but are "rigidly bound by a chain of prior events" (p. 50) of which they may be only dimly aware, but that shape and lend an urgency to what they do. Kubler also refers to *entrances* in discussing the history of art in which the past and present are related through new creations "like a new map reporting unexpected features in a familiar but incompletely known terrain" (p. 88). It seems complete until someone comes along with a vision of changing it once again. Entrances may occur as either social or technical renovation. While art education is in an era with technical renovation, such as the electronic media, we are most assuredly deeply into social change. Such is the nature of transitions in art education.

Art education transitions represent concepts and practices in which prior elements as well as new creations are embedded in propositions or schemata. Transitions are in a sense categories; they are not carved in stone, but reflect the elements of change. From a cognitive perspective, visual/verbal propositions or schemata are the bases for hypothesizing or making sense out of existing phenomena through perception (Neperud, 1988). New information may be accommodated into the propositions; otherwise, there would be no means of acquiring new information unless prior categories existed. Teachers' propositions, expectations, schemata, or hypotheses about art education, interacting with their new experiences, may be modified and accommodated, thus resulting in changed concepts. Art education as a field of study and practice has undergone profound changes reflecting not only adjustments in content and practice, but also the addition of entirely new areas of study, changing attitudes, and new objectives as a result of the questioning and critical attitudes common to educational critiques.

The resultant transitions, combining content and context, ultimately affect how art teachers develop curricula and practices. Content in art and art education is always undergoing change. For example, recognition and valuing of diverse groups, the "other," led to multicultural education and to a new art education content. But multiculturalism has meaning only if the contexts of particular cultural groups are considered, such as their values, customs, and visual imagery. Contextual information related to particular content is essential to understanding the meaning of content. At no other time has this been truer than today. Thus, much of this volume attends to contexts as a means of understanding and creating art education meaning today. Two transitions are examined as representative of areas important to art education today: Whose culture? and Whose knowledge?

WHOSE CULTURE?

Until recently, modernism dominated as the major artistic movement and formalism as the aesthetic associated with it. To a large extent, art education was concerned with understanding and valuing modernist art and artists. Along with classical, medieval, and Renaissance art, this constituted the frame of reference for many art historians, critics, and philosophical aestheticians writing about art. These experts' writings, appearing in most major art survey texts, defined the art that teachers should know as cultural representations, particularly for the discipline-based art education movement. To be cultured was to appreciate and understand the fine art of the Western world, although recent attempts have been made to recognize cultural diversity.

The dominance of modernism was deconstructed by postmodern critiques that laid the groundwork for multiple, contradictory perspectives. Social factors also precipitated changes in dominant monolithic views of art—the valuing of diversity, the questioning of authority and the status quo. All of these influenced changes in the ways of viewing art education. Among art educators, Hicks (1990) argued that "we can only empower a student relative to particular communities of power" (p. 43). She believes that students are empowered not by an awareness of a singular cultural heritage, but by sensitivity to cultural diversity as represented in particular communities.

Unlike the implied dominance of modernist art and aesthetics, Congdon (1989) suggests that "one culture's way of structuring the world cannot be said to be 'better' than another's. From the perspective of cultural pluralism, they are simply different" (p. 180). This questioning of authority in matters of art, aesthetics, and education led to one of the major issues in art education: Whose culture is to be the focus of study? Views of culture, values, and authority contend socially and politically in the struggle for whose meaning is to dominate art education theory and practice.

Freedman, Stuhr, and Weinberg (1989) also recognize important philosophical issues that underlie curriculum issues. "Conceived of as a problem of representation, teaching and learning about culture in a school becomes an epistemological issue tied to interests and power rather than appearing as simply an objective development of curriculum" (p. 52). In referring to the fragments of culture often seen in classroom, such as Indian headbands and the like, they conclude, "While an object may be used to symbolically 'stand for' a people, it cannot represent them" (p. 53). It becomes obvious that art teachers live and work in a world that has changed dramatically, as witnessed by the fragmented, multifaceted culture that has replaced a monolithic dominant culture. Even in the face of a dominant culture with entrenched power, teachers become responsible for providing equity for minorities in classrooms and acquainting students with other struggling peoples as well.

A common misconception among teachers concerned with multicultural art education is that they need to teach about some exotic culture, distant in time or difference from their own; however, teaching about Egyptian culture, for example, usually turns out to be less than multicultural education from a contemporary perspective. What needs to be recognized is that all students have a culture, which may not seem as distinct and different as that of African-Americans or Native Americans, but which nonetheless represents their culture. Students' own ethnic beliefs, values, arts, festivals, and heritage are things to be recognized and valued. Even within most classes of students there are social and gender differences that need to be considered. The cultural differences among dominant and minority student groups, even within a class, need to be recognized so that the entire class is not treated as a homogeneous group, for even subtle class distinctions based on economic factors affect how students are regarded by others. When asked "Whose culture?" the answer is your culture, my culture, and the culture of others.

WHOSE KNOWLEDGE?

Around this question revolve contentious issues representing a major transition in art education. One of the most obvious issues has been the discipline-based versus social/multicultural art education debate. Much has been written about this both in support of and in opposition to either position. What I would like to discuss here is the matter of ideology that underlies contending issues. The beliefs that we have constructed around the meaning of our world differ according to ideological position, which Eagleton (1991) defines as follows:

> Ideology is essentially a matter of meaning; but the condition of advanced capitalism, is one of *non-meaning*. . . . Consumerism by-passes meaning in order to engage the subject subliminally, libidinally, at the level of visceral response rather

than reflective consciousness. In this sphere, as in the realms of the media and everyday culture, form overwhelms content, signifiers lord it over signifieds, to deliver us the blank, affectless, two-dimensional surfaces of a post-modernist social order. (pp. 37–38)

Eagleton sees education in these circumstances as a technological apparatus rather than as critical self-reflection. He believes that to be successful ideology must be linked both practically and theoretically. "It must extend from an elaborated system of thought to the minutiae of everyday life, from a scholarly treatise to a shout in the street" (p. 48).

While ideology lurks in the background of contending issues in art education, it often seems that most art teaching is concerned with technological application within the art classroom in terms of immediate student reception. I would argue that the matter of ideology must be unearthed as an elaborated system of thought as well as at the praxis level. Answers to the question, Whose knowledge? will not be forthcoming or will be obscured if the meaning of the ideology is not uncovered beneath the surface of seeming reality.

TRANSITIONS IN TEACHING ART

The teaching situations for art teachers today are very different from those of even a decade ago. Changed circumstances both within and outside schools have brought new pressures to bear on teachers and students alike. Single parent families, problems with drugs and alcohol, racial tensions, and poverty are but some of the social variables defining the circumstances in which many children grow up today (Weis, 1990; Willis, 1990). Children and youth experience not only physiological and maturational changes in "growing up," but also the social influences of their diverse environments.

Teachers see the result of these influences in behavior that doesn't always mesh with their formal education preparations and goals. In effect, teachers and students often live in different worlds with conflicting goals and behavior (Brake, 1980; Duncum, 1990). Even in art classrooms, long considered the bastions of freedom, student interests, and relief from academic studies, students are increasingly exhibiting signs of disinterest and alienation. Art teachers need to understand not only the changing content of art education, but also the circumstances, or context, surrounding content, and the interactions between content and context.

The dynamics affecting contemporary art education mean that art teachers no longer have the comfort of dealing with formal instruction that does not recognize social and environmental implications. Instead they are often thrust into situations with uncertainties, and tensions that become a part of teaching about art. To be successful today, art teachers need to understand the problems and issues affecting their students and the many reforms designed to improve teaching. This means that they are constantly faced with questions such as these as they wrestle with social and educational realities.

1. How can I teach a class about art, including the making of art, and still respect individual student views and values?
2. How can I teach toward diversity in classes containing several ethnic and social groups?
3. How can the dilemma of teaching toward particular values be resolved, while recognizing the insights provided by deconstruction and critical appraisal of accepted assumptions and beliefs?
4. Why should art education be concerned about extending its curricular focus to include environmental design issues, crafts, indigenous art, etc., that do not fit the existing definitions of fine art?
5. How can the arts of "others" be recognized and valued without reducing them to mainstream interpretations through the semantic structures employed in describing, interpreting, and valuing art?

These are all problematic areas for which there are no immediate solutions, but which teachers can be prepared to grapple with by understanding something of the changes that art education faces today. Without an understanding of the contradictory forces that are shaping the contemporary world and the contexts surrounding our students, methodological and nonadapting teachers are left isolated in a world that is very different from that of their students. Accordingly, teachers need to understand not only the traditional art and aesthetic content, but also how contexts transform tradition. Central to understanding the relationships of content and context are several persisting transitions.

One can be optimistic about the future of art education if art teachers and future art teachers make a serious attempt to understand the changes in art, aesthetics, pedagogy, students, and the society of which they and their students are a part; teachers will understand that art education is a continual struggle over meaning of art. Meaning is not simply given through the content of art, but it involves understanding the dynamically complex context in which art is created and used. Transitions represent the core concerns of contemporary art education that accommodate traditions and change representing content and context. This volume will examine how art teachers can come to grips with transitions in art education today in a postmodern era.

The three parts of this book—Shifting Views of Art Education in Educational Context, Aesthetic Context, and Culture and Community: Context of Art Teaching—address the changes that have been occurring in art education, how contexts have affected art education content, and forward-looking developments that recognize transitions such as whose culture and knowledge.

CONCLUSIONS

There is little doubt that ours is an era of changes in which we are witness to a kaleidoscope of events that shift before our eyes. At first glance, it might seem that the art teacher is continually buffeted about in the social and aesthetic hurricane of current events. But we need neither to preach universal aesthetic truths nor to skip from one relativistic social revelation to another. An alternative scenario recognizes and makes sense out of changes and reconstructs new approaches to art education. We are always in a transitional stage, but this recognition allows us to intentionally recognize and accommodate both traditions and change in a new reconstruction through recognizing and engaging students in a search for meaning.

Transitions in art education are reflective of both content and context. What we call content, whether it be design principle, the study of the things that people create, or particular aesthetic value, is historically and contextually situated, which means that context is always present in what we choose to label content. Based on recent changes in art, aesthetics, society, and cultures, there are several transitions of immense importance to art teachers today. The following chapters address the major transitional concerns as they cut across art education today. The authors of these chapters give an authoritative account of the contemporary views shaping art education and reflect on the content and context of art education in a manner that will assist art teachers to *work with students and community* in crafting practices and programs that recognize contemporary realities.

REFERENCES

Apple, M. (1982). *Education and power.* Boston: Ark Paperbacks.

Apple, M. (1986). *Teachers and texts: A political economy of class and gender relations in education.* New York: Routledge & Kegan Paul.

Brake, M. (1980). *The sociology of youth culture and youth sub-cultures.* London: Routledge & Kegan Paul.

Cherryholmes, C. (1985). Theory and practice: On the role of empirically based theory for critical practice. *American Journal of Education, 94,* 39–70.

Congdon, K. (1989). Multi-cultural approaches to art criticism. *Studies in Art Education, 30*(3), 176–184.

Congdon, K. (1994). *NAEA research task force: Questions on context*. Orlando: University of Central Florida, Art Department.

Duncum, P. (1990). Clearing the decks for dominant culture: Some first principles for a contemporary art education. *Studies in Art Education, 3*(4), 207–214.

Eagleton, T. (1991). *Ideology, an introduction*. New York: Verso.

Efland, A. (1990). *A history of art education: Intellectual and social currents in teaching the visual arts*. New York: Teachers College Press.

Feldman, E. (1967). *Art as image and idea*. Englewood Cliffs, NJ: Prentice-Hall.

Freedman, K., Stuhr, P., & Weinberg, S. (1989). The discourse of culture and art education. *Journal of Multicultural and Cross-cultural Research in Art Education, 7*(1), 38–56.

Gablik, S. (1991). *The reenchantment of art*. New York: Thames & Hudson.

Garber, E. (1990). Implications of feminist art criticism for art education. *Studies in Art Education, 32*(1), 17–26.

Giroux, H. (1983). *Theory and resistance in education: A pedagogy for the opposition*. South Hadley, MA: Bergin & Garvey.

Greenberg, C. (1990). Modernist painting. In H. Risatti (Ed.), *Postmodern perspectives: Issues in contemporary art* (pp. 12–19). Englewood Cliffs, NJ: Prentice-Hall.

Habermas, J. (1990). Modernity versus postmodernity. In H. Risatti (Ed.), *Postmodern perspectives: Issues in contemporary art* (pp. 54–66). Englewood Cliffs, NJ: Prentice-Hall.

Hagaman, S. (1990). Feminist inquiry in art history, art criticism, and aesthetics: An overview for art education. *Studies in Art Education, 32*(1), 27–35.

Hart, L. (1993). The role of cultural context in multicultural aesthetics. *Journal of Multicultural and Cross-cultural Research in Art Education, 10/11*(1), 5–19.

Hicks, L. (1990). A feminist analysis of empowerment and community in art education. *Studies in Art Education, 32*(1), 36–46.

Hutcheon, L. (1989). *The politics of postmodernism*. New York: Routledge.

Jencks, C. (1986). *What is post-modernism?* London: Academy Editions.

Korzenik, D. (1990). Women doing historical research. *Studies in Art Education, 32* (1), 47–54.

Kramer, H. (1990). Turning back the clock: Art and politics in 1984. In H. Risatti (Ed.), *Postmodern perspectives: Issues in contemporary art* (pp. 110–117). Englewood Cliffs, NJ: Prentice-Hall.

Kubler, G. (1962). *The shape of time*. New Haven, CT: Yale University Press.

Lippard, L. (1990). *Mixed blessings: New art in a multicultural America*. New York: Pantheon Books.

Logan, F. (1955). *Growth of art in American schools*. New York: Harper & Brothers.

Marshall, B. (1992). *Teaching the postmodern: Fiction and theory*. New York: Routledge.

May, W. (1989). Teachers, teaching, and the workplace: Omissions in curriculum reform. *Studies in Art Education, 30*(3), 142–156.

McFee, J. (1961). *Preparation for art*. Belmont, CA: Wadsworth Publishers.

Neperud, R. (1988). A propositional view of aesthetic experiencing for research and teaching in art education. In F. Farley & R. Neperud (Eds.), *The foundations of aesthetics, art, & art education* (pp. 273–319). New York: Praeger.

Pearse, H. (1992). Beyond paradigms: Art education theory and practice in a postparadigmatic world. *Studies in Art Education, 33*(4), 244–252.

Rogoff, B. (1990). *Apprenticeship in thinking: Cognitive development in social context.* New York: Oxford University Press.

Russell, C. (1993). The context of the concept. In J. Natoli & L. Hutcheon (Ed.), *A postmodern reader* (pp. 287–298). Albany: State University of New York Press.

Sandell, R. (1991). The liberating relevance of feminist pedagogy. *Studies in Art Education, 32*(3), 178–187.

Sullivan, G. (1993). Art-based art education: Learning that is meaningful, authentic, critical and pluralist. *Studies in Art Education, 35*(1), 5–21.

Turner, R. (1990). Gender-related considerations for developing the text of art instructional materials. *Studies in Art Education, 32*(1), 55–64.

Weis, L. (1990). *Working class without work: High school students in a de-industrializing economy.* New York: Routledge.

Willis, P. (1990). *Common culture.* Boulder, CO: Westview Press.

Wolff, J. (1981). *The social production of art.* New York: New York University Press.

Wolff, J. (1983). *Aesthetics and the sociology of art.* London: George Allen & Unwin.

Wygant, F. (1983). *Art in American schools in the nineteenth century.* Cincinnati, OH: Interwood Press.

Wygant, F. (1993). *School art in American culture, 1820–1970.* Cincinnati, OH: Interwood Press.

PART I

Shifting Views
of Art Education
in Educational Context

In recent decades meaning in art education is as socially produced and historically conditioned as is meaning in other contemporary inquiry. This assertion immediately reveals a bias that places art teaching and art education curriculum development into ideological and aesthetic contestation. Other educators would protest that meaning in art education is *given* rather than constructed through dialectical dynamics. Within the framework alluded to here, art teaching and curricular practices are situated in a postmodern framework of ideological context and contestation.

Postmodernism has contributed to a fundamental transformation in how a speaker or audience member relates to what is spoken, delivered, or created. The underlying structure and premise of messages, positions, and knowledge are deconstructed in the sense of seeking to uncover the meaning of particular messages. Educational beliefs are no longer accepted as given in text by experts, but are carefully examined in context, which may reveal a hidden message or meaning. In Part I, notions of art education and education are examined from postmodern perspectives to reveal how accepted educational context for art education has been generated and shaped.

In Chapter 1, against a review of major aesthetic orientations, Arthur Efland comprehensively examines models of art teaching. This sets the stage for an examination of aesthetic change and postmodernism, upon which Professor Efland carefully develops the several problems that art teachers face, in effect giving art teachers a thorough grasp of aesthetic and educational changes that shape art education.

In Chapter 2, "Art Education Changes and Continuities: Value Orientations of Modernity and Postmodernity," Karen Hamblen discusses views of change and continuity and then examines how two world views of change and tradition are played out in art education practices, how they influence art education, and how they yield different interpretations of the same event. She sees a continuing dialectic between

23

modernity and postmodernity, between change and continuity, as affecting the shape of art education.

In Chapter 3, "Teachers as Curriculum Developers," Wanda May takes exception to a traditional linear view of curriculum development by examining in 3 vignettes how teachers interact with curriculum. In one of these vignettes, Rachel, a third-year itinerant art specialist, teaches an art lesson. Represented in Rachel's lesson are important topics of her view of knowledge, art, teaching, and learning. As she seeks help in solving curricular and other problems, Rachel enters into curriculum development as collaboration with colleagues in deliberations on professional problems represented in the classroom texture of teaching. May's participatory accounts of teachers' classroom engagements represent and recognize art teachers as curriculum developers through thoughtful inquiry and collegial dialogue. May's view of curriculum development represents a shift to a more contextually situated view of art education than heretofore considered.

Kerry Freedman discusses "Educational Change Within Structures of History, Culture, and Discourse" in Chapter 4. Change is assumed to be an historical and cultural issue; the role of the individual and other change agencies are examined. The discussion of eighteenth-century Enlightenment illustrates how historical considerations are embedded in and still influence our views of society. Against this critique of change, history, and culture, the reader has a framework for understanding the differences that exist among major views of art education within social and cultural contexts.

A reading of the chapters in Part I reveals that the major transitions run through the shifting views of art education. Embedded in all chapters is the question of whose knowledge and culture provide the predominant focus and the major assumptions that underlie several forms of art education. The point to be made is that the major transitional concerns represent structures for considering and differentiating art education ideas and practices, a useful framework for making sense out of the complex and changing nature of contemporary art education.

CHAPTER 1

Change in the Conceptions of Art Teaching

Arthur D. Efland

Monroe Beardsley (1958) opened his book on aesthetics with the remark that "there would be no problems of aesthetics . . . if no one ever talked about works of art" (p. 1). Of course, talk about art has gone on for thousands of years, resulting in a long history of argument about its nature, its cognitive status, and its value in human affairs. Teachers of art deal with many of these problems on a daily basis. If their building principal regards art as a dispensable frill, they live with the consequences of its disputed status in a direct and painful way. What people believe about art and its value is likely to affect whether it is taught or not. Moreover, theories of art have changed over time, paralleling changes in art styles and the status of the arts in social affairs.

In this chapter I review the theories that have played a dominant role in art education throughout this century, giving examples of the types of curriculum and styles of teaching they have inspired. Second, I look at curriculum questions posed by the transition in aesthetic theory from modernism to postmodernism. Modernism itself increasingly is being described either as a period style whose time has ended or as a movement in decline. New thinking about art has appeared, which attempts to account for the art forms that have appeared in the 1970s and 1980s, and the question confronting curriculum designers is whether, and if so how, to modify art teaching to reflect this new situation.

MAJOR ORIENTATIONS IN AESTHETIC THEORY

I begin by assuming that theories and philosophies of art play a role in determining the character of art instruction. I offer four examples to help identify the character of this influence.

25

In 1872 Walter Smith taught children to draw by copying elementary geometric forms arranged in a progressive order of difficulty, leading eventually to the more complex forms in nature such as flowers and the human figure. His pedagogy was based on the idea that art is an imitation of nature, which depends for its "acquirement" on the "faculty of imitation" (p. 46). Smith did not teach just any kind of drawing. As he put it:

> The kind of drawing which the state of Massachusetts requires that its citizens shall have the opportunity of studying, is called "Industrial Drawing;" and wisely so called for in that lies the justification of its public action in the matter. (p. 42)

He justified the teaching of drawing at public expense because it enhanced the virtue of industriousness. The purpose of art teaching was not grounded in aesthetics at all, but in economics. Aesthetic theory identified the method of teaching, that is, the exercise of the faculty of imitation, a pedagogy that I will later argue is congruent with a *mimetic* theory of art, the belief that a work of art represents or reflects some aspect of nature.

In 1899 Arthur W. Dow introduced an art curriculum based on certain elements of beauty that he believed were found in all works of art: lines, shapes, tones, colors, and textures, and the underlying principles by which these are organized. His lessons consisted of simple landscape compositions based on such principles as "repetition," "variation," "opposition," or "transition." His practice was grounded in *formalism*, the belief that works of art are composed of elements and principles, and that sensitivity to this underlying structure enables one to understand, appreciate, and apprehend the beauty of form (Dow, 1899/1913).

Dow tried to maintain art in the schools in an era dominated by social Darwinism, by demands for scientific educational practices and social efficiency. His thinking was guided by a process akin to scientific reductionism in which a phenomenon is analyzed in terms of a more fundamental level of reality that can be found beneath its surface. In his case he reduced the extraordinary complexity of art to a set of universal, teachable principles.

Unlike Smith, Dow did not attempt to justify his method by reference to the social context. Indeed for many formalists the social context was quite irrelevant, for beauty needs no justification and demands to be perceived on its own terms. Formalism was well suited as a philosophy of art since in its pure form it advocated an art without representational content or social messages. Art replete with social criticism might well have been unwelcome in an era of dominance by business interests (Callahan, 1962).[1]

In 1928 the progressive educators Harold Rugg and Ann Shumaker advanced their ideal of the *child-centered* school. They stressed a new art method known as *creative self-expression.* They described art lessons where children were encouraged to experiment with various art media to produce original objects. Copying and imitation were discouraged. This practice is congruent with an expressive aesthetic that claims that works of art are the self-expression of artists, to be judged by their creativity or originality. Like many other teachers committed to this view, they also believed that growth in self-expression enabled the child to grow in an emotionally healthy way.

Rugg and Shumaker (1928) portrayed the field of education as divided into camps, a liberal left and a reactionary right. The right was dedicated to the "doctrine of discipline" (p. 34), to "logical thinking, power of sustained intellectual effort, the retention of classified knowledge" (p. 35). The left, like themselves, was dedicated "to the continuous growth of the child, . . . freedom, initiative, spontaneity, vivid self-expression" (p. 35). The conflict was between repressive tradition and personal liberation.

They believed the child-centered school was for children of all social classes. Yet Rugg was strongly influenced by his association with New York's Greenwich Village intelligencia, a well-educated, upper-middle-class elite, made up of artists and writers, responding to pressures of urbanization. Those pressures were restrained by "a Puritan attitude of mind" (Rugg & Shumaker, 1928, p. iv), as they put the matter, coupled with an aggressive materialism that put the needs of things before the needs of people. Creative self-expression in this context was more than an art method; it was also a vehicle for individual freedom. Ironically, most immigrant and working-class families refused to send their children to the kind of progressive schools these writers advocated in their book (Cremin, 1964).[2]

In 1935 Melvin Haggerty discussed art in a new way, as a way of life, a potent instrument for improving the life of the common man. Art in the home, in dress, and in community improvement projects served as art activities rather than the study of grand masterpieces with all their eliteness and remoteness. "Art in daily living" was the slogan for this new approach. These practices were grounded in *pragmatic* theory, where art is an instrument to be judged by its effectiveness in solving the practical, aesthetic problems affecting the life of the viewer. We can understand readily the appeal of this view of art in an era dominated by economic depression and war.

What is clear from these examples is that the impetus for change in educational practice came in large part from socially perceived needs. In some cases the need was clearly articulated, as with Smith in 1872. The social basis for Dow's pedagogy was not stated, but was part of the educational scene within which he worked. Equally clear is the fact that each of the aforementioned pedagogies was grounded in certain core beliefs concerning the nature of art. Each differed in its aesthetic orientation. Smith's view of art was grounded in the belief that all art is a representation of natural form. Dow believed that it was the formal structure of the object that determined whether it was art or not. Rugg saw the originality of creative expression as the factor that determined the value of art, while Haggerty saw art in pragmatic terms, as an instrument for improving daily life.

To the question of the role played by aesthetic theories in art teaching, we can answer that it bears directly on the *method* of teaching and *content* of instruction in each case. Current practice is a blend of these orientations in aesthetics. Quite accurately, we can say that our past lives on in the present.

MODELS OF ART TEACHING

In what follows, several models of art teaching are introduced. Each is based on the aesthetic traditions already implied by the above examples. Coupled to these traditions are notions of how learning takes place, the nature of society, and a vision of education's role in society (Joyce & Weil, 1972).[3,4] The aesthetic theories fall into four major groupings based on the scheme used both by the *Encyclopedia Brittanica* (1974) and in classifications of aesthetic theories offered by Abrams in his book, *The Mirror and the Lamp* (1958). Both describe mimetic, pragmatic, expressive, and formalist theories.[5]

The models are more than theoretical possibilities; they were historical realities as well. Teachers actually implemented practices based on these beliefs about the nature of art. Moreover, differences in beliefs also served as bases for disputes among generations of art teachers.

Although practices in art teaching received their sanction in aesthetic theory, it is important to recognize that the purposes for art teaching were supplied by the social milieu. What might not be readily apparent, however, is the fact that every aesthetic theory also harbors certain social views as well.

A teacher embracing the notion of creative self-expression is likely to believe that the child's innate desire for expression is in danger of being thwarted by social pressures demanding conformity. The teaching task consists of ways to free the child from inhibitions that block this natural desire for expression. Ideas about liberation from social repression are deeply embedded in the matrix of expressive aesthetics. This may explain why expressionism as an art theory accompanied the rise of an avant garde movement that often stood in opposition to the status quo in society.

On the other hand, a teacher who sees art as imitation and copying is more likely to believe that art learning is acquired by imitating the behavior of others. To learn in this tradition is to come under the control of various stimuli provided by the teaching situation. The model implies that the behavior desired in the student has been determined by the teacher or the culture. Imitation and copying are the preferred methods of teaching and learning in

TABLE 1.1 Aesthetics, Learning Theories, and Their Implied Ideologies

Aesthetic Theory	Learning Theory	Implied Ideology
Mimetic Art is imitation	Behaviorism Learning is by imitation	Traditional morality: social control
Pragmatic Art is instrumental	Learning is instrumental	Social reconstruction
Expressive Art is self-expression	Psychoanalytic Learning is emotional growth	Personal liberation
Formalist Art is formal order	Cognitive Learning is concept attainment	Technocratic control by experts

traditional societies striving to sustain valued traditions. In contrast to the first example, this aesthetic is grounded in notions of control.

A teacher holding a pragmatic view of art would likely hold an instrumental view of learning. Knowledge, including art knowledge, is experience having instrumental value that enables individuals and social groups to adapt to a changing environment. The learning task involves intellectual reconstruction as new knowledge changes previous understandings of the world. Encountering new experiences, including new art, is transactional in nature, which may result in the reconstruction of social reality, and the ideology of social reconstruction is one that would accommodate to change.

Finally a teacher possessing a formalist view of art is likely to embrace a cognitive view of learning in which one forms cognitive structures using concepts, principles, criteria, and vocabularies—the language used to talk about art and the manipulation of the elements of form in making art. Objects would acquire their special status as art by the presence of distinctive structural attributes. Through acquisition of cognitive structures, learners come to possess the structure of art as a body of knowledge. To possess this enables one to conduct disciplined inquiry in art. In its deference to expertise, the model implies an elitist, or technocratic, view of society. Table 1.1 describes the relationships among various aesthetic theories, learning theories, and their implied social views.

Each of these models is now presented in more detail. Each aligns a theory of art with a compatible educational theory. Similarly, each is linked with compatible social views. Each will display differing contents, activities, approaches to instruction, and methods of evaluation. The following is the prototype used for each model.

Mimetic-Behavioral Model

This model is suggested by the union of mimetic aesthetics and behaviorally based conceptions of learning, the idea that learning is known by changes in behavior. Common to both is the notion of imitation, that is, art is imitation while learning is *by* imitation. The teaching process presents the student with models to imitate; student learning is discerned as new behaviors are noted in the learner's repertoire. Instruction utilizes specific stimuli placed in the learning environment by the teacher, who controls what is presented, the sequence, level of difficulty, frequency, and intensity. These stimuli can take the form of demonstrations of skills to be mastered. When the student acquires the designated skill, he or she is rewarded by the teacher. For example, academies of art since the seventeenth century have awarded prizes for good performance. Successful teaching places the student under the control of the stimulus situation.

In traditional mimetic theories the artistic process is the result of inspiration from outside forces, either natural or supernatural. Ancient Greeks talked about the muses inspiring the artist, or artists acting under the control of spiritual forces. The power of the artist is revealed in the convincingness of the subjects represented in his or her art. The power of teaching in behavioral theory is seen in the convincingness of demonstrations that bring the student under control. Traditional mimetic theory discusses pleasure as the likely response to works of art, while behavioral approaches to instruction discuss the process of reinforcement to secure learning. Positive reinforcement is experienced as pleasurable. Traditional mimetic theories do not place value in art as art. If art imitates goodness, it is good, but if it imitates evil, it then is evil. Similarly, behaviorists like Skinner talk about the value-neutrality of their instructional approach. Behavior modification can shape good or bad behavior.

To implement the model each behavior to be acquired by the learner is described in a series of detailed objectives. These are not limited to skills but can include perceptual discriminations that can be made among stimuli. An example of a skill defined by an objective might be the following: "Using the medium of charcoal the student will prepare a nine-step gray scale including black and white." An example of perceptual discrimination might be an objective like, "The student will be able to distinguish Picasso's analytical cubism from synthetic cubism." Values and attitudes might be inferred by behavior changes, as, for example, increased museum attendance might be cited as evidence that art is more highly esteemed than was the case prior to instruction. Although behavioral psychology was formulated in the twentieth century, it aligns quite well with mimetic aesthetics, which is one of the oldest philosophies of art.

This model is not merely speculative but has been part of traditional practice from the days of the academy and in schooling practices common in the nineteenth century. To be sure, these early practitioners would have described their psychology of instruction as "exercising the faculty of imitation" rather than in current behavioral terms, but the early methods were not dissimilar from those used in current practice. Current practice, however, differs in its use of precise and systematic analysis of learning tasks and by the systematic use of reinforcement.

Pragmatic-Social Reconstruction Model

This model is suggested by themes connecting pragmatic aesthetics with the view that education is an instrument for social reconstruction. In both cases art and education have instrumental value. Learning is the process of constructing knowledge through one's encounters with the environment, and such knowledge has instrumental value. Learning about art is like learning anything else. That is, one constructs knowledge of art by encountering artistic problems through personal and social living. The learning task involves the intellectual reconstruction of knowledge as new experience alters or confirms previous views of the world.

A striking parallel exists between this view of knowledge and the ways artists work as described in Dewey's *Art as Experience* (1934) where the artist is characterized as being involved in the reconstruction of his or her experience in the process of making a work of art. Similarly, the viewer having "an experience" with a powerful work of art may alter his or her view of reality as a consequence of the encounter.

The above views of art and education are derived from Dewey's theory of intelligence in which successive experiences may cause the learner to revise or reconstruct his or her view of reality. A number of psychologists (Kilpatrick, 1961) referred to themselves as transactional psychologists because they described all learning in this way. They demonstrated how we may interpret experience wrongly on the basis of partial or limited encounters in our perception of phenomena, only to revise our understanding with further experience.

Teachers with these views would not impart formally organized knowledge but would organize learning around life-centered situations. The understandings we formed would be based on successive experiences where new knowledge may cause us to revise old understandings. Learning is thus a reality check. Truth is not absolute but emerges out of successive encounters, and its social utility is tested by whether it enables individuals and societies to adapt to changing circumstances. If our interpretation of reality is faulty, our response to change may not be successful, but if our responses are guided by assumptions that approximate the truth, we increase the probability of successful adaptation. A pragmatically oriented teacher would organize instructional resources for problem solving, and the evaluation of the instruction would be in terms of success experienced by students and teachers alike.

Content in this model would be expressed in terms of problems to be solved where art knowledge becomes a potential instrument in problem solving. Activities would take the form of occupations such as gardening, interior decoration, setting up window displays of merchandise, poster and advertising design, and the like.

Like the previous model, this one is not merely speculation. It was widely espoused in the 1930s by those progressive educators who identified with social reconstructionism. Many used art in teaching the social studies, while the social studies themselves underwent reconstruction around problems society was then facing in the years of the Great Depression and World War II. The definitive example of art education as social reconstruction can be seen in Haggerty's *Art a Way of Life* (1935) and in accounts of the Owatonna Project.

Expressive-Psychoanalytic Model

This model is suggested by themes connecting expressive aesthetics where art is the product of the artist's imagination and person-centered education, where knowledge is a personal construct validated in the feeling life of the learner. Common to both is the view of mind as initiator of learning activities where new constructs, understandings, and insights are made possible by the work of the imagination. Emotions and feelings are felt to play the predominant role in mental life. When the emotions of the artist are given form by the artistic process, they are made accessible to others, and thus art can express ideas, feelings, and emotions in forms that can be publicly shared. It is this public sharing of these privately felt intuitive insights that makes cultural advance possible. Because such forms are products of mental life, they have status as intuitive or subjective knowledge. Art also has value for the individual creator because it enables personal growth to occur. For this reason the arts are therapeutic. Learning in this model is a process of personality integration.

Knowledge as such has no inherent meaning or value except as it is authenticated by the individual in his or her own feeling life. Thus in many ways the construction of one's personal world view is like the creation of a work of art — an act of originality. The validity of one's world view is evaluated not by objective appraisals of reality, but by becoming "tuned in" to reality. An adequate world view permits spontaneity of response. Subject matter competence for its own sake is relatively unimportant.

The value of art, like the value of one's personal world view, is ultimately found both in its originality and in the extent that it leads to personal fulfillment. The unique expression of artists and scientists revitalizes the culture, and conversely the good society is one that maximizes this expression of uniqueness.

Teaching in this model facilitates the self-realization of individuals. The wise teacher does not impose values but permits those of the child to unfold from within. Art is valued in education because artists exemplify in their work the use of personal expression to realize their potential.

Learning is a dynamic process of growth that unfolds from within. The outward expansion of the mind is felt subjectively as freedom, while teacher direction or formal instruction is experienced as coercion or repression. The wise teacher facilitates growth by providing nurturance or emotional support. Effective teachers are good listeners who can empathize with what the child may be feeling.

This model arose during the progressive era and continues to have many adherents. In the era after World War II its leading advocates were Viktor Lowenfeld (1947) and Herbert Read (1945). Advocates of self-expression varied in their teaching methods. Lowenfeld motivated children by having them recall memories and feelings. Other teachers, such as Marion Richardson (1946), used techniques that involved guided imagery to help students visualize their expression in their mind's eye before they began their work. Still others relied on the visual or tactile qualities of media to initiate the flow of ideas.

Formalist-Cognitive Model

This model is suggested by common themes connecting formalist aesthetics and the view of cognition that asserts that learning is the acquisition of cognitive structures. A formalist aesthetic asserts that art objects acquire their status as art by virtue of the structural aspects of the work as an organized entity, and thus it has in common with cognitive psychology the idea of structure as its defining attribute. Rudolph Arnheim (1954) linked formalist theory with gestalt psychology since both dealt with the structure of visual form. Gestalt psychology can be thought of as a theory of perception within cognitive psychology.

The cognitive structures of art knowledge are identified in concepts, vocabularies, and elements of design seen in works of art. Together these provide the wherewithal to make, perceive, interpret, judge, and, ultimately, understand art.

Value claims in formalist aesthetics are described as intrinsic satisfactions. Aesthetic experience has intrinsic value, and it is this quality of mind that distinguishes human cognition from that of other species. Ralph Smith (1986) describes aesthetic experience as "worthwhile experience" (p. 21) in need of no further justification. Most views of education that rely heavily on a cognitive interpretation of learning would tend to argue that the value of knowledge is also intrinsic, that is, education is valued for its own sake, not for the economic or social advantages that may accrue to the learner. Smith argues that art teaching should provide cognitive concepts and understandings not for their sake alone, but because they enable one to have commerce with exemplary works of art known for the excellence of the aesthetic experience they provide, works inaccessible without this knowledge.

Teaching in this model should provide students with the requisite skills and conceptual content to make art and to understand the art of others, and it should also provide students with procedures that enable them to make disciplined inquiries into art.

Teaching methods should facilitate student inquiry by discovery and experiment. They should facilitate concept attainment by enabling students to form generalizations about their experience. They should provide situations that would enable students to speculate about unknowns and, by testing hypotheses, to know that these are ways to enlarge upon the understandings one forms about art.

Evaluation should be done in terms of concepts attained. This includes a knowledge of the forming processes used to make art. For example, a student might know the fact that warm colors advance and cool colors recede, but one should evaluate to see if the learner can apply this knowledge to interpret the meaning of a painting, or use this understanding to create a specific effect in a work of art, and so on.

This model came into prominence during the curriculum reform movement of the 1960s with the cognitive views of learning developed in the writings of Jerome Bruner. He was quick to see the parallel between what he termed "the structure of the disciplines" and the Piagetian explanation of learning as the acquisition of cognitive structures. Art educators based their curriculum proposals on various definitions of the disciplines (Efland, 1987; Smith, 1987). Since 1984, this model also has experienced renewed prominence in the current rise of interest in discipline-based art education (Greer, 1984).

AESTHETIC CHANGE AND POSTMODERNISM

The aesthetic theories heretofore discussed have played an important role throughout the era of modern art and are deeply embedded in today's practices of art teaching. Modernism began with the rejection of mimetic art and with the introduction of expressionism and formalism to justify the changes taking place in art. Starting in the late 1970s and early 1980s, however, a number of art and literary critics concluded that these theories could no longer elucidate the forms of art then beginning to appear. In 1985 Kim Levin described the art scene in the following way:

> Something did happen, something so momentous that it was ignored in disbelief: modernity had gone out of style. It even seemed as if style itself had been used up, but then style — the invention of sets of forms — was a preoccupation of modernism, as was originality. The tradition of the New, Harold Rosenberg called it. At the start of the '70s there were dire predictions of the death of art by modernist critics and artists. By now it is obvious that it was not art that was ending but an era. We are witnessing the fact that in the past ten years modern art has become a period style, an historical entity. The modernist period has drawn to a close and receded into the past before our astonished eyes. (p. 1)

From Suzi Gablik's (1984) point of view, more was at stake than a change of style; the art world was beginning to enter a period of confusion over the aims and purposes of art.

> The overwhelming spectacle of current art is at this point, confusing not only to the public, but even to professionals and students, for whom the lack of any clear or validating consensus, established on the basis of common practice, has ushered in an impenetrable pluralism of competing approaches. (p. 14)

For Gablik modernism was committed to the notion of a self-sufficient art, with aesthetic experience seen as an end in itself — that the only way to preserve its truth was by maintaining its distance from the social world, by staying pure. When artists could no longer find meaning in the social world, they sought it in themselves, and the attitude of "art for art's sake" was essentially a "forced response to a social reality that [they] could no longer affirm" (p. 21). The retreat into self-expression, and the resulting proliferation of novel forms that followed, worked against the possibility of a unified style.

Early modernism, in Gablik's view, was a search for new social and spiritual values in a world dominated by materialism, and modern artists were a part of an avant-garde dedicated to this quest. Late modernism, as reflected in the circle of artists who emerged around the critic Clement Greenberg, such as Helen Frankenthaler, Morris Louis, and Jules Olitski, saw no transcendent, higher, social, or spiritual purpose to art. Art's meaning was reduced to an aesthetic one: "The real problem of modernity has proved to be the problem of belief — the loss of belief in any system of values beyond the self" (Gablik, 1984, pp. 29–30).

As modernism became "purer," its subject matter was reduced to mere preoccupation with form, and as a result the number of people to whom it would appeal decreased. From its inception with the first abstract art and the formalist doctrines of Clive Bell and Roger Fry, modernism tended toward elitism — an art for the few who could derive aesthetic satisfaction from formal relationships alone.

Moreover, theories like expressionism and formalism existed in a special relationship to modern art, which was less true of previous art, for one could be moved by a Raphael seemingly without a theory to explain why. With the advent of modernism, theory became essential to inform the viewer how to look at this new art. Without theory a right reading of the work was not possible.

In postmodern thought, this reliance on theory has gone still farther and deeper, for now the work of art can exist *only* in and through its interpretations. Now the possibility of there being a right reading or interpretation has given way to the prospect that there may be multiple interpretations of the meaning of a work of art. Indeed, some recent critical theories, such as the deconstructionist view, assert that each viewer constructs his or her own set of meanings in a work. The more extreme deconstructionists would even question the belief that the work is created by the artist at all! For example, Stanley Fish (1980) argued that the work of art is a construction of each perceiver, who may create a set of quite different works whose meanings differ markedly from each other and from the meaning intended by the actual artist.

With differing interpretations possible, how does one decide which one is true? David Carrier (1985) suggested that the truth of a critic's argument depends on the persuasive power of his or her rhetoric, on his or her ability to persuade the reader, implying that truth has less to do with a correct reading of the intrinsic features of the work than with the argument supporting the work. This idea was brought home forcefully in his description of how art criticism functions in the world.

> The critic's rhetoric is a way of inducing beliefs in art-world people, and when critics succeed, most people come to believe their claims, which therefore are true. This account may seem outrageous to those who believe that critics merely draw attention to significant features of artworks. . . . What transforms the way the audience receives the work is how a critic talks about it. This change in the nature of artistic rhetoric is important. Michaelangelo could "with the terrible power of his art," Vasari says, "move the hearts not only of those who [had knowledge of painting] . . . but even those who had none." The Renaissance viewer was moved by seeing the work. (pp. 200–202).

Carrier's illustration of how critics influence the art world is supported by Arthur Danto's (1981) conclusion "that there cannot be an art world without an art theory" (p. 135).

> So it is essential . . . that we understand the nature of an art theory, which is so powerful a thing as to detach objects from the real world and make them part of

a different world, an *art* world, a world of *interpreted things*. What these considerations show is that there is an internal connection between the status of an artwork
and the language with which objects are identified as such, inasmuch as nothing
is an artwork without an interpretation that constitutes it as such. (p. 135)

CONCLUSIONS

The art teacher who tries to deal with developments in the contemporary arts
faces a number of problems. First, there is the problem of the sheer plurality
of the new art forms, each more challenging than the modernist styles of the
early part of the century.

Second, the newer criticism and theory attempting to explain this recent
art are both complex and voluminous. Modernist art theory was grounded in
expressionism and formalism; postmodern aesthetic theories, by contrast, are
grounded in doctrines that stray into the sociology of art and the art world.
Postmodernism, "is the somewhat weasel word now being used to describe
the garbled situation of art in the '80s. It is a term nobody quite fully understands, because no clear-cut definition of it has yet been put forward" (Gablik,
1984, p. 73). Under the more recent label of neo-expressionism, the recycling
and recombination of former styles suggest that the succession of styles that
has been underway since the impressionists of the last century is now out of
control. "Postmodernism is much more eclectic, able to assimilate, and even
plunder, all forms of style and conflicting values" (Gablik, 1984, p. 73).

Third, in place of a definitive postmodern theory there is a general dis-
comfort with many of the assumptions on which modernism and many premodernist styles were premised, especially the notion that artistic progress
is a function of stylistic transformations, each of which nullifies past artistic
endeavors—the incessant demand for newness, originality, and novelty.
Gablik and Carrier raise questions about the art world as an institution, the
ways it operates to promote and market new artists and their works. Others
question the assumption that art should concern itself with formal organization for purely aesthetic purposes; finally, the notion that art is a precious
commodity, to be venerated by people with education and taste, is called into
question. The older notion that art is an autonomous, self-sufficient realm
preoccupied with aesthetic issues and values totally separated from the social
world, is being replaced by the idea that works of art and the philosophies
used to explain them are related to each other and also to the culture and
society that give rise to them.

Fourth, a postmodern curriculum would not necessarily discard or replace modernist or premodernist theory and practices. Mimetic, pragmatic,
expressive, and formalist aesthetics would have their place in the critical ap-

prehension of art for they do elucidate certain kinds of aesthetic values in certain kinds of art. However, one now needs to ask prior questions like the following: "In what social or cultural context does formalism or expressionism function as a true theory?"[6]

Just as postmodern art may quote from popular culture or from past art forms, so it would seem that the theories used to elucidate this art would continue to have a place in the learner's understanding, if for no other reason than to acquaint him or her with theory as it existed in the consciousness of past artists. Older theory can be recycled just as some of today's artists recycle imagery from older art or from popular culture. It would also be the case that no single theory from the past could be taken as true theory but could be viewed as provisional explanations regarding the nature of art and its value.

Fifth, when modernism appeared in the early decades of the century it was "full of dictates about what art could, or could not, be" (Gablik, 1984, p. 73). Art had to be a new and original expression; it had to move away from representational images in favor of abstraction, for example. It had to be self-expression if it was to be anything! Many of these assumptions found their way into the teaching of art and continue to dominate the teaching of art today. Generations of art teachers condemned copying and imitation as practices inimical to good art and learning, yet many contemporary artists such as Andy Warhol, used factory-like methods of production to ensure that multiples of the same image would be exact copies. Generations of art teachers worked to motivate children to be original in their production of art. These assumptions need to be looked at once again to see if they still have validity in the present context.

Sixth, this suggests that in the current state of affairs an eclectic approach to an art curriculum is mandated, in spite of the fact that it invites contradiction and inconsistency. A noneclectic curriculum is possible only when one model of art teaching is privileged as being true, a situation that cannot exist as long as the present pluralism is characteristic of the art world.

If the putting together of such rival conceptions were for the purpose of illustrating the idea that art has had varied meanings and values that are openly contested by groups of artists, critics, and their publics, then this becomes a valid purpose for representing these in instruction, for to understand art at this time is to understand that people hold radically different beliefs about art. The curriculum may well have contradictory contents but it is constrained by the requirement to present these views with deference to their development in history. History serves as a control on a random or naive eclecticism. Eclecticism is not a value in itself but is invoked to enable the learner to understand what it means to live and work with contending conceptions of aesthetic value.

Each of the aforementioned theories would lead the curriculum maker to differing content and goals — content and goals that are part and parcel of the contradictory nature of art itself — and to the conclusion that this is a way of representing the diversity of art.

Seventh, it could be argued that an art curriculum reflecting the conflicting diversity in the nature of art, would not be eclectic at all; it would simply represent the state of art at the present time. Understanding this diversity and its historical and social bases is the challenge confronting the learner and the curriculum maker alike.

Finally, it is clear that a postmodern art curriculum — even one dedicated to serious studio practice — will require a fuller understanding of critical and historical studies than may have been true in the past, because they are inextricably interwoven into the practices of postmodern artists. Without aesthetic inquiry, history, and criticism, both modern and postmodern art will remain a closed book to future students.

NOTES

1. Callahan's *Education and the Cult of Efficiency* describes the period between the 1890s and World War I and shows how educational administrators increasingly adopted the model of corporate efficiency as the means for organizing and evaluating educational systems. It was not uncommon to liken the school to the factory.

2. Carolyn Ware's study of Greenwich Village during the 1920s noted that the progressive schools founded in lower Manhattan were intended for poor children, but most immigrant and working-class families preferred to send their children to public or parochial schools. Commenting on this finding, Cremin noted that they soon became the schools for the children of intellectuals, artists, and writers.

3. This section is based on two earlier papers (Efland, 1979a, 1979b). Although the argument is essentially the same, the reader will see differing pairings of aesthetic theories with views of learning. In this chapter I have made an attempt to identify the social views implied by these different aesthetic theories.

4. For conceptual assistance I found Joyce and Weil's *Models of Teaching* (1972) to be useful. Although they identified dozens of educational models, they divided them into four main groupings, behavior-modification, social-interaction, person-centered, and information-processing theories. In place of *information-processing* I used the more inclusive term *cognitive*. These groupings aligned with the four main groups of aesthetic theories: mimetic with behaviorism, pragmatic with social-interaction, expressive with person-centered, and formalist with the cognitive view. These became the basis for my pairings.

5. Abrams actually used the term *objective aesthetics* instead of *formalist aesthetics*. The *Brittanica* uses the term *formalist aesthetics* in place of *objective aesthetics*. Since most contemporary writers identify modernism with formalism, I felt that this term would be easier to identify in this chapter.

6. This idea was suggested by a conversation with Michael Parsons.

REFERENCES

Abrams, M. H. (1958). *The mirror and the lamp: Romantic theory and the critical tradition*. New York: W. W. Norton.

Arnheim, R. (1954). *Art and visual perception*. Berkeley: University of California Press.

Beardsley, M. (1958). *Aesthetics: Problems in the philosophy of criticism*. New York: Harcourt, Brace.

Brittanica, Encyclopedia. 15th ed. (1974). *Propedia, Part Six. Art, Division I. Art in general*. Chicago: Brittanica Encyclopedia, Inc., p. 211.

Callahan, R. (1962). *Education and the cult of efficiency*. Chicago: University of Chicago Press.

Carrier, D. (1985). Art and its market. In R. Hertz (Ed.), *Theories of contemporary art* (pp. 193–205). Englewood Cliffs, NJ: Prentice-Hall.

Cremin, L. (1964). *Transformation of the school*. New York: Vintage Books.

Danto, A. C. (1981). *The transfiguration of the commonplace*. Cambridge, MA: Harvard University Press.

Dewey, J. (1934). *Art as experience*. New York: Minton, Balch.

Dow, A. W. *Composition*. (1913). New York: Doubleday Doran. (Original work published 1899)

Efland, A. (1979a). Conceptions of teaching in the arts. In G. L. Knieter & J. Stallings (Eds.), *The teaching process & arts and aesthetics* (pp. 152–186). St. Louis: CEMREL, Inc.

Efland, A. (1979b). Conceptions of teaching in art education. *Art Education, 32*(4), 21–33.

Efland, A. (1987). Curriculum antecedents of discipline-based art education. *Journal of Aesthetic Education, 21*(2), 57–94.

Fish, S. (1980). *Is there a text for this class? The authority of interpretive communities*. Cambridge, MA: Harvard University Press.

Gablik, S. (1984). *Has modernism failed?* New York: Thames & Hudson.

Greer, W. D. (1984). Discipline-based view of art education: Approaching art as a subject. *Studies in Art Education, 25*(4), 212–218.

Haggerty, M. (1935). *Art a way of life*. Minneapolis: University of Minnesota Press.

Joyce, B., & Weil, M. (1972). *Models of teaching*. Englewood Cliffs, NJ: Prentice-Hall.

Kilpatrick, F. P. (1961). *Explorations in transactional psychology*. New York: New York University Press.

Levin, K. (1985). Farewell to modernism. In R. Hertz (Ed.), *Theories of contemporary art* (pp. 3–12). Englewood Cliffs, NJ: Prentice-Hall.

Lowenfeld, V. (1947). *Creative and mental growth*. New York: Macmillan.

Read, H. (1945). *Education through art*. New York: Pantheon.

Richardson, M. (1946). *Art and the child*. Peoria, IL: Charles A. Bennett Co.

Rugg, H., & Shumaker, A. (1928). *The child-centered school*. New York: World Book.

Smith, R. A. (1986). *Excellence in art education: Ideas and initiatives*. Reston, VA: National Art Education Association.

Smith, R. A. (1987). The changing image of art education: Theoretical antecedents of discipline-based art education. *Journal of Aesthetic Education, 21*(2), 3–34.

Smith, W. (1872). *Art education scholastic and industrial*. Boston: James Osgood.

CHAPTER 2

Art Education Changes and Continuities: Value Orientations of Modernity and Postmodernity

Karen A. Hamblen

Change has been interpreted as serendipitous, as tightly linked to causal factors, as controlled by whimsical gods, or as part of an overall grand plan. Change is inextricably related to time and our consciousness of being. The perception of change gives a sense of the passage of time and signals intervals and continuities. Without an awareness of large and small events of change, time would be of a singular, unbroken weave. Conversely, without perceived similarities and patterning among events, time would consist of discrete, unrelated occurrences. It is the linking of events of change that provides continuity and allows for predictions and the stability of built traditions. As Kubler notes in his book, *The Shape of Time* (1962), time is patterned and takes shape through changes and continuities. Although the events of change that populate time serve to punctuate existence, it is the value given to those events of change that provides meaning and significance to experience. In this chapter, the changes and continuities of art education will be discussed as they relate to the values given by modernity and postmodernity.

INTERPRETATIONS OF CHANGE AND CONTINUITY

Finding causal links among ostensibly disparate events marks the dawning development of the child's awareness of self and the possibility for purposive behaviors. Likewise, on the societal scale, causal links among events provide opportunities for social planning—from the concrete need to plant crops in the spring so that they can be harvested in the fall to more abstract planning involved in population control policies so that in future years adequate food supplies will be available. Linking events is part of the human need to explain, if not forecast, experience. Causal links have been forged between events in all areas of human activity. Rain will fall because of complex atmospheric changes or because a ritual dance has been performed—and, in times of draught, both explanations may be given credence. In attempts to explain stylistic characteristics and periods of change in art, links have been made between art and economic, religious, and political systems. Linkages have been made between agricultural production and abstract art, hunting activities and naturalistic art, social dislocations and a proliferation of artistic styles (Kavolis, 1968). In an attempt to explain recurring similarities among artistic events over time, Wölfflin (1950) proposed that art passes through classical and baroque styles in a spiral cyclical manner. According to Focillon (1948), major styles have an internal development consisting of archaic, classical, mannerist, and baroque stages. Change in art and in society has been interpreted as cyclical, dialectical, developmental, oscillating, undulating, and evolutionary (Kluckhohn & Strodtbeck, 1961; Roucek & Mohan, 1972; Schapiro, 1962).

How change and the meaning given to change are explained is itself part of the value system of a culture and, hence, varies throughout time and space. Recent changes in art education theory and practice—and proposed practice—have been linked to teacher accreditation requirements, student demographics, economic conditions, philanthropic support, art agency policies, the back-to-basics movement, reform reports, and so on. One might tease out any one or more of these factors and link them to art education changes. However, such a structural analogic approach, commonly used in the sociology of art, needs to be tempered by the value orientations taken toward social factors of influence (Abell, 1957; Kavolis, 1968). The presence of any given condition or factor is no indication of what its influence actually will be. For example, it is not the presence of any particular economic system that influences art, but rather the value orientation—positive, negative, or neutral—that is taken toward the economic condition (Abell, 1957). Moreover, according to Marxism, the social class that has power to confer value and significance is a crucial consideration.

Social factors can be emphasized, minimized, or ignored in terms of their impact on change. Current reform movement publications funded by governmental agencies appear to have helped fuel the fires of change in art education. However, dramatic changes in student demographics, such as the influx of immigrants, appear to have had little impact, as evidenced by the lack of curricula tailored for such populations. In art education the value system of modernity has acted as a selective lens, focalizing on some factors of possible influence and defocalizing on others.

At this time in the history of art education, the value systems of modernity and postmodernity influence theory and practice as well as give shape to many of the issues that are now being debated. Modernity and postmodernity pervade a variety of institutions of society and have great explanatory power for a range of social phenomena. Modernity and postmodernity, respectively, are descriptive of change and traditionalism, academic and local knowledge, industrialized and nonindustrialized economies, masculine and feminine interpretations of behavior, and low context (rational) and high context (vernacular) cultures (Hall, 1977).

In this chapter, change in art education will not be discussed as a function of discrete factors and events, but rather as part of philosophical world views that themselves influence how change and continuity are perceived, interpreted, and given meaning. Any theory or explanation of change and continuity is itself subject to the vicissitudes of changing values, attitudes, and beliefs about change and tradition. The purpose here is to examine how two world views of change and of tradition are evident in art education practice, how these two world views have themselves influenced art education events, and how they can offer very different interpretations of a given event.

The values of modernity are those of change, progress, and an eschewing of tradition. The values of postmodernity are those of tradition, continuity, and conservative change (Bowers, 1987). Just as no one aesthetic theory is explanatory of all types or aspects of art (Weitz, 1962), a value system serves to allow for the exploration and explanation of some aspects of reality while defocalizing on others. The value systems of modernity and postmodernity, as expressed in art education and as frameworks for examining the field, are, separately, only partial explanations within the shape of time. In concert and in a dialectic relationship, however, they allow for the expression and the examination of both change and continuity.

ART EDUCATION CHANGE AND CONTINUITY

Histories dealing with an overview of the field of art education often focus on the implementation of major programs and the formulation of distinctive education theories (Hamblen, 1985a). Within such histories, art education is punctuated by a progression of events, from Walter Smith's Industrial Drawing of the late 1800s, to the Picture Study Movement around the turn of the century, to the Child Study focus of progressive education, and so on (Logan, 1955). Major movements are often designated by descriptive phrases with capitalized letters that come to stand as summarizations of complex assumptions and actions. Characteristics are cited to indicate contrasts among the theoretical bases of different movements, and changing social conditions and cultural values may be linked to such art education movements. For example, the Picture Study Movement was made possible by technological, photographic advances and was influenced by idealist philosophical tenets on the moral benefits to be gained from trafficking with the beautiful (Stankiewicz, 1985).

It becomes possible to interpret art education as a series of improvements when history is seen as consisting of events of change and difference. The belief that change signals a more correct fit to some ideal is especially true for contemporary developments in art education. Events of the more distant past can be tolerated or dismissed as adequate for their own time. The drawing exercise books of the last century take on a certain quaintness or collectible preciousness. From a modernist perspective, change within the present takes on a moral imperative to correct inadequacies of the past. There is, for the present, an assumption of improvement and correctness, and a certain optimism greets each new program development. Needless to say, such optimism is often short-lived, and, in the give-and-take of program implementation, theoretical frameworks quickly lose their original clarity of focus.

Considering curricular and theoretical movements to be improvements is predicated on seeing them as significant changes and as possessing major differences from the past. However, in surveying the history of art education from the vantage point of the mid–1970s, Lanier (1975) was prompted to write that the more art education changes, the more it stays the same. In particular, Lanier noted a continuing emphasis on instruction in studio production, to the exclusion of more conceptually, verbally based modes of understanding and appreciating art. For example, despite major differences between Smith's strident workbook exercises involving careful renderings of a predrawn example and Lowenfeld's open-ended creativity explorations, Smith and Lowenfeld did have in common the belief that the making of art constitutes the essence of art instruction and understanding. Since the inception of formal art instruction in this country, studio production has constituted its core, and attempts to change this have meet with varying degrees of criticism, if not indignant outrage suggesting that a moral percept is being violated.

While Lanier (1975) points out a major configurational continuity in art education, other continuities can be found within the details of our history. Foreign competition prompted the Massachusetts Board of Education to hire Smith in 1871 to bolster, through art education, the design capabilities of industry in the United States (Logan, 1955). Today, economic competition with the Japanese has resulted in back-to-basics education movements and a commensurate call in art education for specific goals and objectives that can be efficiently tested. Art education changes have been prompted by wars, explorations of outer space, and worldwide economic depressions. Individualism and the psychological underpinnings of artistic expression have surfaced throughout our history in the linking of classroom art instruction to the activities of the adult artist, the therapeutic benefits to be accrued from art activities, the assumed singularity of a child's creativity, and so on. The modernity values of individualism, subjectivity, creativity, and an overthrow of tradition have constituted a powerful continuity in much of art education's history. Continuity and tradition have characterized our history in the sense that art education change often has been a reinterpretation of past practices and also in the sense of providing links to community, context, and cultural values. The art workbooks of the 1920s and 1930s suggest that the progressive education movement and its commensurate Child Study research often placed the individual's experience, within the context of community and social responsibility through classroom activities, on crafts and folk art and on public displays of art that would improve the design of the community and the well-being of its citizens.

Art instruction in the 1930s provides a powerful example of the interplay that develops between change and continuity and between the world views that subsequently have been termed modernity and postmodernity. The Owatonna Project is often cited as an example of how art can be part of the fabric of life and part of the built environment (Logan, 1955). This project serves as a prototype for collaboratives among philanthropic foundations, academic institutions, community groups, and individuals. In this sense, the Owatonna Project exemplifies the values of postmodernity's contextualism, pluralism, and tradition. This project, however, developed out of the values of modernity in that it was a product of intervention by academic experts who rationalized the artistic process and predefined and codified artistic behaviors of production and response. Although the Owatonna Project's unit of concern was the community and the contextualized values within that unit, it also was imbued with modernity's optimistic belief in progress and in the supremacy of the individual's free choice. The Owatonna Project emanated from the belief that change can be institutionalized and that rational change constitutes an improvement in the human condition.

In art education programs themselves, that is, in their characteristics and operating assumptions, one can find the values of modernity and postmodernity. One also can find the values of these two world views in the relationship of programs to each other, that is, in whether particular programs constitute a major change from the past or whether they retain significant similarities. Except in the unblemished world of theory, programs do not present any one world view, but rather tend to incorporate multiple, often conflicting, assumptions that may be weighted in a particular direction. Such a weighting allows us to form generalizations, albeit often ignoring conflicts within the details.

CHARACTERISTICS OF MODERNITY AND POSTMODERNITY

Modernity

Modernity has its origins in the philosophical beliefs of the Enlightenment, in the production modes of industry, and in the hierarchical relationships of bureaucratic society (Bowers, 1974, 1987). The unit of action in modern society is the autonomous individual. Abstract, theoretical knowledge is given the highest accolades, with concrete, sensate, and nonverbal forms of knowing considered to be of lesser value, if not suspect. Knowledge and human activity, from the personal to the public, are rationalized and put into hierarchical relationships in which greater value is given to that which is abstract, theoretical, and/or capable of being quantified. In the hierarchical, bureaucratic, and specialized world of technological innovation, there is a reliance on expert knowledge.

Modernity is characterized by a pervading optimism that with the proper tool or intellectual process, all problems ultimately can be solved or, at the very least, controlled. Technological processes and rational intervention are used to solve an array of technical as well as human problems. Gouldner (1979) believes that this optimism in ultimate success results in a continual tinkering with social institutions — and, of course, with commercial products that are part of the planned obsolescence that fuels technological innovation. Commercial products are never allowed merely to exist; products as mundane as Tide laundry detergent are continually reformulated and heralded as *new* and *improved*. This fascination with new, improved versions applies also to ideas. It is a fascination that denigrates the past and tradition and calls into question previous assumptions and actions. The continual need to evaluate, update, and improve is endemic to the educational system wherein the success of a school is judged by the number of specialized programs it has instituted and the extent to which student test scores exceed the national mean.

Modernity is characterized by change, whether stylistic, behavioral, or institutional. The twentieth century has seen a veritable kaleidoscope of philosophical *isms,* scientific paradigm shifts, and art style changes. In the mid-twentieth century, the merit of an art form often was attributed on the basis of how much it differed from the past and its extent of innovation. Art history commonly has been taught as consisting of a series of artistic landmarks in which previous artistic inadequacies have been overcome by the adoption of a more so-called sophisticated style. In this sense, art influences art, and art is a series of self-influencing, *sui generis* events that operate within their own system of logic and purpose (Gombrich, 1969). Such interpretations of artistic change are part of the Western tendency to interpret time as linear and progressive, wherein previous events are conquered or eradicated by the *new* (Malraux, 1949).

The modernist sees history as a series of events that will eventually culminate in an endpoint of perfection — thus, the endless discussions in the 1960s as to whether art had exhausted itself, whether there were any other stylistic frontiers to be conquered, whether conceptual art was the *ne plus ultra* of art history, and so on. In Gablik's book aptly titled *Progress in Art* (1977), we are reminded of how imbued art history and educational psychology are with the idea of change and, more important, with change being equated with improvement and progress. In this sense, changes become linked in a greater and grander plan than their singular existences might seem to merit. The underlying morality of a seeming endless frenzy of change is that of an implicit belief that improvement is being accomplished. Change gives a sense that *something* is happening, irrespective of what the something might be or its value. Much as the Victorians had a horror of empty space in their architectural interiors, modernists abhor a sameness of events. Change can come to be valued for its own sake. At its extreme, modernity fosters change without a morality.

Postmodernity

The emphasis on change and improvement is the major, overarching way in which modernity is expressed in art education and the lens through which the history of art education often has been interpreted. More specifically, creativity, self-expression, individualism, and formalistic aesthetics are some of the modern characteristics readily found in art education theory and practice. In contrast, collaborative art projects, the study of community and ethnic arts, and environmental design responsibilities are expressive of the values of postmodernity. Postmodernity embodies the values of social pluralism, ethnic diversity, tradition, and contextualism. Local knowledge and the input of non-experts are valued, in contrast to the rationalism and technological expertise valued by the modernist. Concrete experience, folk wisdom, and tradition play a role in the postmodernist's world and his or her decision making. Reality to the postmodernist is composed of many different social, historical, and personal worlds, with the meaning and significance of these worlds contextually relevant and variable.

Although *postmodernity*, as the term indicates, postdates modernity, the above-cited characteristics do apply to events predating the last several decades. Ruralist, populist, traditionalist, and, in some respects, socialist movements contained the seeds of postmodernism, and during the last century a distrust of centralist, nationalistic, and industrialist tendencies surfaced in grass-roots movements that are compatible with postmodernity. To the modernist, individualism was seen as an antidote to various forms of economic and political repression. In the 1960s and 1970s, however, doubts were raised as to the efficacy and morality of change and uncensored individual action. In postmodernism, the individual acts within the context of social and ecological responsibility. In the 1960s some of the results of unbridled change became evident in the form of ecological disasters, dwindling natural resources, military escalations, and so forth. The optimistic anthem of modernism, that "everyday everyone was getting better in every way," was replaced by a belief that change needs to be tempered by reference to tradition and that there is no necessary grand progression of improvement, but rather small-scale accomplishments applicable to localized contexts and communities.

Configurations and Details

The complex interplay and dialectic between change and continuity, as they are expressed in the value systems of modernity and postmodernity, provide one means of examining the shape of time in art education. This dialectic is expressed in the relationship between the overall configuration of art education events and the details within that configuration. In studying artists working in traditional modes, Andre Malraux (1949) notes that, although overall composition and subject matter might conform to academic requirements, in hidden symbology and in the details of brushstrokes one can see the artist's individuality or the hints of a new style. In the details, socially and aesthetically censored ideas can be abridged. For example, Rembrandt's early work contains hints of spiritualism that would pervade his later work and result in his artistic ostracism—as well as his ultimate fame. Conversely, in the details of artwork that signals a new style, can be seen vestiges of the past. For all its innovative features, Picasso's *Les Demoiselles d'Avignon* still retains numerous time-honored conventions. Just as a new technology often is used or understood in the manner of the technology it replaces, for example, the car as a horseless carriage, change in art incorporates the old and is understood in terms of what it ostensibly has replaced. In this sense, the new incorporates the old in its details, and, conversely, the traditional contains the seeds that forecast its own demise. This same relationship between overall configuration and details applies to art education changes and continuities. It is in the details of new art education programs that doubts and qualifications often are expressed that may substantially alter such programs.

CURRENT EVENTS, CHANGES, AND CONTINUITIES IN ART EDUCATION

Currently, the most discussed and publicized program in art education is discipline-based art education (DBAE), as formulated by the J. Paul Getty Trust

(1985). Although developed from the aesthetic education theories and programs of the 1960s and 1970s, DBAE purports to offer a break with the past, especially in regard to studio instruction. Proponents of DBAE propose that art instruction consist of sequenced content in the four areas of aesthetics, art criticism, art history, and art production; such instruction is to be implemented district-wide, and student outcomes are to be closely evaluated. The modernity values of change, rational planning, and accountability are evident in the overall configuration of DBAE (Hamblen, 1985b, 1987). However, within its details and within some actual instances of implementation, DBAE retains strong ties to past art education practices and assumptions. For example, the initial revolutionary nature of instruction being shared among the four content areas appears to have been recognized in terms of what this would portend for studio instruction. Not surprisingly, this feature of DBAE surfaced as the focus of major criticisms (London, 1988). Subsequent prescriptions for DBAE allow studio production to retain its primacy by acting as the integrating core for instruction (Eisner, n.d.). Teachers who have assumed that they have always included aesthetics, art criticism, and art history in their studio-based programs will, undoubtedly, be reassured by the legitimacy of a program that purports to be a radical change yet retains strong ties to the status quo and traditional practices.

Through the fine-tuned lens of tradition, DBAE, in its details, retains strong ties to studio instruction, to an emphasis on technique, to formal design qualities as the basic content of art, and to Western fine art. In many cases, these characteristics are themselves part of modernity's value system, yet they have, through their continuity, come to form a solid core of tradition in art education. Through the larger lens of modernity, DBAE presents standardized content, teacher-proof materials, top-down decision making, and a reliance on experts for curriculum development, guidance, and evaluation.

MacGregor (1988) believes reinterpretations of DBAE, if not resistances, to be a function of the distance one is from the control center of DBAE policy making. The extent to which DBAE will represent a clear-cut change from the past and will be developed more or less in its theoretical purity is directly proportionate to one's proximity to power over DBAE policy, definitions, and implementation. Conversely, the extent to which DBAE will be ignored or implemented with major continuities to other programs will be directly proportionate to the extent one is distanced from power. Local control, social pluralism, and aesthetic contextualism also work to adulterate DBAE's modernist characteristics (Congdon, 1987; jagodzinski, 1987).

A primary objection to current DBAE proposals and programs is that they do not encompass the study of a range of art forms and thereby do not take into consideration the aesthetic diversity of the world, let alone that of our pluralistic society (Lederman, 1988). The most vocal critics believe that DBAE does not take into account the creative impulse in the quest for predictability of outcomes and accountability via instructional sequencing (London, 1988). Related to this criticism is the belief that DBAE will defocalize the importance of art production and the continuity it provides to art appreciation and understanding (London, 1988). Also, DBAE has been faulted for too closely resembling the content and methods of instruction used for subjects within general education (Hamblen, 1987).

Areas of resistance are not to be discounted in any program existing in an hierarchical structure. Recent literature from DBAE policy makers suggests that concessions to some of these criticisms are forthcoming inasmuch as it is proposed that DBAE be accommodative to local conditions and interpretations (Eisner, n.d.). It is worthy of note that the above-cited criticisms of DBAE hinge specifically on an opposition to modernist values and/or a support of postmodernist continuities and contextual considerations.

CONCLUSION

Ironically, it is now postmodernity that represents change and requires a re-thinking and readjustment of the entrenched value system of modernity; modernity, while thriving on and embodying change, has itself become a taken-for-granted and predictable tradition. Modernity, which in the past thrived on throwing off the mantle of tradition, has created its own continuities of change, individualism, and rationalization. Today, attempts to substitute modernity with the stability and traditionalism of postmodernity are seen as revolutionary. Modernity's continuation of a series of changes appears to give some sense of security that it is "business as usual." Any scurry of activity can be considered legitimate and purposeful. The proliferation of educational programs, fact-finding studies, educational reports, institutes, conferences, and seminars can easily give art educators a sense that something is being accomplished.

To paraphrase Lanier (1975), change is tempered by tradition, and tradition is modified by change. Hausman (1987) believes that DBAE theory, although possibly signaling major changes for the field, was formulated as a conservative response to major social changes. Change itself is relative in magnitude. In the 1950s, differences between Lowenfeld's and d'Amico's theories of creativity were matters of debate. Through historical distancing, such differences today seem relatively minor. Any analysis of change and continuity relationships must place these relationships in the context of cultural or professional values, magnitude of change or continuity, variable interpretations, and contingent events.

In theory, DBAE has characteristics highly similar to subjects taught in general education and is legitimated on the basis of its modernity values of change, standardization, predictability, and quantifiable outcomes (Hamblen, 1985b, 1987). Conversely, DBAE is being reinterpreted and resisted on the basis of postmodernity values of tradition, local control, and cultural pluralism. It does not signal a paradigm shift in the sense of providing a totally new way of thinking about art instruction. Rather, DBAE represents a dialectic between change and continuity, between modernity and postmodernity. Furthermore, DBAE is not unusual in its dialectic nature. Relationships between change and continuity and between overall composition and detail afford a means of dialectic analysis for all art education theory and practice. The practicalities of putting theory into practice and the embeddedness of change in past assumptions result in there being no complete, pure paradigm shifts. Which part of the dialectic might predominate in any given instance is dependent on whether change or continuity is relegated to the details — and the particular world view lens one uses for analysis.

REFERENCES

Abell, W. (1957). *The collective dream in art: A psycho-historical theory of culture based on relations between the arts, psychology and the social sciences.* Cambridge, MA: Harvard University Press.

Bowers, C. (1974). *Cultural literacy for freedom: An existential perspective on teaching, curriculum, and school policy.* Eugene, OR: Elan.

Bowers, C. (1987). *The promise of theory: Education and the politics of cultural change.* New York: Longman.

Congdon, K. (1987). Occupational art and occupational influences on aesthetic preferences: A democratic perspective. In D. Blandy & K. G. Congdon (Eds.), *Art in a democracy* (pp. 110–123). New York: Teachers College Press.

Eisner, E. W. (n.d.). *The role of discipline-based art education in America's schools.* Los Angeles: The Getty Center for Education in the Arts.

Focillon, H. (1948). *The life of forms in art* (2nd ed.). New York: Wittenborn, Schultz.

Gablik, S. (1977). *Progress in art.* New York: Rizzoli International.

The J. Paul Getty Trust. (1985). *Beyond creating: The place for art in America's schools.* Los Angeles: Author.

Gombrich, E. H. (1969). *Art and illusion: A study in the psychology of pictorial representation.* Princeton, NJ: Princeton University Press.

Gouldner, A. W. (1979). *The future of intellectuals and the rise of the new class.* New York: Seabury Press.

Hall, E. T. (1977). *Beyond culture.* Garden City, NY: Anchor.

Hamblen, K. A. (1985a). An art education chronology: A process of selection and interpretation. *Studies in Art Education, 26*(2), 111–120.

Hamblen, K. A. (1985b). The issue of technocratic rationality in discipline-based art education. *Studies in Art Education, 27*(1), 43–46.

Hamblen K. A. (1987). An examination of discipline-based art education issues. *Studies in Art Education, 28*(2), 68–78.

Hausman, J. (1987). Another view of discipline based art education. *Art Education, 40*(1), 56–60.

jagodzinski, j. j. (1987). Toward an ecological aesthetic: Notes on a green frame of mind. In D. Blandy & K. G. Congdon (Eds.), *Art in a democracy* (pp. 138–163). New York: Teachers College Press.

Kavolis, V. (1968). *Artistic expression — A sociological analysis.* Ithaca, NY: Cornell University Press.

Kluckhohn, F., & Strodtbeck, F. L. (1961). *Variations in value orientations.* Evanston, IL: Row, Peterson.

Kubler, G. (1962). *The shape of time: Remarks on the history of things.* New Haven, CT: Yale University Press.

Lanier, V. (1975). Objectives of art education: The impact of time. *Peabody Journal of Education, 52*(3), 180–186.

Lederman, A. (1988). Art for the real world. In J. Burton, A. Lederman, & P. London (Eds.), *Beyond DBAE: The case for multiple visions of art education* (pp. 78–86). North Dartmouth: Southeastern Massachusetts University.

Logan, F. (1955). *The growth of art in American schools.* New York: Harper.

London, P. (1988). To gaze again at the stars. In J. Burton, A. Lederman, & P. London (Eds.), *Beyond DBAE: The case for multiple visions of art education* (pp. 26–41). North Dartmouth: Southeastern Massachusetts University.

MacGregor, R. (1988). Curriculum reform: Some past practices and current implications. In *Issues in discipline-based art education: Strengthening the stance, extending the horizons* (pp. 117–126). Los Angeles: Getty Center for Education in the Arts.

Malraux, A. (1949). *The creative act* (S. Gilbert, Trans.). New York: Pantheon Press.

Roucek, J. S., & Mohan, R. P. (1972). An essay on the developments and implications for the sociology of art. *International Journal of Contemporary Sociology, 9*(4), 214–230.

Schapiro, M. (1962). Style. In S. Tax (Ed.), *Anthropology today: Selections.* Chicago: University of Chicago Press.

Stankiewicz, M. A. (1985). A picture age: Reproductions in picture study. *Studies in Art Education, 26*(2), 86–91.

Weitz, M. (1962). The role of theory in aesthetics. In J. Margolis (Ed.), *Philosophy looks at the arts: Contemporary readings in aesthetics* (pp. 48–60). New York: Scribners.

Wolfflin, H. (1950). *The principles of art history: The problem of the development of style in later art* (M. D. Hottinger, Trans.). New York: Dover.

CHAPTER 3

Teachers as Curriculum Developers

Wanda T. May

This chapter addresses the serious, difficult work ahead of us if we want to reconceive what curriculum development can mean and consider more responsive ways to create worthwhile curricular "texts" or experiences in art education. You will meet different teachers grappling with curriculum development in terms of the kinds of opportunities they try to create for themselves and their students in the arts. Because my orientation to curriculum is interpretive and critical, my analysis relies heavily on fieldwork in several art and music classes, conversations with teachers and students, collaborative "workings" and interpretations of these lived texts and dialogues, and the meanings *teachers* attach to their work.

I will draw on several case studies of teachers' experience to anchor my interpretation of curriculum development.[1] This approach reflects how I believe we should center teachers in any discussion of curriculum development. What we can understand about curriculum development is shaped by the interplay of language, power, and meaning (Bowers & Flinders, 1990; Cherryholmes, 1988; Foucault, 1980; Lather, 1991; Rorty, 1989). Our understanding also is shaped by our narratives of experience and critical reflection on them in a personal and social context (Boud, Keogh, & Walker, 1985; Connelly & Clandinin, 1988; Willis & Schubert, 1991). Thus, it would be foolhardy for anyone interested in curriculum development *not* to listen carefully to teachers; to pay close attention to what they say, do, and experience; and to try to understand how they interpret curriculum situated in their own practice.

Staging the text in this particular way, I hope to accomplish two things: (1) demythologize traditional, rationalistic approaches to curriculum development; and (2) provoke readers to reflect on their *own* experience as curriculum developers—as writers, art teachers, and/or with other art teachers—to re-examine what curriculum development could mean.

First, I will present different conceptions of curriculum development, with the teacher as figure and curriculum development as ground. For example, I will not argue about what constitutes worthwhile content in an art curriculum and how this content should be organized in a written curriculum. My focus will be more on what *teachers* interpret as worthwhile curriculum questions and the ways in which they engage in curriculum development in their everyday practice.

Then, I will present three vignettes of teachers engaged in curriculum development, moving from an individual art teacher, to two art teachers discussing their curriculum, and finally to three music teachers in their planning sessions. None of these vignettes depicts traditional images of teachers engaged in curriculum development (e.g., participating in curriculum committees or writing/revising a curriculum guide). In the first vignette, we will learn about Rachel and her efforts to frame and act on a curriculum problem in her fifth-grade art class. We will live in Rachel's head and classroom for a while to understand curriculum development as theorizing and developing *personal practical knowledge* (Connelly & Clandinin, 1988).

Building upon the personal dimensions of curriculum development, the remaining two vignettes illustrate curriculum development as *collaboration*. The purposes, social relations, and potential effects of teachers' collaborative work are compared in the deliberations of teachers across two settings. The first illustrates contrived collegiality between an experienced art teacher and a less experienced one. The second illustrates a more genuine form of collaboration ensuing from the sustained work of three music teachers.

In the final section, I suggest alternative ways that curriculum development can be fostered by those who work with teachers and also point out some of the ethical dimensions of this work. I conclude with the assertion that when curriculum development is viewed as professional development—or sustained, critical inquiry into one's own practice and a group's collective practice in a particular setting—we will have appropriated to teachers the power to create meaningful art curricula for themselves and those engaged in and touched by their efforts.

CURRICULUM DEVELOPMENT AS PLANNING-ON-PAPER

How a teacher articulates his or her image of art, pedagogical wisdom, propensities, and assumptions about what it means to learn art in unit/lesson plans and behavioral objectives, I don't know! Fortunately, when I was an art teacher, I wasn't required to submit daily lesson plans. Had these been required, I would not have had enough time left to act on my inclinations and invest energy in those professional activities that felt more authentic and responsive to me and my students. My curriculum was lived in my love of art and relations with children more than it was meticulously mapped in advance or sketched in detail. It felt right for me and my kids, but I don't know that I could *argue*—theoretically, eloquently, or convincingly—why it was right or best in principle, without persistent self-reference to us in real time and place. I couldn't assume that what I did would be feasible or right for anyone else. Even today, I can't imagine how my curriculum could be described adequately on paper, much less recommended for others.

Traditionally, curriculum development has been equated with *planning*, or something that teachers must do prior to instruction or teaching their lessons. For example, we continue to insist that preservice teachers write unit and lesson plans, prescribing those components and a format that we believe a good plan or lesson should have to promote students' learning. We believe, rightly or wrongly, that novice teachers need prepared scripts to refer to, to feel more secure in an already complex situation called learning to teach. We believe that they need to know how to write such plans because these most likely will be demanded of them "out there." Further, many art supervisors and principals expect experienced art teachers to do likewise, to record their intentions on paper so that their coverage of content can be monitored and the teachers can be held accountable to some external document or agreements made by others. Lesson plans are perceived as necessary tools for substitute teachers in teachers' absences. Even so, most administrators admit that teachers' plans are not carved in stone because teachers are autonomous professionals, apt to make changes for legitimate, pedagogical reasons.

Next, we call it curriculum development when we ask teachers to serve on curriculum committees to create or revise a written curriculum intended to influence more than a single classroom. The products of such labor not only are used as general guidelines for teachers to determine what should be taught at which grade levels. They also are used to hold educators accountable and to support their responsiveness to policies critically influenced by public expectations and hierarchical mandates from various levels beyond an individual classroom or school.

This conception of curriculum development as planning-on-paper is narrow, even in the most traditional sense (Tyler, 1949). Curriculum *development* involves implementation, evaluation, and modification as well as planning. Development suggests that something is always in process or progress, even though periodically we need a sense of closure or accomplishment. The most traditional curricularist, sensitive to the realities of teaching diverse learners in diverse contexts, perceives curriculum development as a sustained, cyclical enterprise, something that will and should be mediated, adjusted, and continually refined by teachers. Most traditional curricularists, then, would agree that curriculum *development* hardly ends with plans committed to paper. *Plan-*

ning ends there perhaps, congealed and concretized for future scrutiny, reference, and revision.

Whereas the above conception of curriculum development acknowledges the contingencies of teaching and teachers' professional autonomy, the expectation is that a written document—commercially produced, committee-generated, or teacher-made—will be the primary referent for teachers to use in developing curriculum and for others to use in evaluating what is taught and learned. This myopic focus on written plans and guidelines as the curriculum, and the creation of such plans as curriculum development, is where we must part company with tradition!

First, despite all arguments resting on teacher involvement, ownership, or professionalism, asking teachers to produce traditional documents decenters them and their students. What to teach and why are stripped of their personal and pedagogical significance, context, and enactment. Developing curriculum in a detailed, written format is constrained, highly rationalized, unnatural-feeling, and artificial compared with the everyday realities, opportunities, and contingencies of teaching. Articulating goals and objectives on paper does not reflect the more complex, subtle dimensions of teachers' images of practice, decisions, or likely justifications for their particular actions. Their commitments and theories are situated in the exigencies of practice and in the stream of their lived experience. Who teachers are and what they experience and do in their daily practice is curriculum development—not writing curriculum guides or unit/lesson plans. However, it is mere routine if teachers do not reflect on, scrutinize, or savor their experiences. Thus, development should be viewed as an intentional, sustained effort to inquire and understand what art and teaching/learning art mean.

When paper plans are the primary referent of *others'* understanding or judgment of what is taught and learned (e.g., principals, parents, policy makers), these judgments will be partial and misinformed, for the same reasons as above. Curriculum is a situated event, emerging as it happens in the dynamic context of classrooms and schools (King, 1986). Curriculum plans (prior to the actual event), which ignore the participation of learners in these events, or assess narrow outcomes related only to intentions without examining their mediation, can never be a complete account of the curriculum.

Finally, no matter how elegantly written or well-articulated a curricular text is, how persuasively it is packaged, or how efficiently it is implemented and used, it is an arbitrary text scribed within a *context*. Some choices were made; others were not. Some voices were included; others were not. Its form and message(s) will not guarantee universal meaning and interpretation by all writers and readers (Foucault, 1980; Hamblen, 1985). There is no such thing as the "right" interpretation or fidelity in such matters. Readers and users will impose their own unique meanings on texts. The possible meanings will be mutually defined by the institutional and sociopolitical context of readers, writers, and users, and their relations.

In summary, relying on written curriculum as the primary referent for curriculum development activities, or to determine what is taught and learned, is misguided and miseducative. While situating ourselves in classrooms may give us a better vantage point, this will not tell us *all* that is taught and learned. Our knowledge will always be partial, incomplete, and contestable, however acquired or constituted.

CURRICULUM DEVELOPMENT AS "WHAT COMES WITH THE TERRITORY"

I define curriculum broadly as "what students have an opportunity to learn — and not." Students learn from what is omitted and ignored as much as from what is presented and emphasized. Eisner (1985) coined such omissions the "null" curriculum. For example, although almost all students say they enjoy art and learn many things, as early as first grade many say that art is not as important as other subjects, particularly reading and math (May, 1985). This perception persists for many throughout schooling (Goodlad, 1984) and adulthood, and school is not the only culprit that influences the perceptions and sustains them. However, much of this is due to the slighting or omission of the arts in the school curriculum and to what students learn (or do not learn) when art is excluded or marginalized. Although the reasons for this marginalization are beyond the scope of this chapter, most of us understand that legitimacy, interests, support, and contestations within and among disciplines and their loose connection to school subjects have a long sociopolitical history (Efland, 1990; Freedman, 1987; May, 1989). Finally, hidden and null curricula also operate within the boundaries of art classes where students have opportunities to develop *particular* understandings and ways of knowing or experiencing art, and not others (Johnson, 1985; May, 1987).

Opportunities to learn (and not) are created and influenced by an art teacher's understanding of art as a way of knowing and a worthwhile area of study; his or her decisions and actions in art class; what interests, understandings, and experiences students bring to class; the communities and cultures represented by students and teachers in a given context, and how these are acknowledged and interact; and the structural and cultural contexts of institutions (allocation of time and resources, social roles and relations, institutional rites and rituals).

The above areas represent Schwab's (1969) four "commonplaces" of the curriculum: subject matter, milieu, learner, and teacher. These commonplaces are an inescapable set of interacting factors that often occur in statements about the aims, content, and methods of curriculum and also figure prominently in teachers' discourse and practices. For example, it is difficult to consider *what* to teach without also considering one's particular students, the social context, and which instructional strategies would best help these particular students experience art. It is difficult to consider a particular pedagogical strategy (e.g., cooperative learning) without seriously considering what it is one wants students to experience and how they might respond to this social arrangement. Thus, there is much more to curriculum and the making of curriculum than subject matter.

While there are numerous influences on what students have an opportunity to learn (and not), a key influence is the teacher. It is the art teacher who constructs, presents, selects, negotiates, mediates, and evaluates what students learn as art in schools. It is the teacher who makes learning meaningful and memorable (or not). More broadly, however, it is the teacher — as an adult and professional — who assumes many roles and responsibilities in educating others about the arts. These activities occur in the most obvious context of teaching K–12 students, to working on curriculum committees, serving as a mentor teacher with student teachers, educating parents about one's program, lobbying for policies or legislation that promotes the arts, team teaching, sharing an idea for an art activity with a classroom teacher, or teaching art in a community center, museum, summer camp, or senior citizen center.

All of the above endeavors are opportunities to learn — not only for those with whom the teacher interacts, but also for the *teacher*. Again, no matter how autonomous teachers perceive their decisions or work, teaching ultimately is a public, moral endeavor. In a variety of ways, teachers create and mediate art curricula. They construct curriculum reflexively in the contexts of classrooms, schools, and communities as students themselves. They rely on their past experiences and personal images of art. They do what comes professionally and what goes with the territory. All of these activities are opportunities for the teacher to teach *and* understand art. How teachers perceive and choose to participate in such activities will contribute to their conception of curriculum development and their identity and place in it.

CURRICULUM DEVELOPMENT AS DELIBERATION

The above distinctions alone neither adequately reflect nor help us to address the complex nature of teaching and learning art, the practical dimensions and social context of our work, or the language we use to describe what we do, have done, should have done, can do, want to do, and ought to do, and why. We respond to concrete situations that make circumstantial demands on our practical and moral perception (Buchmann, 1988; Reid, 1978; van Manen, 1982).

Curriculum development is a professional activity fraught with contradictions and critical choices. Despite the contradictions, thoughtful teachers (those who do not approach teaching routinely as a job) develop the disposition to reflect, consider, choose, and act in ways that are more likely to benefit students than not. Such benefits not only include meaningful things experienced in art. They also include equitable outcomes in terms of who gets to learn what kinds of things, and with what potential personal and social consequences. Our work should help others see and act in the world imaginatively and compassionately.

I view curriculum development, then, more as *deliberation* than as some formulaic procedure disconnected from the serious reconsideration of aims and purposes as well as the possible consequences of our actions for those in our care (Dewey, 1904; Gauthier, 1963; Greene, 1978; Reid, 1978; Schwab, 1969; Walker, 1990). Deliberation occurs inside an individual's head as well as among colleagues creating or acting upon their decisions. This deliberation may or may not result in a document such as a curriculum guide or unit/lesson plan. Even when it does, the document does not adequately reflect what I have defined as curriculum or curriculum development.

In deliberation, our decisions and actions are grounded in the practical and a view of the possible, in what we believe will work and what we believe is worth knowing and pursuing, or what we believe is true, beautiful, good, and just. Some of our beliefs are more tacit than others, and most hardly mirror any formal theory external to our own experience. Nevertheless, our personal histories, social situatedness, current circumstances, and confidence in tomorrow or a "next time" all merge to help us choose and act, more or less thoughtfully, in relation to others in the present.

What, then, does deliberation look and sound like in practice? What does embodying one's curriculum feel like? Teachers' personal practical knowledge involves more than decision making or problem solving because their decisions and actions are tethered to their lived experience as persons with unique histories (Connelly & Clandinin, 1988).

VIGNETTE #1: CURRICULUM DEVELOPMENT AS DEVELOPING PERSONAL PRACTICAL KNOWLEDGE

I now introduce Rachel, an elementary art teacher, and her efforts in curriculum development. This analysis is based on a case study where I observed and participated with Rachel twice a week for several months in 2 second- and 2 fifth-grade art classes (May, 1990). Together, Rachel and I wanted to under-

stand better her beliefs and practice as an art teacher through multiple opportunities for her to reflect, experiment, and do what she perceived would be
most authentic for her and her students. Although her other art classes were
going fairly well, near Thanksgiving (and tears), Rachel said she had a problem, which she defined as "discipline," with her fifth-grade classes.

It was Rachel's third year as a part-time, itinerant art specialist teaching
nearly 400 students in two elementary schools, 3 days a week. Art classes are
once a week in 45-minute periods, conducted in a room designated as "the
art room." Fifth graders are seated four to a table, with six rectangular tables
arranged in a "hexagon" within the classroom space. Despite a quiet arrival
in the hall, students enter the room noisily and fight over chairs. Even though
Rachel devised a seating chart and there are assigned seats, she may or may
not check this chart or insist that all students sit in their assigned seats. She
knows most students by name because she has worked with them for 2 years
in this school.

Rachel begins most art lessons by showing students two contrasting
prints (e.g., Cezanne and Van Gogh), small or calendar-sized, related to the
art concepts she will present (e.g., warm/cool colors, cityscape/landscape).
Most often, she asks students to describe what they see in each print and to
compare them. Sometimes, she asks students to interpret: "What do you
think is going on in this painting?" "How does this painting make you feel?"
or "How do you think the artist felt about X?" She rarely asks students *why*
they think, feel, or believe what they say, or asks them to elaborate.

Many students are not attentive during this presentation, poking each
other, rolling pencils, or kicking each other under their tables. Rachel's presentation is punctuated with polite "sh-sh's" and "You need to listen so you'll
know what to do." The presentation, with questions and answers, usually lasts
about 10 minutes, never includes a demonstration with the media students
will be using, and ends with, "Who has an idea of what he or she might do
today (in relation to warm colors, line, etc.)?" A few students volunteer what
they might create in their art work; most do not. These ideas are not explored
any further but are accepted at face value.

Distribution of materials takes some time because not all of the materials
are out or set up. While a few students begin their art, most wait and wait for
their materials. Even after all students receive their materials, many remain
off-task and become increasingly disruptive throughout the period. Some ask
what they are supposed to do. Several say they "can't think of anything to
make." Rachel may move one or two of the most disruptive students to work
by themselves. At some point during the period, three or four students will
throw paper wads at each other or pencils over the drying line stretched diag-
onally across the room. At least two students will get into a verbal or physical
fight, will be attended to by Rachel, separated, and talked to privately about
their behavior after the class is dismissed.

Students work approximately 10 to 15 minutes making an art object, with Rachel rotating around the room assisting individual students, and students getting out of their seats to seek Rachel's attention. When patiently attending to an individual, Rachel does not seem to notice three students chasing each other around a table or two boys having a mock sword fight with their scissors across a table. Student talk, while making art, rarely relates to the lesson, manipulation of materials or tools, experimentation, or interpretation and evaluation of efforts or work. Most of the students' artwork is disappointing in terms of demonstrating what most students at this grade level are capable of creating; idea development and elaboration; technical skill; care and appropriate use of materials and tools; and perseverance. Most students do not seem challenged by the lesson or materials and express little satisfaction with what they have accomplished or made; few seem curious about what their peers created.

Rachel announces "cleanup time." Cleanup takes 15 to 20 minutes, with increasing chaos. Rachel turns the lights on and off periodically to get attention, but noise subsides for only a minute or so. Art class often runs over the allotted 45-minute period, with the classroom teacher waiting patiently and silently at the door for her students. Students suddenly become quiet upon exiting the art room, and no noise can be heard from the hallway as they return to their classroom.

Rachel's Discovery of Her Image of Art

After Rachel disclosed she had a discipline problem in the 2 fifth-grade art classes, we went to a nearby restaurant after school to engage in one of many conversations about her beliefs and practice as an art teacher. We agreed to tape the conversation so that we would have a record to reflect upon for future conversations.

Rachel: There's always been this struggle for me [as an artist] with where your ideas come from and what's important to you. "Why do you do this if you don't have anything interesting to say?" It's always been kind of a struggle in my own art, getting that established, because I felt really inferior at times with that . . . grappling with that question . . . . I haven't had a lot of help with that at all, and I felt like that was a real key thing that you deal with [as an artist]. I've had life drawing and painting that was . . . a way to get at material, but not a way to get at what it is that drives you to do it.

Wanda: So, the motivation behind it?

Rachel: Hm-hm.

Wanda: Is that why you've focused a lot in your teaching on [students] "getting ideas"?

Rachel: Yeah, I think it's really important to have your own idea and being motivated by that. But, how do you get—I mean, there are things that drive—that turn that wheel [points to head]. Getting that going is not just automatic. Certain things have to be sort of talked through or sparked, and in a group, I think you can really work at that—at least, address it initially.

Wanda: Is this why—I know a lot of times you show kids visuals . . . , but I rarely see you show other kids' examples that they've done, or your own, or actually cut the thing out and do it [demonstrate].

Rachel: Yeah.

Wanda: Are you afraid of stifling their own ideas?

Rachel: Yeah, a little bit. I have done that [shown examples], but it's been the wrong way. . . . Last year, a lot of kids cut out the one *I* did. Well, that was frustrating to me. It was because I didn't show them *other* ways to do it.

Wanda: But, it's an interesting dilemma about how to help kids get ideas.

Rachel: Hm-hm. . . . Maybe that comes in with the trust. . . . If I had more trust in what—how they could—you know, if I had more structure and trust in what they could do, I would . . . [Long pause]. I use some things, I think, for structure and control that aren't really usable that way.

Wanda: Like what?

Rachel: The idea thing. I think if they have an idea as they're sitting down waiting for their materials, that's on their mind—not using their scissors or glue or whatever they might get into.

Wanda: But, you do tend to resist doing examples for them or showing them examples [student-made or teacher-made]. You could have four or five things and then put them up [out of sight, after viewing and discussing them].

Rachel: That's true. That's another way of evaluation, too.

Wanda: That you could evaluate?

Rachel: For *them* to evaluate . . . what it is I'm approving of.

Wanda: That this is appropriate, and this isn't? This is a good idea because . . . this is a good idea because . . . ?

Rachel: Right.

Wanda: Sometimes, I think they might have trouble coming up with an idea. The subject matter is too open.

Rachel: Yeah, you're right . . . because it has in my past only come from me. I haven't had the luxury of having it be stimulated. I don't think I have in my whole art education had that sort of stimulation. It's a good point. I'm thinking maybe I'm frustrated with that, and yet I'm perpetuating that in what I do!

Later in this conversation, I learned more about Rachel's preparation in art education and how she perceived her experience in terms of the program adequately stimulating her ideas for *teaching*. She said that her methods courses focused primarily on projects to do, not on the many ways teachers might structure students' learning, activities, materials, and time. Also, there seemed to have been some mystique perpetuated in the program concerning what art teachers should do that nonspecialists cannot: "[You were supposed to have] these wonderful creative ideas that you've thought of that are so different from all these teachers that have the same of everything."

Then, we discussed Rachel's most vivid memories of art when she was an elementary student. Rachel recalled the art objects she made as a kindergartener and elementary student. She remembered sketching outside with charcoal, doing plaster casts and painting and carving them, making art objects out of cans, and what her art objects looked like in great detail. She also remembered the ambience of these activities.

> It was very wild. I remember kids all over the place, but I remember being really into it . . . . I remember being around a lot of chaos and activity when I was doing it. It seemed wild compared to other classes.

Rachel remembered the objects she made and the social context of making art more than art *content* or "big ideas," such as the elements of design, or art history, and *why* people should learn these things, or what these ideas help people understand or do.

The Problem with "Getting Ideas" as a Curricular Image

Rachel's image of art as "getting ideas" was persistent but vague, and it had visible consequences for her students. Most were baffled and frustrated without much information. They didn't seem to be "getting ideas" well enough to express them in art.

Rachel suddenly recognized that her image of art as "getting ideas" actually promoted student *frustration* rather than learning or understanding. She construed showing examples or demonstrating as "evaluation" or as a structural device rather than as trying to understand what students were experiencing or learning. She distinguished "getting ideas" from projects, procedures, and techniques. While she should have been most knowledgeable about procedures, demonstrating techniques, and how to use materials (given what she said she *did* learn in university courses), Rachel rarely included this in her own teaching. Why?

Rachel's abiding image of art as "getting ideas" was problematic because she was unclear about where ideas come from. Even so, once these sources of ideas might be identified, how do you assess their appropriateness and pedagogical worth in teaching youngsters? To Rachel, was knowledge received or reflexive? Private or public? Did it occur in a vacuum inside one's head, or was it socially constructed and mediated? There is much ambiguity here. Rachel's metaphorical language of *"getting* ideas" suggests that she perceived knowledge (ideas) as external, separate from the knower, artist, or student, given her references to motivation or "stimulation." Legitimate sources of ideas and methods to stimulate them among students remained a mystery to Rachel, even though she told students that artists get their ideas from observation and imagination (derived from Chapman's *Discover Art,* 1985).

Contrary to her metaphorical language, Rachel seemed to have a romantic view of the creative process in terms of where ideas come from and how they get developed: After private independent reflection and imagination, and with little or no influence or stimulation from others, artists think of unique ideas and make unique art objects that communicate something of importance to them. Despite alluding to the importance of teachers being able to "spark" or motivate students' ideas in a group, or students' capacity to do so themselves, in reality, Rachel seemed to think that getting ideas occurred internally in the reflective mind of the individual artist. Thus, Rachel interfered as little as possible in helping students get ideas — or telling them what to make, how to make it, and why.

Without much direction from her teacher preparation program, what would stimulating or "getting ideas" look and feel like to Rachel in a *teacher's* practice (rather than an artist's practice)? In this one conversation, Rachel recognized that she was using "getting ideas" as an unsuccessful control device, naively expecting fifth-grade students to be self-disciplined, quietly and productively reflecting on what they would create without much direction, while they patiently waited for their materials.

Finally, Rachel recalled that art in kindergarten was "wild," "chaotic," and exciting. Despite art activities seeming wild, Rachel remembered being able to concentrate as a kindergartner on making cherished objects. Thus, Rachel may have had more tolerance for disruption in art class than some of us would as teachers. She remembered being able to create art, no matter what was going on around her, and perhaps she believed her students were capable of doing likewise.

Rachel's Curriculum Deliberations as Theorizing

Rachel's exploration of "getting ideas" as her image of art was a form of theorizing. So was her framing of the perceived problem and actions taken to address this problem. In the thick texture and complexity of everyday practice, curriculum development often means identifying, framing, and reframing perceived problems and trying to respond to them so that teaching and learning proceed less problematically toward the goals one has in mind. It took Rachel several weeks to say she had a problem in her fifth-grade art classes, and then she identified this as a "discipline" problem. On the surface, this certainly seemed to be the case.

After initially identifying discipline as the problem, Rachel proposed many different reasons (premises and hypotheses) for this problem and then acted from these different frames of reference to resolve the problem. At first, Rachel reasoned that students' misbehavior in art class was understandable and forgivable when compared with overly rigid classrooms, whether or not her premise was grounded in evidence. Thus, she framed the problem as *context*. Rachel viewed art class as potentially therapeutic for students in the greater scheme of things, and she was willing to tolerate dysfunction. Students needed to "blow off," "relax a little," even though Rachel surmised that students would have difficulty adjusting flexibly to different teachers' expectations. However, Rachel began to understand that her decision *not* to act or impose more structure had mushroomed beyond her control. She was now unable to teach art in the fifth grade.

Rachel then reframed the problem as the *students*. She thought students saw art as "merely play time" and that they weren't taking her or art seriously enough. Thus, her premises shifted from "milieu" or school context to blaming the students (the victims) for their misbehavior. Without changing her curriculum or any other instructional strategies, in mid-October Rachel created and posted rules for the art room and firmly went over these with students. She sought advice from two colleagues—one, a classroom teacher, and the other, an art specialist in another school. Rachel borrowed from these teachers two commercial books on assertive discipline and double-checked the school's discipline policy. (Although she seemed to have a good relationship with the principal, and the principal was just across the hall and within earshot of the chaos, Rachel did not seek her assistance, nor did the principal drop in informally, observe Rachel's teaching, or ever offer any helpful advice.) Rachel did not implement any of the ideas she acquired, except for posting new rules and distribution/cleanup duties. Doing this much, however, forced Rachel to make some changes herself, which she quickly realized were necessary in carrying out her new plan. She *had* to have materials out and better organized so that students could then assume these new responsibilities.

When the above actions did not work very well, Rachel then reasoned that the problem was not having enough minutes in an art period to accomplish what needed to be done (a viable premise). She entertained the idea of lobbying the principal and staff for more minutes per period, reframing the problem as a *contextual* one. Believing this is a legitimate concern of all art teachers, I offered to do a time-on-task analysis for Rachel for several art periods and grade levels to provide her with data if needed to support her case. The results suggested to Rachel that her request for more time was unreasonable (at this point anyway). When seeing her lessons documented in real time, Rachel responded, "No, I've gotta get a better handle on the time I already have! It shouldn't take *this* long to distribute supplies and clean up! This is ridiculous!" Thus, Rachel reframed the problem as an organizational one within her pedagogical control as *teacher*.

When it took more time than expected to see a significant change in student behavior, Rachel hypothesized that students were unruly in art class because they had all their "special" classes scheduled on the same day (P.E., music, and art), with art scheduled in the afternoon (another viable explanation). Students "had no structure at all" on the day that art class was scheduled. Thus, Rachel reformulated the problem as a *contextual* one beyond her control, unless she requested art classes be rescheduled during the week.

Interestingly, among all of these premises and reframing of the problem, what was to be learned and students' interests, abilities, and needs rarely came up in Rachel's discourse. She did not examine or critique students' art after class; find their work particularly underdeveloped for fifth graders (as I did privately); talk about how students had or had not met her goals (beyond on-task behavior); focus on what was to be learned in a particular lesson and share some visible criteria for meeting her goals; or notice what most students struggled with repeatedly, week after week. Rachel seemed unable to make significant connections among subject, teacher, learners, and context/milieu. She continued to view these dimensions of curriculum in isolation from one another. Until we talked, she also seemed unaware of her curricular image of art as "getting ideas," what kinds of experiences as a learner and artist may have contributed to her image, and how this image was being articulated in her practice and understood — or misunderstood — by her students.

While Rachel's image of "getting ideas" persisted, this image was so fuzzy that it gave her little guidance in figuring out what to teach, how to foster students' ideas in the classroom, or how to judge her own success and that of her students in this regard. What kinds of artistic ideas did Rachel want students to get or develop, and why? *This* was the problem — not discipline! This was the central curricular question, and it wasn't a technical, managerial question at all. Had Rachel had a clearer image of what she meant by "getting ideas" — or the kind of content, concepts, issues, and activities that would foster this understanding — she might have known better ways to organize time, materials, and activities toward this end.

As we try to reconceive more meaningful forms of curriculum development in art education, we must encourage teachers' deeper reflections, felt dilemmas, and critique, not just positive discourse or vague images that blur the realities of their experience. Some features of pedagogical life and the autobiographical narratives written by teachers transcend school subjects and give us provocative things to think about with respect to our own practice (Holly, 1984; Hunt, 1987). Teacher lore and practice-centered inquiry have increased tremendously in recent years, but not in art education. There is very little *art* teacher lore to curl up with, savor, and converse with. Much of our descriptive research glosses over, silences, and numbs with flat surfaces. There are few penetrating questions or multiple lenses and voices to help us move deeply behind the most obvious so that we can emerge, seeing and acting differently.

VIGNETTE #2: CURRICULUM DEVELOPMENT AS "CONTRIVED COLLEGIALITY"

Teaching is noted for its professional isolation. On the one hand, we enjoy our autonomy behind the classroom door; on the other, it can be terribly lonely and frustrating. Research tells us that many beginning teachers like Rachel, even in their fourth or fifth year of teaching, leave the profession altogether or resort to overly conservative, unimaginative pedagogy in order to survive (Wittrock, 1986). What can happen when a less experienced art teacher observes a lesson and converses afterward with a more seasoned teacher? Great things for both teachers, right? Wrong, at least in the following case. Collegiality, cooperation, and collaboration are hardly benign, unproblematic endeavors (Blase, 1991). They are complex, sociopolitical arrangements, no matter who is involved or how and why such relations are initiated or encouraged.

The Case of Anne and Martha: What Does "Following the Curriculum" Mean?

Anne and Martha have taught art at all grade levels. Anne, who has been teaching for about 5 years, is the younger of the two teachers and is assigned to two elementary schools and one middle school. Martha, who has been teaching art for over 20 years, is assigned to two elementary schools, one of which is "shared" with Anne. Although they share this school, they had never spent any time together, much less talked about their curriculum and what they do. Their formal schedules weren't amenable to such discussion. I spent over a semester in Martha's first- and fifth-grade art classes, trying to understand better a highly respected, seasoned art teacher's "wisdom of practice."

Mr. Horton, the principal, asked Anne to observe Martha teaching the lower grades and to talk with her afterward about the art curriculum. He expressed concern that Anne is "not following the curriculum in a sequential manner" and has received complaints from some of the other teachers that she is "teaching over the kids' heads." After observing Martha teach a first-grade art lesson and taking copious notes during the lesson, Anne began their conversation.

Anne: Mr. Horton has told me, "Cover line, line, line, line. Cover shape, shape, shape, shape. Color, color, color. Texture, texture, texture."

Martha: Yeah, but Mr. Horton is not an art person. [Throughout the conversation, Martha tells Anne that Mr. Horton is "probably just trying to be helpful." Later in the conversation, she says, "He understands about the fine arts a little bit, but I don't know if he understands about *teaching* art." In other words, it is the art teacher's authority and responsibility to interpret art curriculum and to know how best to teach art.]

Anne: See, my problem with that, Martha, is that I would like to paint lines one day, paint shapes the next day, paint with sponges the next day. You know, I would like to use the materials as paint, paint, paint, charcoal, charcoal, charcoal, and hit on all the concepts that are in our curriculum that way. But he said, "No, go in order." And I said, "What I'm trying to do is hit on as many concepts as possible and use the *materials* as consistently as possible," which is easier for me doing it . . . if I have all my classes painting that week. That makes a lot more sense to me.

Martha: I think if you explain to him that "I'm emphasizing painting, and I'm going paint, paint, paint," then it doesn't matter to him if you're going line, line, line.

Anne: Oh, really?! [seems quite surprised]

Martha: I think maybe that if you explain to him that "I am doing one thing—I'm working through paint, but I'm using different techniques when I'm using paint." I think maybe he thought you were jumping around—I don't know. I don't see where he could say "line, line, line, line . . .," why he would think that was sequential—

Anne: —He wants me to work sequentially—

Martha: —He looks at our curriculum and thinks we teach line, then shape, then . . .?

Anne: He wants me to be sequential that way. See, I would like to mix colors, day one. Day two, maybe object prints with paint. Day three, paint shapes. Day four, paint stencils. Do four different things with paint, talk about . . . okay, day one might be hot colors, day two might be cool colors—

Martha: —Well, when you talk to him, I think it's very natural, he'll know you're doing something in order, and that you are following some kind of plan—

Anne: — Well, I figured he could see that —
Martha: — and not haphazard —
Anne: — with my lesson plans.

The real crux of Anne's problem soon emerges: not whether or not she knows and teaches art concepts or covers the curriculum sequentially, but that she doesn't know how to relate to younger students. Mr. Horton, Martha, and some classroom teachers already suspected this was the problem, but not Anne.

Anne: "Denny's [restaurant] has orange couches. That's to stimulate your appetite. Color psychologists think that's true." And I joke with the kids about that, and I say, "Who knows, who knows? It's just something to think about." That's what I was telling the older kids. I haven't told the younger kids about Denny's —
Martha: — The young kids would not even know what Denny's is. [Both laugh, and Anne picks up on this clue.]
Anne: The other day, I said to the first grade, "Get out your handout." And they said [looks blank and confused] . . . . And so I have to say, "Pick up the picture with the bird" [waves a paper in the air]. "Remember the paper I gave you? Take this out." That is the really hard part for me — figuring out what they need.

Then Anne mentions that Mr. Horton said she ought not use the word "transparent unless it is going to be a major feature of that lesson or a major feature of your next lesson." Things continue to click for Anne.

Anne: I'm being too, uh, too [pause] . . . complex with them. I can tell by talking to you. See, by talking to you, I can tell in what *ways* I am. Now, the "transparent" — that's not a good example. That was just one little isolated thing that I said one time [in second grade], but —
Martha: — I say you can use "transparent" with kids if you make them really thoroughly understand what it means and *why* you need them to know what it means in this particular case. If you were using cellophane, and you were using it on top of something, and you said this was "transparent material," well, then you explain why because you can see through it as opposed to something that wasn't transparent. But, I think if you're talking about transparent *paint* — watercolor — I'm not sure they're going to understand that. I don't think it'll mean anything to them because to them, it's paint. And it doesn't look — to *them* — . . . they can't see through it.

Anne: It's color to them.
Martha: It's color. It's [being transparent is] not going to mean anything.

Anne reflects on her lack of personal experience with primary-level youngsters as well as in teacher preparation. Martha tells Anne that she probably prefers teaching in the upper grades because that is the level in which she did her clinicals and student teaching, and also because the middle school and high school schedules allow for more lessons per week and, therefore, more continuity from lesson to lesson.

Anne: I understand how they [middle school students] *think* more. I think like a sixth grader. I was thinking about this the other day: "Why do I understand how the older kids think so much better than I understand the little kids?" The little kids really seemed foreign to me when I first got here. I was the youngest by 7 years, and I never babysat much. I always babysat older kids, and I did not hold a baby till I was probably 18. I have not had very much contact with little kids, and it's just very strange for me to say, "Take out your handout," and they go [stares blankly]. You know, they don't *understand* [what "handout" even means].

Anne says she's "read her Lowenfeld" (a developmentally focused art education text), which Martha suggested she reread. "But I still can't know by doing that. I have to know by talking to people like you, and by doing it myself, and by making mistakes, by figuring it out from there. I think that's really how I'm going to learn this stuff." Anne's view of learning to teach is supported by others who view expertise in the practical professions as the situated development of theories-in-action (Schön, 1991). Observing another's practice, talking with a colleague, and direct experience in the classroom are more meaningful ways to construct curriculum than is reading a theoretical text.

Anne referred again to her observation of Martha's lesson.

Anne: You explain stuff a lot less than I do. You say, like, uh [pause, searching through notes] . . ., It was only four words long [pause]. I wrote down what *I* would've said, and it would have been about seven or ten words long. . . . Somebody said, "I didn't get a brush." And you said, "It's coming. It's coming." I would have said, "Well, you have to wait. They're being passed out. Jenny's passing them out. You're going to get two different ones, remember? And we're going . . . ." See? I feel like I have to explain *everything*. I *overexplain* stuff that I don't need to overexplain. That's good [for me to learn] because that gets too much attention, time, and energy.

The wisdom of practice (and lack of it) appeared in Anne's and Martha's final remarks concerning their discourse with students. Martha says she tries to "help students think *they* thought of it" (an idea, concept, term), rather than her telling students everything. "Oh, that's a wonderful way to put that," or "I'm glad you thought of that." Thus, she encourages students to assume authority for their learning.

Martha: You know, you were hoping all along one of the kids would. That's why you had them into it to begin with.

Anne: Sometimes I say, "Wow, you're the only one that figured it out so far" [seemingly pleased with herself and confident in this form of praise].

Martha: "Yeah, you're the only smart one in the class . . . and you're all dumb!"

Martha's last statement was said mockingly as a joke, but the sarcasm in how it was uttered suggested she thought Anne's form of praise inappropriate. Such praise establishes a competitive atmosphere and is a poor way to reward a student's response—at the expense of others. Second, Anne's remark suggested she was the sole authority of art knowledge or had the answers, which students tried to "figure out" or correctly guess. Because Martha's remark was said jokingly and dropped quickly, Anne may have missed the point.

All was not lost, however, as Anne was an astute observer, and she considered several important things in contextualizing her classroom observation. From Martha she learned more about establishing communication and positive relations with classroom teachers and principals by being informative, confident, and organized; trying to figure out individual teachers' classroom rules and modus operandi to fit in and not upset teachers or to confuse students as little as possible; having difficulty being "the new kid on the block" and living up to Martha's reputation; having persons misunderstand what is being taught when they only glimpse 2 minutes of a lesson (e.g., using the word "transparent"); and having others judge her competence when they themselves are incompetent in art or are critical of the wrong things ("Aren't leaves supposed to be green?" or "Do line, line, line.").

All the art teachers I have observed plan their curriculum quite flexibly. Some briefly record what was accomplished (or not) in a lesson for a given class and pencil in next week's box on a calendar, or where to "pick up" and what to move on to. Martha did this sort of critical reflection religiously. Pushing her art cart back to her tiny office between classes, she would recant the previous lesson—who did what; why she did what she did in the flow of the lesson; how certain children responded; what she wanted to attend to more closely next time; what worked, how, and why; and what may have missed the mark. She always situated this lesson in the larger web of the other lessons she was weaving.

Some teachers are more sensitive to the rhythms of the school year in their curriculum development than are others. For example, Martha's wrapping paper lesson on "pattern and design" took place near the Thanksgiving holiday. She told me that she could avoid religious controversy (had this lesson occurred near the Christmas holiday) as well as stereotyped "turkey projects," which she knew most classroom teachers would cover in abundance. Students would wrap their clay objects to give as presents to their families. The point is that in September Martha did not know she would follow a unit on clay with a lesson on pattern and design. She thought of this while firing clay pieces, considering the school calendar, and reflecting on what her first graders had already learned and could now experience in a more sophisticated way.

Rachel, on the other hand, paid less attention to the school calendar, despite her students' sensitivity to it. When they did not finish their paper-bag masks one week, a second grader said, "But next week is November *first*." Rachel responded, "That's okay. I don't see what that has to do with your masks." Halloween would have come and gone; had these students planned to actually wear their masks for Halloween? Thus, it seemed that students often were more adept at envisioning the purposes and social context of art than was their teacher. On the other hand, Rachel focused on symmetry and asymmetry when introducing masks, while her students didn't.

In the school shared by Anne and Martha, the student body was small but incredibly diverse. However, there was little attention to the cultural, critical, and historical dimensions of art. Still, Martha was much more knowledgeable about the art of the students' 101 representative cultures in this small school than was Anne, and she incorporated this cultural interest in several of her lessons. She rarely emphasized the principles of design in such lessons. Martha also was more sensitive to the needs of the relatively high population of hearing-impaired students in this school because she had a deaf child of her own. She taught students about differences and social relations by saying things like, "No, no, he can speak for himself. Don't speak for him. He has important ideas, too, and you don't know what he thinks. *He* knows what he thinks, so listen." Martha also was sensitive to cultural differences in terms of responding to those children whose parents were telling them throughout the school year that art is "women's work." She could draw on comparative examples across cultures and help legitimize what students were learning in art. It didn't appear that Anne was very knowledgeable about such matters or attentive to the subtle textuality of groups or cultural differences.

The Absence of a Shared Language

A revealing clue to the quality of art teachers' relations and collaboration is the language they use. Practitioners' language and the ways they interact with one another say much about their social relations and understanding of curriculum. If teachers do not work or talk together often, there is little shared understanding of the meanings they attach to art and their work. This lack of discourse or a conversational community creates all kinds of barriers to teachers' learning from each other and their developing a cooperative, negotiated understanding of curriculum and their own goals and practice.

Rachel viewed "evaluation" as procedural knowledge. Anne viewed "evaluation" as a distinct lesson segment, an academic exercise that attended to the design features of the products that students had just created, not so much as art criticism in the broader sense, or as she and her students trying to assess what they understood or had learned. She noticed that Martha "didn't get to evaluation either." Both lamented "never having time," but Martha also questioned the value of doing this at the elementary level—at least in terms of having a discrete lesson segment called evaluation. Martha construed "evaluation" much as Anne, but she also interpreted evaluation as something embedded throughout a lesson, as well as student independence and self-assessment in light of their joint goals.

> I don't get too many kids any more who say, "I can't" because I think they know whatever they do is accepted . . . . There are still some kids [new to the school] saying, "Is this good?" The other kids know I will never answer that question. I'll say, "What is it that we were trying to do?" Then I make them tell me, and I say, "Do you think you accomplished it?" I won't say, "Yeah, that's good or that's bad." *They* can make up their minds. I let *them* evaluate.

Thus, Martha conspicuously linked evaluation to the goals or purposes of her lessons and the objectives generated by individual students as well. Again, Martha expected students to assume some authority and responsibility for their own learning.

How Was Anne and Martha's Collaboration Contrived?

I remind readers that Anne and Martha's collaboration was contrived from the beginning because Mr. Horton coerced their conversation. Because of his intervention, Anne was put on the defensive. Anne and Martha's dialogue represents a power struggle over voice, authority, and expertise. The full transcript is replete with both teachers talking at the same time and interrupting each other, neither listening too attentively to the other's concerns or advice. These interruptions are visible to some degree in their dialogue (e.g., the numerous dashes). Little professional trust had been established between them because they had never really conversed before, even informally.

Anne had to struggle to interject what and why she did things the way she did, trying to make sense of what she was doing "wrong" and how she might improve her practice. Martha didn't seem particularly interested in what or how Anne taught beyond the immediate problem: Anne's ineptness in teaching primary-level students and Martha's having to hear the other teachers' complaints. Mr. Horton's action put Martha on the defensive as well, straining her relations with colleagues and the principal — particularly if Anne didn't exhibit much "improvement" in the future. According to Mr. Horton's approach and standards, Anne needed to be "fixed," and Martha was just the person to fix her.

After her conversation with Anne, Martha told me that she was "tired of teaching other art teachers what they should have learned in college" or through "common sense" and experience. She was tired of "playing art supervisor" when none existed any longer after the district's budget cuts. Then she admitted, "Maybe I'm getting burned out. I've seen so many things come and go." Martha reflected (on Anne's idealism and effort to learn), "I just can't get too excited or enthusiastic about bandwagons anymore." While Martha warmed somewhat toward Anne as their conversation progressed, she really was not all that interested in learning from Anne. However, Anne persisted diplomatically with frequent compliments such as, "That's a good idea," "I really admire what you do," and "I'm being too complex with them. I can tell by talking to you."

Anne tried to turn the principal's negative criticism into a more positive opportunity to learn than some teachers might have been able to muster in similar circumstances. Given the feel of this conversation, however, I doubt that Anne will ever seek Martha's advice again unless the principal demands it. And given Martha's negative feelings about mentoring, I doubt that she will ask Anne how she is getting along in the future. It is ironic that Martha loved collaborative work with classroom teachers in her other school but not with an art colleague.

Anne and Martha's collegiality was a contrived form of collaboration. Hargreaves (1991, pp. 54–55) describes contrived collegiality as having the following features: (1) it is *administratively regulated,* that is, it does not evolve spontaneously from the initiative of teachers, but is an administrative imposition that requires teachers to meet and work together (Mr. Horton's request); (2) it is *compulsory,* with little discretion afforded to individuality or solitude (Anne's job was on the line, and she was expected to teach more like Martha); (3) it is *implementation-oriented,* requiring or persuading teachers to work together to implement the mandates of others (to follow "the" art curriculum);

(4) it is *fixed in time and space* (one observation and conversation were perceived to be adequate); and (5) it is *predictable,* that is, it is designed to have relatively high predictability in its outcomes, even though that cannot be guaranteed (e.g., the assumption that Anne's practice would improve).

Collaboration need not be contrived, however, and it can work well when initiated spontaneously among teachers themselves in a climate of trust and shared expertise, and geared toward agreed-upon ends of their own making.

VIGNETTE #3: THE CASE OF CURRICULUM DEVELOPMENT AS SOLIDARITY

In another case study, I learned much from three elementary music specialists who had a more authentic, collegial relationship in curriculum development than did Anne and Martha. This is not to say music teachers are more collegial than art teachers; rather, I happened upon this arrangement accidentally when studying two of these teachers' music classes. The pronoun "we" was used so often in our individual conversations that I soon suspected something rich was going on behind the scenes of music classes.

Esther, Marilyn, and Roberta were meeting in 2-hour planning blocks on Thursdays after school. Each teacher was responsible for teaching approximately 1,100 students per week in 30-minute lessons. They wanted to be within reasonable agreement on what they were teaching by grade level and school, and in terms of what they called a "coherent and defensible" elementary music program. They agreed to use the same one-page lesson plan form devised and revised over time by one of the teachers. This parsimonious form included vocal warm-ups (goal, song, pitch matching/reading, and taking attendance); music concept (performing and creating); and a listening lesson (name of music, composer/performer, goal, teaching strategy, and sequence). These content areas represent much of what discipline-based art educators propose for art curriculum and art teaching.

Like the art specialists, these teachers developed curriculum flexibly, using sketchy lesson plans more as a record of what was presented and omitted than what was to be (an inflexible plan). However, they were more explicit and articulate than the art teachers in their conversations about what they wanted to teach and why, and I think this was due to the conversational community they had developed for themselves. They drew upon each other's knowledge and expertise during their planning sessions for ideas, strategies, and reasons for doing things. Rather than their differences straining their relationship, they strengthened and sustained it.

Esther was expert in developing creative call charts, symbolic visuals to help children "read" the story-like structures of musical literature as they listened. She also promoted student improvisation and knew diverse ways to challenge youngsters' thinking when listening and responding to music as well as when performing and creating it. Marilyn was expert in clever movement ideas, knew a rich musical repertoire from which to draw in teaching concepts, and was skillful in politely keeping the group of music teachers on-task without coercion during their planning sessions. Roberta was resourceful in acquiring musical instruments for students' firsthand examination, borrowing videotapes from the public library, and linking opportunities for talented middle school students to work with elementary students. While trying to standardize their curriculum to some degree by "publishing" their lesson plans for each other and discussing them, these teachers always acknowledged the need to maintain their flexibility as individuals and as a group.

All agreed that they couldn't always "get to everything," just like the art teachers. However, in these planning sessions (as Martha did reflectively and independently), the music teachers monitored the concepts and activities they covered and omitted. They discussed what the trade-offs were and why, talked about what students found particularly problematic and enjoyable, and agreed to refocus (individually and collectively) during the following weeks in ways that maintained continuity and a delicate balance of activities over the long run. They discussed which musical selections and activities best helped students to understand music and to appreciate diverse musical forms in social, cultural, and historical context. Much of this literature and broad but deep understanding of music was inscribed in the teachers' repertories, life experiences, and the polyvocal text they created in their deliberations, not from a textbook or curriculum guide.

According to Schwab's (1969) commonplaces, these teachers focused heavily on content (what about music they wanted students to learn and why) and fairly evenly on students (age-appropriateness, learners' diversity, interests, and responses) and teaching (their own pedagogical knowledge and expertise). There was little reference to milieu or context. This is ironic since the music teachers' workplace constraints were oppressive and far exceeded those of the art teachers in terms of pupil–teacher ratio and length of class periods. Further, the experienced music curriculum was of primary interest to Esther, Marilyn, and Roberta in their deliberations. In some ways, this focus is ironic because when one thinks of "planning," one imagines talk that focuses primarily on future content or events to be presented, not those experienced in the present and past. However, a close analysis of audiotaped transcripts of the music teachers' planning sessions for a semester revealed this irony of "presentism" and "historicity" in planning. The analysis also revealed a number of persistent themes and topics in their professional talk, which are summarized below.

The music teachers spent a great deal of time in their deliberations discussing the music curriculum in terms of content: the vertical and horizontal articulation of the curriculum across grade levels, along with coverage and balance. However, these questions were virtually impossible to address without continual reference to the prior knowledge and experiences brought to the curriculum by both teachers and students. While the teachers tried to synchronize their expectations and the content presented across each grade level (horizontal articulation), their deliberations almost always included responsive revisions in the process. Such revisions were provoked by the teachers' close attention to the students they were currently teaching at particular grade levels, the students' diversity, what they seemed interested in, and what was happening in class. Typically, these revisions moved in the direction of planning more challenging, interesting things for students to think about and do, regardless of the grade level.

One of the most important themes of the music teachers' deliberations was their close, abiding attention to the vertical articulation of their curriculum. For specialists who teach several grade levels, this is a very important dimension of curriculum to keep in mind, but it often gets undermined in the curriculum presented or experienced because of various constraints, such as professional isolation, a hectic schedule, short class periods, and the large number of students typically taught. Attention to this continuity forced the music teachers to think about students' experiences at the moment, over time, and in a particular context. Each teacher seemed very interested in what their efforts might "add up to" in the long run. They conceived of this in a spiraling curriculum that increased in sophistication and complexity over time. They thought critically about making linkages; avoided unnecessary repetition and redundancy; created depth over breadth by deciding what was important to learn "as a whole" at the elementary level; and attended to balance (not emphasizing one dimension of music learning over another).

How best to design and organize a curriculum both horizontally and vertically must be addressed by all educators. This is an extraordinarily difficult thing to do. But teaching at all grade levels and planning together made this persistent curriculum dilemma and its pedagogical implications all the more visible and problematic to these music teachers. The teachers skillfully used what was presently going on their music classes—the experienced curriculum—and what had gone before to guide their immediate decisions and long-range planning.

Another significant theme in the music teachers' deliberations was teaching/learning. The teachers' conceptions of musical knowledge and pedagogy hinged critically on their many honest attempts to understand students' understanding and experiences in the classroom. Teaching was viewed as learning, a lifelong project constructed not only in the classroom but in life and in relation to others. These teachers blurred the boundaries between teaching and learning, who is a teacher or learner, and when and where teaching/learning occurs. Like the art teachers, the music teachers drew upon their autobiographies in determining how best to teach/learn particular aspects of music and why some aspects of music were downright mysterious or difficult for them personally to teach/learn. They asked each other questions and demonstrated pedagogical strategies. They shared copies of draft lesson plans and other resources and responsibilities ("I'll call him and order the recorders for us"; "I'll make copies of that for you"; "I'll give you my set of call charts"). While these teachers occasionally did discuss their constraints and issues related to classroom management and organization, these topics rarely came up.

Much was at stake for Marilyn, Esther, and Roberta. Only 3 years prior to my conducting this study did the district hire music specialists by reinstating music in the elementary curriculum. However, this threesome seemed to be off on the right foot. Because they deliberated about their curriculum in this sustained collegial way, their differences enhanced the overall music curriculum, and there was little confusion about what this music program was about in this district or in the specialists' classrooms. What had been accomplished or learned and what was to be taught were negotiated by these three teachers on a sustained basis. These agreements were communicated more easily to principals, classroom teachers, and students. They built solidarity in their professional discourse and a firm base from which to argue for more resources and reasonable working conditions for themselves in the future.

Hargreaves (1991) would define the music teachers' collaboration as genuinely collegial. Their deliberations were spontaneous and voluntary, instigated and defined by them. They created their own professional community. Collaboration was viewed as enjoyable, productive, and professional; these teachers never hinted that this effort was an infringement on their time or autonomy. Their collaboration was development-oriented, demonstrating little interest in implementing others' mandates or applying others' theories/conceptions of music to their own practice. Development was created and pursued for its intrinsic worth. Finally, their planning was pervasive across time and space, not defined or regulated by those external to their classrooms. They created their own opportunities and flexible schedule for planning. They had no arbitrary "deadline" to meet because they viewed their deliberation, curriculum development, and professional development as ongoing and integral to their work as professionals.

Much can be accomplished in curriculum development. However, there must be visible expectations and tangible support for teachers to engage in pedagogical conversations of their own making and concerns for this to occur on a sustained basis. We have to remember that our deliberative texts are created in a context. This leads us to the promise and pitfalls of treating curriculum development as staff development.

POSTMODERN READINGS AND APPROACHES
TO STAFF DEVELOPMENT

Teachers develop curriculum, and things get taught and learned—whether or not institutions promote and support professional dialogue and collegiality among teachers. Schools, districts, and universities are sociopolitical arenas where collective decisions must be made and acted upon in the interest of educating the masses. Sometimes, however, if not often, we forget to educate ourselves in the process. As I have argued elsewhere (May, 1989, 1994), the construction of art knowledge and efforts to reform curriculum/practice must acknowledge these sociopolitical arenas and address the persistent constraints that impinge upon our collective work—not just the work of teachers. We are in a unique position to choose, struggle for, and justify more meaningful opportunities for teachers to learn than we currently practice in our various roles and positions as "teacher educators."

In university art education programs, district offices, and staff development programs, we cannot expect to educate knowledgeable, reflective, critical art teachers if the opportunities we provide them and our own pedagogy do not embody a spirit of inquiry, a sense of community, and an ethic of care. When we work with teachers in our varied roles and contexts, we are "doing" curriculum development or staff development and fostering a particular view of knowledge, teaching, and learning. How effective we are in such endeavors depends on the values we proffer and the social relations we create with teachers in the name of "supporting" them/us in professional development.

Huebner (1966) suggests that different values can be emphasized in curriculum development activities, knowingly or unwittingly. For example, in our discursive practices we could reflect the following kinds of values: (1) *technical* (emphasis on employing a means–end rationality, measured mastery, stating objectives in behavioral terms, management); (2) *political* (looking for ways that peer, community, and administrative support are taken into consideration); (3) *scientific* (trying to find out more about what we have learned from research related to teaching/learning art in particular); (4) *aesthetic* (if and how a search for beauty, integrity, form, and learning for learning's sake pervade deliberations); and (5) *ethical* (how social relations in teaching/learning processes are perceived and valued).

Postmodern educators would argue that the above values—and the discursive practices typically associated with these values—do not occupy such tidy spaces or categories. Rather, they overlap and conflict in messy, complex ways. For example, it is obvious that the boundaries between political and ethical values are not all that clear or clean-cut. And it is difficult to imagine technical or aesthetic values having no political or ethical context, connection, or consequence. Further, it might be difficult for art educators to separate what Huebner distinguished as scientific and aesthetic. Postmodern educators would agree with Huebner's assumption that knowledge is partial, incomplete, contested, and value-laden; therefore, our deliberations will reflect those characteristics.

Postmodern educators would go further by saying that knowledge is shaped by the interplay of language, power, and meaning. Values — what we often take to be knowledge and the "underbelly" interests of our deliberations — are constructed in social relation and in personal/social contexts that have a history (May, 1992). Therefore, our values aren't so "hidden," "personal," or "relative" at all. A critical reading of the "texts" or discursive practices we create in particular contexts can suggest what kinds of knowledge and social relations are valued, how these get constituted, why, and to what effects for all involved (Atkins, 1986; Cherryholmes, 1988). The vignettes presented earlier illustrate the many ways teachers immobilized, energized, and empowered themselves (and their students) through their own deliberations. Those teachers who were more conscious of their decisions/actions, self-critical, and keenly interested in interpreting the multiple ways students constructed and interpreted the curriculum, created more openings, opportunities, space, and choices for themselves as professionals. They recognized that knowledge is negotiated and co-constructed in social context and assumed agency in developing the kind of curriculum they desired to construct.

Now, let me make this postmodern interest in the "nexus" of power/knowledge more explicit by situating curriculum development in one final case: weekly art staff meetings. What are staff meetings for, and for whom are they really intended? As part of a 2-year study (May, 1985), I attended the weekly art staff meetings of one art supervisor and 10 elementary art specialists who taught in a large, midwestern school district. This program served only third and fourth grades, but nearly 6,000 students! Because of the large number of students and small number of specialists, third and fourth graders received art only once a week and then only one semester a year. And because of budgetary constraints, art was taught by classroom teachers in the first and second grades as well as the fifth grade. (In grade 6, other art specialists were hired to teach "unified arts.") This program was critical in that it provided the first formal opportunity for students to study art with qualified art specialists. So, whatever teachers deliberated (or did not deliberate) as their curriculum would have a profound effect on what 6,000 students learned in/about art. (Given the structural arrangements of this program, some might argue that there would be no "significant" impact on students' learning, positive or negative. But the results of my study suggest differently.)

In these weekly staff meetings, curriculum development and professional development were virtually nonexistent in this group's discursive practices. Ironically, teachers and their abiding interests were decentered in their own staff meetings, and both they and their supervisor contributed to this marginalization. The teachers established and maintained this by privileging the supervisor's discourse and managerial/technical interests in most meetings. For example, the bulk of these meetings was spent with the supervisor distributing travel vouchers, reminding teachers of upcoming exhibits, and deciding who would "cover" face painting in a local arts and crafts fair and who would hang students' work at the board of education offices. These are the unrelenting, necessary tasks and duties that go with the territory of any art specialist. We all know this. However, this persistent technical interest and its ethical effects really hit home when I observed the supervisor ask these teachers to paint, during their staff meetings, hundreds of "placements" for an upcoming, state-level art education meeting—which none of these teachers themselves had paid inservice days to attend as conferees and professionals! "Why," I asked myself, "didn't the art teachers protest or try to change this, as unhappy as they obviously were about not being able to attend this conference?" The art supervisor was warm, accessible, reasonable, and supportive, and the teachers seemed to view her in this way, too.

One reason it may have been easy for these teachers to accept their lot on this particular occasion and the overriding technical emphasis of staff meetings was that the supervisor always actively participated in these technical tasks herself. She, too, painted placements. She, too, helped mat and hang students' work. She was "one of them," so to speak, no better, no worse, and willing to contribute to the common cause. Second, every art teacher knows that these kinds of tasks have to be done by someone. If we don't do them, we risk losing visibility and political support for our program, which also translates into our already marginal position and status. To resist or do otherwise could be professional suicide! So perhaps these teachers felt bound to duty and their service ideal, as unpleasant and time-consuming as these tasks typically are.

Third, over the years, this group had developed a shared, tacit understanding of what staff meetings should be like and entail, and how to participate in them. As staff meetings go, these professionals knew of no other way to conduct themselves, except for deciding what time and day of the week their meetings should be scheduled so that all could attend. Fourth, it is easy to perseverate in managerial/technical concerns when one works under the extraordinary constraints most art specialists do. It is difficult to sustain one's energy and to be reflective under those very conditions that force one to worry about managing and organizing time, materials, and students in different schools. If we aren't effective, efficient managers, again we risk our jobs, which already are insecure, no matter how good or committed we are as teachers. Finally, I believe this technical interest held sway in the staff meetings because neither the supervisor nor the teachers were involved in any kind of field-based inquiry or change initiatives that might have provoked their questions — or a different kind of discourse. These teachers were barely able to talk about media and art forms, much less theoretical or pragmatic concerns regarding their curriculum, pedagogy, and students' learning.

Despite the obvious, negative effects of these staff meetings for teachers and students, I saw marvelous openings and possibilities in this setting. For example, by interviewing and questioning teachers privately, I learned that all of them perceived "presenting" and pedagogical discourse at staff meetings as the most meaningful part of these meetings — that is, if and when such discussions were allowed and there was time. Teachers said they wanted more dialogue to "share ideas," "to see how other teachers do things," and to address their practical concerns. One teacher suggested she would like to have "more inservice training by artists and art educators to broaden my horizons and make teaching more interesting and stimulating to myself and the students." Another desired "time off for art teachers to attend art-related conventions or a planned group to the local art museum — a half day off (to do things together)." They were asking for the same kinds of collegial opportunities that several of the other teachers described in this chapter created for themselves. Yet, they didn't ask their supervisor, who might have been responsive to their concerns and even creative in her response.

My research in five of these teachers' classrooms provoked their questions — privately. Teachers found students' reported experiences of their curriculum provocative and replete with surprises. For example, students had very diverse conceptions and interpretations of the meaning of "realistic" compared with those the teachers presented — or thought they did. This led the teachers to question task structures, the micropolitical context of the classroom, and what "content" means, or the many ways this can be interpreted by students in art class. Realistic content, subject matter, and artistic forms had been emphasized across teachers' lesson plans and enacted curricula over other legitimate forms of artistic expression, and the teachers seemed quite surprised and unnerved by this finding.

The art teachers were very interested in what students had to say about which were their favorite/least favorite lessons and which they perceived to be the easiest/most challenging, and why. Again, the teachers seemed surprised that students could express themselves beyond "It's fun" or "I dunno, I just like it" and elaborate on their reasons. Teachers were impressed by students' insightfulness, honesty, humor, and sophistication. And finally, I think these teachers were intrigued by how one could learn a lot of interesting things by observing art lessons, taking scratchy notes, analyzing lesson plans, chatting with teachers and students, asking questions, and simply "hanging out." While teaching *in situ* is complex, demanding, and fast-paced, some teachers have figured out ways to pay closer attention to what is going on, to the subtlety, nuance, and thick texture in their classrooms, and can discern what is meaningful in the blur of their practice.

These are the kinds of questions that art teachers could ask themselves (and their students) anytime they wish, and in a variety of ways! What would help teachers generate questions about their own practice and students' learning? One way might be through collaborative inquiry, such as the kind Rachel and I engaged in. Most university art educators and researchers are familiar with diverse genres of inquiry and methods. They can serve as mentors, helping teachers generate and refine their questions of interest and assisting them in data collection, analysis, and interpretation. They could teach both art supervisors and teachers how to engage in action research and support them in data collection/analysis and multiple ways to interpret these "data" or the texts and stories they generate from such inquiry.

To diminish the asymmetrical relations that already exist within and across institutions, university researchers' data, meaning-making, and actions, however, must be as open to teachers' interpretation and critique as the other way around. Not only would this promote more equitable social relationships, it would make the collaboration itself (members' differences, relations, and negotiations) more central to the inquiry. None of the members' interests should become peripheral or subordinate to those of others, nor should the quest for answers and "final solutions" become privileged over the questions—or the open-endedness (mindedness) of inquiry. Instead, we need to explore more fitting views of theory, research, and practice in the teaching profession, leaving concerns about contamination and subjectivity to scientists (Carr & Kemmis, 1986)! Feminist scholars recommend this (Lather, 1991), as do others who propose we inscribe and report our inquiries differently to make our work more accessible to each other and open to interpretation (Barone, 1987).

The work of university professors, artists, supervisors, principals, and community members could assume a different meaning in terms of teacher education and staff development. Art staff meetings could become a professional forum for curriculum development based on teachers' goals and inquiries into their practice. Most staff development programs focus on importing external innovations or correcting "teacher deficits" rather than celebrating the potential of teachers to define their own learning and create their own meanings (Bolin & Falk, 1987; Howey & Vaughn, 1983). If many art teachers are isolated professionally, how can we build a conversational community? How can we create quality time together in staff meetings, coursework, inservices, public classrooms, or even potlucks? How can we help ourselves imagine our possibilities and then act on those opportunities that imagining and inquiring usually present?

Together, we have the capacity and expertise to suggest a variety of conceptual frameworks and tools we can use to analyze playfully and critically our images of art, professional discourse, university/school policies and practices, collaborations, and what we and our students are learning/experiencing. In order to do these things well, we must be conscientious students of our own practice, much like Dewey put forth in 1904. We need conversation to bring our practice and its consequences to the foreground. We could witness and testify to the heretofore invisible and unspeakable. Rather than recoil from the complexity and ambiguity in our work, we should celebrate the fact that we do not have art curriculum/teaching nailed down once and for all—and never will.

There is much that is disturbingly unaesthetic and oppressive in the life-world of art teachers and in the persistent view that curriculum is an object or a text external to teachers. All teachers deserve to feel creative, cherished, competent, and empowered to co-construct their curricula in the tapestry of their lives and work. Our challenge is to create opportunities for more meaningful forms of curriculum development than a written curriculum. We need to better understand those curricular texts we create, mediate, and embody in our classrooms, language, and experience. Like any text or work of art, these texts are open to interpretation and rich with possibilities for all who can see and feel.

NOTE

1. A version of this chapter was previously published by this author as a technical report entitled *Art/Music Teachers' Curriculum Deliberations* (1990). Most of the case studies reported here, unless otherwise noted and referenced, were funded primarily by the Office of Educational Research and Improvement, U.S. Department of Education. The opinions expressed in this chapter do not necessarily reflect the position, policy, or endorsement of the Office or Department (Cooperative Agreement No. G0098CO226).

REFERENCES

Atkins, E. (1986). The deliberative process: An analysis from three perspectives. *Journal of Curriculum and Supervision, 1*(4), 265–293.
Barone, T. (1987). Research out of the shadows. *Curriculum Inquiry, 17*(4), 453–459.
Blase, J. (Ed). (1991). *The politics of life in schools: Power, conflict, and cooperation.* Newbury Park, CA: Sage.
Bolin, F., & Falk, J. (Eds.). (1987). *Teacher renewal: Professional issues, personal choices.* New York: Teachers College Press.

Boud, D., Keogh, R., & Walker, D. (1985). *Reflection: Turning experience into learning.* New York: Nichols.

Bowers, C., & Flinders, D. (1990). *Responsive teaching: An ecological approach to classroom patterns of language, culture, and thought.* New York: Teachers College Press.

Buchmann, M. (1988). *Practical arguments are no accounts of teacher thinking: But then, what is?* (Occasional Paper No. 119). East Lansing, MI: Institute for Research on Teaching.

Carr, W., & Kemmis, S. (1986). *Becoming critical: Education, knowledge and action research.* Philadelphia: Falmer Press.

Chapman, L. (1985). *Discover art.* Worcester, MA: Davis Publications.

Cherryholmes, C. H. (1988). *Power and criticism: Poststructural investigations in education.* New York: Teachers College Press.

Connelly, F. M., & Clandinin, D. J. (1988). *Teachers as curriculum planners: Narratives of experience.* New York: Teachers College Press.

Dewey, J. (1904). The relation of theory to practice in education. In C. McMurry (Ed.), *The third yearbook of the National Society for the Study of Education* (pp. 9–30). Chicago: University of Chicago Press.

Efland, A. (1990). *A history of art education: Intellectual and social currents in teaching the visual arts.* New York: Teachers College Press.

Eisner, E. (1985). *The educational imagination.* New York: Macmillan.

Foucault, M. (1980). *Power/knowledge.* New York: Pantheon Press.

Freedman, K. (1987). Art education as social production: Culture, society, and politics in the formation of curriculum. In T. Popkewitz (Ed.), *The formation of the school subjects: The struggle for creating an American institution* (pp. 63–84). New York: Falmer Press.

Gauthier, D. P. (1963). *Practical reasoning: The structure and foundations of prudential and moral arguments and their exemplification in discourse.* Oxford, U.K.: Oxford University Press.

Goodlad, J. (1984). *A place called school.* New York: McGraw-Hill.

Greene, M. (1978). *Landscapes of learning.* New York: Teachers College Press.

Hamblen, K. A. (1985). The issue of technocratic rationality in discipline-based art education. *Studies in Art Education, 27*(1), 43–46.

Hargreaves, A. (1991). Contrived collegiality: The micropolitics of teacher collaboration. In J. Blase (Ed.), *The politics of life in schools: Power, conflict, and cooperation* (pp. 46–72). Newbury Park, CA: Sage.

Holly, M. (1984). *Keeping a personal-professional journal.* Geelong: Deakin University Press.

Howey, K., & Vaughn, J. (1983). Current patterns of staff development. In G. Griffin (Ed.), *The 82nd yearbook of the National Society for the Study of Education* (pp. 92–117). Chicago: University of Chicago Press.

Huebner, D. (1966). Curricular language and classroom meaning. In J. Macdonald (Ed.), *Language and meaning* (pp. 8–26). Washington, DC: Association for Supervision and Curriculum Development.

Hunt, D. E. (1987). *Beginning with ourselves: Practice, theory and human affairs.* Toronto: OISE Press.

Johnson, N. (1985, April). *Teaching and learning in art: The acquisition of art knowledge in an eighth grade class.* Paper presented at the annual meeting of the American Educational Research Association, Chicago.

King, N. (1986). Recontextualizing the curriculum. *Theory into Practice, 25*(1), 36–40.

Lather, P. (1991). *Getting smart: Feminist research and pedagogy with/in the postmodern.* New York: Routledge.

May, W. (1985). *What art means to third and fourth graders: A two-year case study.* Unpublished doctoral dissertation, Ohio State University, Columbus.

May, W. (1987). Student responses to media: Implications for elementary art curriculum. *Studies in Art Education, 28*(2), 105–117.

May, W. (1989). Teachers, teaching, and the workplace: Omissions in curriculum reform. *Studies in Art Education, 30*(3), 142–156.

May, W. (1990). *Art/music teachers' curriculum deliberations* (Elementary Subjects Center Series No. 22). East Lansing: Michigan State University, Institute for Research on Teaching and Learning of Elementary Subjects.

May, W. (1992). Philosopher as researcher and/or begging the question(s). *Studies in Art Education, 33*(4), 226–243.

May, W. (1994). The tie that binds: Reconstructing ourselves in institutional contexts. *Studies in Art Education, 35*(3), 135–148.

Reid, W. (1978). *Thinking about the curriculum: The nature and treatment of curriculum problems.* Boston: Routledge & Kegan Paul.

Rorty, R. (1989). *Contingency, irony, and solidarity.* New York: Cambridge University Press.

Schön, D. (Ed.). (1991). *The reflective turn: Case studies in and on educational practice.* New York: Teachers College Press.

Schwab, J. (1969). The practical: A language for curriculum. *School Review, 78*(1), 1–23.

Tyler, R. (1949). *Basic principles of curriculum and instruction.* Chicago: University of Chicago Press.

van Manen, M. (1982). Edifying theory: Serving the good. *Theory into Practice, 21*(1), 44–49.

Walker, D. (1990). *Fundamentals of curriculum* (selected chapters). New York: Harcourt Brace Jovanovich.

Willis, G., & Schubert, W. (Eds.). (1991). *Reflections from the heart of educational inquiry: Understanding curriculum and teaching through the arts.* Albany: State University of New York Press.

Wittrock, M. (Ed.). (1986). *Handbook of research on teaching: A project of the American Educational Research Association.* New York: Macmillan.

CHAPTER 4

Educational Change Within Structures of History, Culture, and Discourse

Kerry Freedman

A consideration of the ways in which people theoretically represent change is important when investigating change in art education. It is important because, although theories are usually developed to describe reality, they often work in ways that influence the construction of reality. The theoretical models people use to categorize, organize, and talk about social life make only certain conceptions of what happens possible and contain certain assumptions about how people think and act.

Theories representing change have various forms that imply particular arrangements of power and processes of transformation. For example, some theories represent change as taking place over a period time. In others, such as theories represented by top-down models of social change, time is not represented as a fundamental issue. A top-down model is unidirectional, linear, and immediate. It presents change as descending from greater to lesser levels of authority and taking place in a smooth, nonresistant fashion. This model, like many models of change, draws upon certain theories of psychology and scientific management that do not attend to complex social interactions. Such models obscure the social interests and conflicts that play important roles during periods of reform (Popkewitz, 1984).

Popkewitz (1984) examines the assumptions underlying two other conceptions of change: center-to-periphery and decision making. The center-to-periphery model begins with results of empirical research that are translated to build taxonomies for educational practice. The model is derived from a systems approach to schooling, which carries with it the assumption that social life is like an organism with progressive, linear patterns of growth. This representation of change supports the belief that knowledge can and should be formally reduced, then used to prescribe action. The decision-making model shifts attention away from expert research and onto the practical decisions made by teachers. This model also carries the assumption that a selected and closed group of people will cause change to occur and that changes are initiated by professional expertise; however, in this case, the group is made up of practitioners. Both of these conceptions of change, while seeming to have different arrangements of power, focus on process as independent from social life. They represent change as an ahistorical, value-neutral process, obscuring the values and interests that underlie educational reform.

The conception of change discussed in this chapter contains the assumption that change in art education, like other social change, must be considered an historical and cultural issue. Even when the time seems relatively short, the assumptions and activities that are part of change are conditions of time and place. I will argue that change emerges within an historical and cultural structure that provides the possibilities, vehicles, and limitations for what educators think and do, and that understanding this structure enables us to gain insight into educational practice.

Conceived of in this manner, change involves certain sociocultural continuities, such as systemic and discursive frameworks, that interact and build on each other. The chapter will explore these aspects of change on three levels. First, the historical and cultural structure that maintains constancy and is a medium for contemporary change will be discussed. Second, debates in sociology and cultural critique about power, progress, and agency that have shaped recent conceptions of educational change will be summarized. This summary will provide a foundation for understanding some of the contradictions inherent in modern education that have resulted in ruptures in structural continuity and promoted institutional transformation. Third, the example of reform in art education will be presented as an historical process shaped by discourses of scientific rhetoric.

HISTORICAL POSSIBILITIES FOR CHANGE AND CONSTANCY

Traditional American mainstream historical writing tends to support the idea that particular individuals control political, economic, and social conditions. This writing is based on the assumption that an individual is capable of "changing the course of history," which suggests that a moment in an individual's life may, in a sense, be isolated from the rest of time. From this perspective, actions and events seem to be discrete bits of time, independent of the historical and cultural frameworks that make them possible, and outside the medium of time and space that suspends them.

An alternative perspective of historical change is to focus on long periods of time as historical structures of consciousness (Braudel, 1969/1980). From this perspective, structure dictates certain constancies over time, providing people with, and being reflected in, collective subjectivities or ways of thinking. Sociohistorical structure tends toward similarity over time by shaping the consciousness of individuals, who then influence others. In part, the influence occurs through the maintenance of values and ideals, such as individualism, embedded in the structure. At the same time, such structure contains elements of transformation. For example, in a sociohistorical structure that maintains the idea of individualism, difference will emerge and initiate change.

In order to understand historical and cultural structure in relation to daily life, we must consider the character of the relationship between continuities and discontinuities that are provided for by such structure and result in stasis and change. Sociologist Anthony Giddens (1979, 1987) approaches this relationship by distinguishing between structure as deep and unobservable, and system as surface and apparent. For Giddens, structure underlies systems, such as institutions or polities, which maintain certain behaviors within them. Structure is the unconscious or "absent totality" that provides the framework for consciousness and the explanation for systemic inventions. For Giddens, the mechanisms through which people see and develop an understanding of change are at the systemic level because we become aware of change only when something in particular has changed. That is, people tend to see change as occurring when something is replaced by something else. However, the change is never a complete replacement and occurs in relation to what came before. Therefore, change emerges as a transformation of, or within, a system.

While Giddens' conception of social structure and system aids in understanding conceptual locations of change, it does not attempt to explain what happens at sites of their convergence (Layder, 1985). Forces at the sites of convergence between structure and system provide direction for social transformations and shifts in consciousness. These forces may be thought of as discourse formations (Foucault, 1972). A discourse formation is a group of conceptually continuous statements bound by the historical and cultural settings in which the formation is realized. These formations have parts that are definable, such as a body of rules, and parts that are not, such as the ways new interpretations of words or theories develop as they are used in new times and places.

Without a consideration of these converging forces, the explanatory character of social and historical contexts is diminished because the contexts become mere patterns of behavior (Layder, 1985). To understand the importance of context to structural convergence as an initiator of change in our time and place, we must look at our culture as an anthropologist looks at other cultures, as problematic and informative. As part of the problematizing, the next section will examine certain arrangements of power and the notions of progress and agency.

DECENTERING THE INDIVIDUAL: CONCEPTIONS OF POWER, PROGRESS, AND AGENCY

In the past few decades, social theory has included new perspectives of change derived from diverse frameworks such as neo-Marxist theory, feminist theory, and French semiotic and poststructuralist analysis. Two related and common concerns of the new perspectives are pertinent here. First, there is a shift in focus from the surface behaviors of people to deeper linguistic constructs. For example, Michel Foucault (1970) focuses attention away from the idea that social change is a natural process and a generalizable condition, toward the transformation of a particular, cultural and historical context that maintains its structure, but shifts certain aspects of social life. He focuses not on the individual as agent, but on sites of contestation in the control of knowledge and discourse (Dreyfus & Rabinow, 1983). Although discourse maintains structure, promoting constancy, power arrangements shift and new social patterns emerge through discursive conflicts. For example, people can be excluded or included through discourse. They can gain power by adopting a discourse viewed as legitimate by people who have power.

Second, a debate about the relationship of individuals to historical structure has been underway. The new vision of the location of individuals rejects the essentialism and logocentrism of the traditional approach to history and brings the notion of the subject as initiator of change into question (Aronowitz & Giroux, 1985). From this perspective, the subject is decentered; either there is no subject or there are collective subjectivities located in certain positions in the social structure, none of which completely controls social change.

These positions illustrate the debate about the notion of agency, which concerns whether individuals intend and act freely. The notion is problematic because we live within rule-based systems that reflect discursive relations, not our own personal being. Actions become possible only after their possibility has emerged; that is, people's actions must first be made possible by larger structural considerations. The conceptual structure of a time and place shapes people's unconscious and the systems that define consciousness through which we construct reality (Berger, Berger, & Kellner, 1973). Therefore, change must occur, at least in part, through a redefinition of self that is directed by the possibilities provided by discursive forces.

The concept of agency also contains the assumption that the interests and actions of individuals will improve their situation; that is, action is conceived of as serving some progressive purpose. However, the assumption of progress is problematic because what improves a situation for one group may worsen it for another. People often do not know or agree upon what will improve a situation, and the outcomes of their actions do not always fulfill their purposes; actions produce unintended, and often undesirable, results. Also, the actions of individuals continue past the events themselves into conflicts with and oppositions to the original intent. Regardless of our actions and intentions, meanings emerge that we do not control.

The debate about structure and agency focuses on the problem of decentering the individual while maintaining the belief that we are able to improve our lives. Structural Marxism provides a perspective that shifts attention from the subject and represents social transformation as emanating from contradictions inherent in a structure (Althusser & Balibar, 1986). Marxist theory represents the proletariat as the agent of change, and change as necessarily based on historical, economic relations. Rather than supporting the idea that individual agents take voluntary action that produces change, this theory focuses on the existence of predetermined structures containing contradictions that instigate change. In his theory of communicative action, Jurgen Habermas (1979, 1984) represents social transformation as a function of linguistic structure and moral development. Transformation emerges from cultural contradictions tied to moral positions in advanced industrial countries where complex rationalities for economic organization have developed (Habermas, 1976). These perspectives reflect the complex relationship between shifts that occur at various social locations, beliefs about what is possible to change in a society, and the notion of how change occurs in that society.

When considering the complex character of social transformation, it is helpful to view structure and agency as a duality, rather than a dualism (Giddens, 1987); that is, to consider agency as inherent to structure rather than in contrast to it. Social transformations occur, reflecting values and meanings that emerge through systemic experience within social structures. In other words, we do not construct meaning personally or arbitrarily; rather, different social locations within systems provide different experiential opportunities for different groups. It is because various groups live within the same structure that individuals within and across groups may be able to generally understand one another, but it is the different experiential opportunities that provide crises between and within groups.

The perspective of change involving the stability of long-term cultural structures that maintain certain contradictions, resulting in crises and transformations of social systems, will aid in the later discussion of art education reform. The next section contextualizes the later discussion by focusing on some of the structural dimensions of the eighteenth-century Enlightenment that continue to influence social life.

THE ENLIGHTENMENT AS A STRUCTURE
FOR STABILITY AND CHANGE

An historically contextualized consideration of contemporary change may begin by focusing on the project of the Enlightenment.[1] A philosophical debate emerged in Europe during the seventeenth and eighteenth centuries about the character of knowledge, nature, and culture. This debate provides structure for some contemporary thought.

Knowledge had a natural form and content that had been masked by corrupt clergy and greedy aristocracy. From this perspective, these authorities had constructed culture artificially and imposed it on individuals in order to maintain their positions of power. The French Revolution and other responses to authoritarian regimes placed tradition in crisis by representing in vivid form the cultural (not natural and necessary) character of politics and social arrangements. The crisis focused on the new idea that men (specifically) had natural civil rights, including a right to knowledge and freedom from political oppression.

The eighteenth-century rationalist perspective represented men as having existed before history and as having constructed society. However, enlightened philosophy also impressed human qualities on nature (Eagleton, 1983). In contrast to culture, which was thought to be based on belief and interest, enlightened knowledge was considered rational, disinterested, and scientific.[2] Scientific knowledge was to direct people to live naturally and humanely. Men were newly supposed to be logical, free-willed, and able to control their own destiny. The enlightened man was to act progressively to improve society and to maintain individual freedom.

A profound disillusionment has been voiced internationally in recent cultural critiques about the limitations of reason as conceived in the Enlightenment project, resulting in what Richard Bernstein (1986) has called "the rage against reason." The disillusionment emerged as internal contradictions in the enlightened vision became increasingly realized. In part, the realization was theorized through analyses of new technologies of social control, which are often psychological and subtle in character (Foucault, 1970). Concerns now exist that such technologies may be even more insidious than the physical controls they replaced, because psychological control is viewed as scientific (and therefore natural and disinterested).

An example of the contradictions in the assumptions of progress in the Enlightenment was the representation of women's place in nature and culture (e.g., Jordanova, 1980; Schwartz, 1984). Enlightened knowledge was not for women. The conception of nature was fundamental to the ways in which reason and culture were understood in relation to women. Women presented a dilemma for enlightened thought because, at one level, women were believed to be more natural and uncivilized than men. This was thought to be proven by women's ability and assumed desire to give birth and women's assumed irrationality. On another level, women were supposed to socialize men so that they could live happily in a communal situation, considered to be in opposition to man's natural tendencies. A woman was to provide a family and home that would be dependent on a man, but also make him dependent on her (Schwartz, 1984).

The pervasive conflicts in gender relations since the early Enlightenment may be considered an example of how internal contradictions in historical and cultural structures promote social transformations while maintaining structure. While individuals were conceptualized as agents of change, the idea of natural free will contained conflicts because only certain types of people were considered "individuals." The struggle to destroy authoritarian institutions contained the assumption that each person was to be a free actor, implying that individuals could act on all possibilities. However, being an individual meant something different for people of different races, classes, and genders.

Since the eighteenth century, much of the Enlightenment structure has been maintained, but has been ruptured by responses to contradictions, such as the movement of women into domains previously inhabited only by men. At one level, what it means to be a woman has been transformed by the requirements of thinking and acting consistently with male social systems in order to gain power. At another level, the systems themselves have been transformed through the crisis of women's transformation (Douglas, 1977).

Educational Reform and Institutionalized Progress

Because education contains and reflects pervasive qualities of the larger social structure, it reproduces structural conditions. Education is founded on a rule-based professional discourse of administration, teaching, and learning that promotes cultural reproduction (Bourdieu & Passeron, 1977). Therefore, educational reform generally involves a conscious and collective effort to transform an institution that will remain fundamentally the same. For example, although public school reform discourse states that reforms will benefit all, the discourse often has fulfilled only the interests of certain socially dominant groups. Recent critical analyses have provided evidence of mechanisms embedded in such discourse that specifically maintain and reproduce the socioeconomic dimensions of structure (e.g., Apple, 1986). These mechanisms work by systematically promoting compliance with the interests of industry and the State in an effort to produce an efficient labor force and sociopolitical consensus.

Directed by such mechanisms of cultural reproduction, school reform in the United States in the late nineteenth and twentieth centuries has particularly engaged two styles of knowing: production and bureaucratic (Freed-man & Popkewitz, 1988). These styles of knowing have focused reform on tinkering with a system rather than a "major overhaul," a technization and abstraction of knowledge (which provide the opportunity to think of practice as being separate from theory), and a sense of fractured or multiple (including bureaucratic) roles to be played by people in general, and teachers in particu-lar. The styles of knowing represent a structurally shaped consciousness that responds to conflict by seeking consensus. As a result, issues of educational reform become part of public discourse to promote the approval of previous social and economic transformations (Popkewitz, Pitman, & Barry, 1986). Therefore, although individual educators may profess a desire for reform to promote leadership in cultural transformation, the system tends to follow so-cial change, promoting stability by maintaining a focus on functionalism and "agreed upon" knowledge.

However, part of the reproduction of structure is the reproduction of its internal contradictions and it is these contradictions that act as catalysts for systemic ruptures and discontinuities. Within a pervasive conceptual frame-work, changes in discourse emerge that respond to contradiction and trans-form curriculum and teaching. In the following sections, the relationship be-tween pervasive and transformative discourses in educational reform is illustrated through an analysis of the historical use of scientific rhetoric in art education.

Social Agendas and the Functions of Scientific Rhetoric in Education

Part of the general functional rationality of the production and bureau-cratic focus of modern education is a scientific rhetoric that has provided the conceptual horizons for reform discourse and has been used, in part, to over-come conflict. The Enlightenment project helped to shape contemporary ideas about the value and form of scientific thought in the development of all public systems. In the process of a general cultural rejection of the meta-physical from such systems, scientific rhetoric became increasingly important in the construction of answers to questions concerning curriculum and in-struction.

Scientific rhetoric is not science per se. Rather, it is an element of certain professional discourses, including educational discourse, that exemplifies some common beliefs about the structure, applicability, and certainty of sci-ence. The rhetoric carries with it the assumption that social life may be sys-tematically tested like the physical world. From this perspective, it is assumed that through testing, objective truths will be discovered and measured, or at least untruths will be revealed. It is further assumed that science progressively moves toward truth by achieving better methods, technologies, and data or by paradigmatic shifts that better provide a description of reality. Finally, scientific rhetoric is considered universally applicable, not only to the physical world it was intended to describe, but to the social world where it is used to prescribe.

Scientific rhetoric does not carry with it a representation of the play of scientific ideas against a structural background of time and place. It does not, for example, represent science as involving an historically constructed ideology entailing power relations influenced by politics, economics, and social struggles (Aronowitz, 1988). Rather, the rhetoric is considered neutral and self-contained, unattached to historical crises and social transformations.

One way to consider the dynamics of scientific rhetoric in relation to curriculum is to focus on the work of Michel Foucault. Foucault (e.g., 1970, 1972) has provided a discussion of how historical representations of human beings have become mechanisms of control. He has explained the human sciences as producing "regimes of truth" through the transformation of subjectivity into an object of study. Through the objectification of the subject, the sciences have redefined what it means to be human.

Historically, the human sciences have taken forms Foucault calls "technologies of the self." These technologies are ways of thinking about the control and possibilities of social life. Change often has been embodied in new technologies to maintain social control.

Foucault represents the human sciences as being constructed through an interplay of discursive relations. These relations are represented in the discourse we use to, for example, construct models of social change. Even the notion that such models can exist, either theoretically or in reality, is dependent on the possibilities provided by particular forms of discourse. Discursive practices govern action by providing the structures of rationality that make certain thoughts and actions reasonable. What counts as truth is determined by the discursive relations of a particular discipline. In education, scientific rhetoric has become a prime factor in the discourse of reform.

SCIENTIFIC DISCOURSE AS SOCIAL REFORM: STRUCTURE AND TRANSFORMATION IN ART EDUCATION

Art education has been shaped by the discursive practices of the human sciences. These practices have determined what may be considered reasonable curriculum content and also have transformed that content. Nondiscursive factors, such as decisions or actions, are formed in relation to and become the elements that sustain discursive activities (Dreyfus & Rabinow, 1983). For example, the decision to accept a certain scientific theory as a framework for art education does not in itself create new concepts or strategies. However, decisions are made based on discursive rules that reflect a historical and cultural structure and result in transformations of institutional and other social systems, such as those of labor and social stratification.

I will now examine how the larger structure of the Enlightenment project has been reflected in the various versions of scientific discourse that have shaped art education. Historical examples will be used to illustrate how, while art education has appeared to change over time, its focus as part of public schooling has been maintained. The illustrations will show how reform in art education has been not merely to enlighten, but to respond to conflicts "in the air" resulting from structural contradictions, such as those concerning individual freedom and issues of race, class, and gender. At the same time, art education has maintained constancy by using scientific rhetoric to support the purposes of an institutional system (public schooling) within a larger social and historical structure (the Enlightenment project).

A History of Scientific Frameworks for Art Education

Scientific rhetoric has been used in schools to legitimate certain economic and social interests and make practice seem objective and ideologically neutral (Apple, 1979). Scientific rhetoric is not a linguistic reproduction of the logic of science or of scientific practices. Rather, it is part of a discourse of rationalization that reconstructs certain, traditional ideals of science, such as objectivity, truthfulness, linearity, progressiveness, and universality, and transforms knowledge and action in schools.

The use of scientific solutions to social problems was part of the structure that made art in mass public schooling possible. When public school art began, in the late nineteenth century, there was a growing general interest and confidence in the utility of science. Science was believed to condemn metaphysics to the past and provide progressive prescriptions for action. There was a focus on the scientific discovery of nature, and anthropology, evolutionary biology, and other sciences had a popular appeal (Noble, 1970). Studies of social life became conceptualized as "scientific" disciplines and the professional social scientist emerged (Haskell, 1977). Art and art education became attached to late nineteenth century scientific rhetoric, in part as a legitimation for work in these fields, important because art reflects changes in cultures, but also because science signified progress.

At least four shifts in the history of art education provide illustrations of how scientific rhetoric has been used to combat social problems and legitimate social transformations. First, public school art was originally based on a science of management that was to discipline the mind and reflected a belief in eugenics. Second, a developmental conception of human capabilities emerged through which normative progress and the notion of talent in children were constructed. Third, art education was used to promote psychological health. Fourth, a contemporary approach to systems theory has guided an information-processing model of curriculum and a new corporate perspective of reform in art education. Each of these orientations involved the use of scientific rhetoric, but their different conceptions of knowledge, reflecting somewhat different structural dilemmas, shaped different representations of art in school.

Industrial Management and Eugenics: A Schooling for Social Reproduction

In the late nineteenth century, a dependence on the scientific expert and manager to construct an art education that would solve social problems developed (Freedman, 1987a; Freedman & Popkewitz, 1988). There was confidence that a scientific common school would promote progress by solving problems of industrial production, such as the necessity for new industries to hire European-trained designers, and resolving social conflicts, such as unemployment among the urban minority and poor. As education became secularized and professionalized, mechanisms of social control were represented as natural, objective, and scientific. Application of the latest expert thinking about labor management was thought to improve education by making it exact and efficient.

Art education became a mandatory part of public schooling to instill designing skills and industrial ways of thinking in urban children. The first state art supervisor and head of the first art normal school, Walter Smith, stated

> The drawing required to be taught in the public schools is *industrial* drawing, not pictorial drawing. It has been so defined in the statute, because the accuracy of workmanship and good taste in design, which sound instruction in drawing imparts to the creators of industrial products, are of general interest and pecuniary value in manufactures, whilst the mental habit which scientific accuracy and love of the beautiful will develop in the minds of all will be a social advantage. (Smith, 1879/1983, p. 226, emphasis in the original)

The drawing education was to socialize common school children to develop a loyalty and responsibility to American institutions and corporate work.

The labor selection and socialization purposes of public art education made it plausible to design curriculum that drew upon a scientific rhetoric in form and content. Curriculum involved a breaking down of concepts and images into what was believed to be their scientific elements. Drawing skills were achieved through repetitive copying of simple, then more complex, adult-drawn examples of geometric designs, maps, "characteristic leaves and flowers arranged according to their botanical orders . . . various zoological forms arranged according to scientific classification . . . [and] technical subjects, such as machinery" (Krusi, 1874/1983, p. 192).

The industrial science approach to schooling reproduced a stratified social system that was thought of as natural. While people could improve their skills and moral values, they were assumed biologically predestined for a certain type of work and social position. Children were taught that there were genetic ceilings on their capabilities.

Coupled with scientific management was the idea that progress would be promoted by the "improvement of the race" through hereditary selection and industrial productivity. Eugenics, which was particularly popular in the United States, was based on the belief that social stratification was a natural result of variance in the innate capabilities of different races, classes, and genders. Eugenics gained credibility, in part, through the selective use of empirical data and statistical analyses (Gould, 1981).

Fundamental to the eugenics movement was an interest in the study of hereditary genius, particularly artistic genius. In schools, even in the late nineteenth century, the few children who might later exhibit artistic genius were not to be "overlooked or misdirected" (Smith, 1879/1983, p. 226). A scientific drawing program was to prepare them for adult artistic production.

Eugenicists claimed that genius was in the blood of northern European men. Blacks and other "races" who made up most of the poor population were not capable of the same intellectual strength. Women, while carriers of their racial heritage, were also incapable of great genius.

Although the factors used to distinguish genius were conceived of as genetically imbued and revealed through scientific analysis, they were actually social and cultural. For example, Galton's (1869) criterion for a diagnosis of genius was an outstanding professional reputation that included an acquisitive "nature" and a desire for prominence (as well as an age of at least 50 years). While critics at the time pointed out that attaining such a reputation depended on a number of social forces, including an education available only to the affluent (Constable, 1905), Galton's thesis supported general beliefs. These beliefs also were fueled by other "scientific" discourse, such as Spencer's theory of social evolution.

The understanding of who should do industrial labor, how they should be managed, and who had hereditary superiority were examples of the use of scientific rhetoric to support existing power arrangements and confront conflicts resulting from structural contradictions. Certain social beliefs were legitimated through a use of methods and procedures designated as reasonable in the scientific community and accepted by other groups. The framework of social beliefs and practices made possible what was considered legitimate science.

To assume that these examples of scientific discourse used to shape and legitimate art education were merely conditions of early public schooling would be misleading. While rejected by the scientific community decades before, eugenics was apparent in commonly used science textbooks at least through 1949 (Selden, 1989), and intelligence testing continues as part of an ideology that seeks to legitimate social stratification (Bowles & Gintis, 1983). A focus on teaching technical proficiency in artistic production remains in art education, and complex understandings of aesthetics and criticism are reduced to the scientific rhetoric of "critical thinking skills" or "decision-making skills."

Instrumental Developmentalism: Psychological Measurement and the Notion of Talent in Children

In the late nineteenth century, while drawing was taught, the production of art was not conceived of as psychological; nor was it generally considered a domain of childhood. Art education required little from the student except a responsibility for repetitive practice and hard work. Art knowledge, as represented in the scientific curriculum of public schooling, was conceived of as universal, objective, and acquired in a testable form.

However, near the turn of the century, art education became influenced by psychological conceptions of individual potential and the notions of natural human development that had emerged during the Enlightenment. Although some researchers denied that normative structures of development existed, and criticized as being antidemocratic the use of statistical procedures to determine innate differences, psychologists such as G. Stanley Hall and Edward L. Thorndike were convinced that norms of inborn potential would be scientifically discovered and used in schools to improve the progress of talented individuals. Hall (1907) stated that this group consisted of middle-class boys.

An element of child study research was the scientific analysis of children's drawings (e.g., Barnes, 1908; Hall, 1911; Sully, 1895). The analysis focused on representational characteristics and formal qualities (such as the use of line, color, and space) that were assumed to illustrate "natural" cognitive development and were interpreted as measures of intelligence. Scientific rhetoric was applied to explain how normal children universally drew objects and represented space in particular ways during certain periods of growth. However, many of the generalizations made about what was natural and normal to all children were based on the analysis of drawings produced by the German children in Georg Kershensteiner's 1905 study. Hall and Thorndike used these drawings and Kershensteiner's descriptive analysis in the development of their theories about drawing. German scientific method was foundational to child study and was brought to the United States by Hall and others who studied the newly emerging experimental psychology in Wundt's pioneering laboratory.

In the context of the social and political milieu of the United States, the new psychology quickly turned to questions of individual differences. However, the scientific conception of individual differences was framed by concerns about the behaviors of social groups. For example, Thorndike was particularly interested in the innate potential for group abnormal and outstanding behavior. His study of individual differences involved a collection of behavioral measurements from an array of quantitative tests. The behavioral tasks were assumed to indicate cognitive capabilities and included tests of drawing (Thorndike, 1913).

Assumed in the early behaviorism was that curriculum content and methods of organization were scientifically isolated variables on which a child's response was dependent. What occurred within the mind was of no importance since the primary function of schooling was to change overt behavior. The focus was on scientifically determined levels of normalcy.

The influence of a rhetoric about normal stages of growth and natural, individual differences in potential transformed school art while maintaining the structural and systemic consistencies of schooling. School was to systematically select and socialize children for work. However, the structural contradictions in the idea of enlightened knowledge for all were reflected in a language of individualism that placed value on some social groups more than others.

Psychotherapy as Artistic Behavior

The conception of "natural" expression in child art represented fundamental beliefs contained in the structure of the Enlightenment project. By the 1920s, progressive education had emerged, drawing upon a discourse of psychotherapy. The progressive schools in New York were private and attended by the children of professional, financially successful people. The therapeutic art education involved procedures, based on Freudian psychology, that were to expel unnatural social oppressions and a mystical conception of cosmology developed by Jung (e.g., Hartman & Schumaker, 1939). The psychology was based on a definition of self, consistent with mainstream values, but considered a universal reality. Artistic behavior was to make public what was personal, but what was conceived of as personal in these children was shaped by their social circumstances.

Although behaviorism developed, in part, as a response to the subjective focus of therapeutic psychology (O'Donnell, 1985), psychotherapeutic rhetoric became integrated with the behavioral focus of public schools. Unlike private schools where the therapeutic focus emerged, public education sought an efficient form of social control (Franklin, 1986). Behaviorism appeared to present an objective alternative to the psychotherapeutic study of what was hidden in the mind. It concerned measurable responses and predicted outcomes and was used to support a testable curriculum; at the same time, art directed by social science was considered a humanizing agent in an increasingly mechanistic and impersonal school system.

As teachers spoke of the art of children as a therapeutic expression, a school art style emerged that was assumed to represent the inner self in a standardized form. While the formal characteristics of self-expression changed over time, certain subject matters, qualities of line, and uses of color were to indicate psychological health. A child's art was not considered expressive if it did not have the appropriate stylistic characteristics. Self-expression was conceived of as natural and scientifically discovered.

By the end of World War II, the therapeutic conception of children's expression through art had shifted. While the early rhetoric focused on social reform through individual adjustment, art education of the 1940s and 1950s sought to develop a mass democratic personality (Freedman, 1987b). The shift was a response to national fears of totalitarianism and preparation for a new international role for the United States. Political tendencies were described as personality traits and mental states. A concern existed that fascism resulted from and propagated an authoritarian personality; a psychotherapeutic form of schooling was needed to prevent such a personality from developing in children. Developing the democratic personality through a scientific approach to art education was considered vital in a world thought to divisively impose unhealthy, undemocratic principles on weak individuals (Lowenfeld, 1947).

The curriculum to develop a democratic personality represented a structural conflict. To talk of expression through art gives the impression that there are free-willed children who act independently and that school is a politically neutral and scientifically healthy place, but the notion of expression involved certain social impositions. While the focus of curriculum was supposed to be on each individual, the manner of expression was represented by groups of children and defined by the scientific authority of a psychology based on normative behavior and shaped by a particular political milieu. Scientific language represented prevalent political beliefs as objective categories of health that could be applied to all schoolchildren.

A Systems Approach: Cognitive Psychology, Corporate Functionalism, and Computer Metaphors

A more recent scientific rhetoric to influence art education is tied to contemporary structuralism. Structuralism, a conception of whole systems based on the assumption that there are discrete parts and that each part defines and is defined by the other parts, has shaped education at least since World War II (Cherryholmes, 1988). In Cherryholmes's (1988) analysis of structuralism in proposals for educational reform, he examines the ways in which schooling is represented. The representation involves a focus on immediate conditions (without reference to the past), on the system rather than the people, on binary distinctions (such as sequence/nonsequence, evaluation/nonevaluation, accountability/nonaccountability, and legitimate knowledge/illegitimate knowledge), and on an illusion of ideological neutrality.

Structuralism in education combined with the rhetoric of experimental psychology, which has become increasingly more concerned with cognition since World War II, the "science" of systems theory, and information processing. As discussed earlier, metaphors of physics and biological systems have long been used for analyses of mental and social conditions. However, since the war, the rhetoric of scientific systems has become incorporated into school art programs through three related frameworks: (1) computer information-processing metaphors, (2) human information-processing models of cognition developed in experimental psychology, and (3) recent approaches to corporate business. These three frameworks of the systems approach have parallel histories, and similar outcomes, but different purposes.

The development of computer models, such as flowcharts, influenced systematic approaches to the conceptualization of complex human activities (e.g., Burrell & Morgan, 1979). In part, the framework emerged from problems of computer programming that sought to simulate human thought processes using the idea of cybernetics. Cybernetics applied to human cognition and institutional practices involves interactive processes and self-correction and, therefore, goes beyond the older model of linear and unidirectional machine processes and management.

The psychological systems framework promotes visual perception and human information processing, considered foundational to aesthetic apprehension and production. From this perspective, curriculum is to teach children when they are "ready" for new information as determined by ongoing processing (e.g., Bruner, 1960). This framework gives the appearance of focusing on individual students because it uses language such as "learner readiness," but curriculum is generalized and students are depoliticized through an emphasis on the psychobiological systems and an assumed common development of thought processes, interests, and attitudes.

The corporate systems framework is intended to organize information, and the "flow" of information, for efficient small-scale production (learning) and large-scale distribution. The corporate framework emerged in art education with a focus on information from certain parent disciplines (e.g., Barkan, 1955).[3] This framework attempts to shape students' thought processes in accordance with a structuralist analysis of professional disciplines that are often incongruous with the lived reality of the professional community.

The use of the systems approach can be seen in examples such as the CEMREL aesthetic education curriculum packages. About the CEMREL curriculum, Beyer (1983) states:

> 1) aesthetic experience is "packaged" in such a way that its meaning and value become transformed into objects to be purchased, consumed, and discarded; 2) aesthetic experiences are useful insofar as they lead to some external objective or end point; 3) the specific activities . . . are relatively standardized or routinized; 4) the evaluation instruments and activities . . . show a high degree of standardization; 5) aesthetic meanings are rationalized, segmented, and isolated; 6) . . . the aesthetic is seen as, in a sense, artificial or unreal; and 7) in acquiring aesthetic knowledge, the student has a passive role. . . . (p. 101–102)

The corporate systems framework may also be seen in the current reform movement in general education and in art education. The national reforms have been concerned with how to develop systems of control on multiple levels to facilitate particular changes. For example, the Getty Trust is the philanthropic funding agent that promotes discipline-based art education (DBAE), supporting the implementation of curriculum that focuses on four art disciplines: artistic production, aesthetics, criticism, and art history. However, in order of a project to be funded by the Trust, the people involved must demonstrate that they are "ready" to be reformed. This can only be demonstrated when the various administrative levels in schools and higher education act as corporate systems.

However, the DBAE reform is not intended only for the people and programs in funded projects. The systems approach to reform requires that change occur at all levels, and the Trust seeks to reform all managerial levels of schooling, the state, and the university. These levels of the system then will work to repair other parts of the system that become inconsistent with the whole. Programs are to be developed to deliver objective, testable results of systemic change that will, in turn, facilitate implementation in other school districts and eventually direct all art education. The perspective involves a sought-after state of equilibrium. Through the reform procedures, curriculum becomes technicized and the content of fluid areas of study, such as art disciplines, is crystalized. Artists, critics, historians, and aestheticians do not require a wealth of knowledge from areas outside the art disciplines to do their work, which is represented as objective, disinterested, and consensual components of a closed system whose purposes do not overlap.

A vital part of this reform focuses on accountability and evaluation drawing upon scientific rhetoric. The primary concern is determining what works. It is assumed that what works in one situation will work in all and that the basis for deciding what works is generally agreed upon. There is little consideration of the relativity of the concept of "what works."

While the Trust has "agency," it began promoting a transformation in curriculum already in motion. The focus on professional disciplines of the fine art community has had currency in art education at least since World War II (Efland, 1987). Also, the Trust's interest in school reform was initiated following, and is politically tied to, the 1970s national reform proposals for general education.

Poststructural and postmodern analyses, such as those of Foucault and Derrida, have made the rules of discourse and the language that we use problematic. While these approaches pertain to what have been called social sciences, they draw upon conceptions of social life not previously considered scientific. Poststructural, postmodern approaches tend not to be linear, positivistic, and progressive. Rather, they make problematic what is represented through and by professional discourse in general and scientific rhetoric in particular, including the belief held dear in education that there are true and objective solutions to well-defined problems. These new forms of analyses provide a possible future for conceptions of change in art education.

Art educators have not always accepted the use of scientific rhetoric in art education. Elliot Eisner's (e.g., 1985) work on educational criticism has been an important response to this foundation. However, the critical work of general curriculum theorists such as Michael Apple, Cleo Cherryholmes, Henry Giroux, and Madeline Grumet has received little attention in art education.

How scientific rhetoric has shaped art education historically illustrates the ways in which structure both limits and provides a medium for educational reform. The rhetoric of science, containing ideals of the Enlightenment project, appears universal, objective, and ideologically neutral. It also seems to be enabling, because it promotes individualism and disciplinary expertise (Gay, 1962). However, it both reflects and hides structural contradictions. Individual agency is conceptualized differently at different times and often promoted in school as an endorsement of reforms already in progress. What was to provide for school improvement has not actually reformed the educational system as much as it has shifted discourse to help reify and legitimate social transformations already in place.

CONCLUSION

Schooling provides a medium for many people's hopes for both change and cultural reproduction. In the United States, public schooling often has been looked to for ways to improve society. Educational reform movements continue to reflect the progressive spirit on which public schooling was built and, at the same time, reflect a desire to conserve the way things have been done in the past and the consciousness that made the past possible.

The historical examples given here bring to light some of the complexities of these and other contradictions in the pervasive structure, system, and discourse. When considering change in art education, the subtle and often hidden ways in which structure resists change become vital to analysis. Also vital to consider are the ways in which discourse makes some things possible. Overcoming the educational mechanisms of cultural reproduction is difficult, as is determining which of these mechanisms to maintain and which to reject; however, the general stasis of education has been confounded, at times, by reform efforts. At such times, alternative discourses have developed, and although change may not have occurred with the desired speed or completeness, the reform discourse has illustrated the conflicts of consciousness it seeks to remedy.

NOTES

1. Theorists refer to the consciousness of the age as "the Enlightenment project" because the work of many people in many disciplines converged to form the philosophical tenets of enlightenment.

2. Conceptions of science in the early Enlightenment were different from contemporary ideas. Then, science focused to a greater extent on formal logic than on empiricism.

3. Although such a focus implies that disciplines in the professional art community, which are generally considered opposed to the rhetoric of science, would direct art education, this has not largely been the case. As information from art disciplines becomes part of public school curriculum and teacher education, it is transformed by the interests of schooling and shaped by the pervasive scientific rhetoric. For example, research in art education doctoral programs has focused heavily on psychological questions since these programs began three decades ago.

REFERENCES

Althusser, L., & Balibar, E. (1986). *Reading capital*. London: New Left Books.

Apple, M. W. (1979). *Ideology and curriculum*. London: Routledge & Kegan Paul.

Apple, M. W. (1986). *Teachers and texts: A political economy of class and gender relations in education*. New York: Routledge.

Aronowitz, S. (1988). *Science as power: Discourse and ideology in modern science*. Minneapolis: University of Minnesota Press.

Aronowitz, S., & Giroux, H. (1985, Fall). Radical education and transformative intellectuals. *Canadian Journal of Political and Social Theory, 9*(3), 48–63.

Barkan, M. (1955). *A foundation for art education*. New York: Ronald Press.

Barnes, E. (1908). Child study in relation to elementary art education. In J. Haney (Ed.), *Art education in the United States* (pp. 101–132). New York: American Art Annual.

Berger, P., Berger, B., & Kellner, H. (1973). *The homeless mind*. New York: Vintage Books.

Bernstein, R. (1986). The rage against reason. *Philosophy and Literature, 10*(2), 186–210.

Beyer, L. E., (1983). Aesthetic curriculum and cultural reproduction. In M. W. Apple & L. Weis (Eds.), *Ideology and practice in schooling* (pp. 89–113). Philadelphia: Temple University Press.

Bourdieu, P., & Passeron, J. (1977). *Reproduction in education and society*. London: Sage.

Bowles, B., & Gintis, H. (1983). IQ in the United States class structure. In H. Giroux & D. Purpel (Eds.), *The hidden curriculum and moral education: Deception or discovery?* (pp. 229–266). Berkeley, CA: McCutchan.

Braudel, F. (1980). *On history* (S. Matthews, Trans.). Chicago: University of Chicago Press. (Original work published 1969)

Bruner, J. S. (1960). *The process of education*. Cambridge, MA: Harvard University Press.

Burrell, G., & Morgan, G. (1979). *Sociological paradigms and organizational analysis: Elements of the sociology of corporate life*. London: Heinemann.

Cherryholmes, C. H. (1988). *Power and criticism: Poststructural investigations in education*. New York: Teachers College Press.

Constable, F. C. (1905). *Poverty and hereditary genius: A criticism of Mr. Galton's theory of hereditary genius*. London: Arthur C. Fifield.

Douglas, A. (1977). *The feminization of American culture*. New York: Doubleday.

Dreyfus, H. L., & Rabinow, P. (1983). *Michel Foucault: Beyond structuralism and hermeneutics* (2nd ed.). Chicago: University of Chicago Press.

Eagleton, T. (1983). *Literary theory: An introduction*. Minneapolis: University of Minnesota Press.

Efland, A. (1987). Curriculum antecedents of discipline-based art education. *Journal of Aesthetic Education, 21*(2), 57–94.

Eisner, E. W. (1985). *The art of educational evaluation*. London: Falmer Press.

Foucault, M. (1970). *The order of things: An archaeology of the human sciences*. New York: Vintage Books.

Foucault, M. (1972). *The archeology of knowledge* (A. M. Sheridan Smith, Trans.). New York: Harper Colophon.

Franklin, B. (1986). *Building the American community: The school curriculum and the search for social control*. London: Falmer Press.

Freedman, K. (1987a). Art education as social production: Culture, society and politics in the formation of curriculum. In T. S. Popkewitz (Ed.), *The formation of school subjects: The struggle for creating an American institution* (pp. 63–84). London: Falmer.

Freedman, K. (1987b). Art education and changing political agendas: An analysis of curriculum concerns of the 1940s and 1950s. *Studies in Art Education, 29*(1), 17–29.

Freedman, K., & Popkewitz, T. S. (1988). Art education and social interests in the development of American schooling: Ideological origins of curriculum theory. *Journal of Curriculum Studies, 20*(5), 387–405.

Galton, F. (1869). *Hereditary genius*. New York: D. Appleton.

Gay, P. (1962). *The Enlightenment: An interpretation* (Vols. 1–2). New York: Knopf.

Giddens, A. (1979). *Central problems in social theory*. London: Macmillan.

Giddens, A. (1987). *Social theory and modern sociology*. Stanford, CA: Stanford University Press.

Gould, S. J. (1981). *The mismeasure of man*. New York: W. W. Norton.

Habermas, J. (1976). *Legitimation crisis*. Boston: Beacon Press.

Habermas, J. (1979). *Communication and the evolution of society*. Boston: Beacon Press.

Habermas, J. (1984). *A theory of communicative action*. Boston: Beacon Press.

Hall, G. S. (1907). Education: A life-long development. *Chautauquan, 47,* 150–156.

Hall, G. S. (1911). *Educational problems* (Vol. 2). New York: D. Appleton.

Hartman, G., & Schumaker, A. (Eds.). (1939). *Creative expression: The development of children in art, music, literature and dramatics*. Milwaukee: E. M. Hale.

Haskell, T. L. (1977). *The emergence of professional social science: The American Social Science Association and the nineteenth century crisis of authority*. Urbana: University of Illinois Press.

Jordanova, L. J. (1980). Natural facts: A historical perspective on science and sexuality. In C. MacCormick & M. Strathern (Eds.), *Nature, culture and gender* (pp. 42–69). Cambridge: Cambridge University Press.

Krusi, H. (1983). Manual for teachers. In F. Wygant (Ed.), *Art in American schools in the nineteenth century* (pp. 191–195). Cincinnati, OH: Interwood Press. (Original work published 1874)

Layder, D. (1985). Power, structure and agency. *Journal for the Theory of Social Behavior, 15*(2), 131–149.

Lowenfeld, V. (1947). *Creative and mental growth: A textbook on art education*. New York: Macmillan.

Noble, D. W. (1970). *The progressive mind, 1890–1917*. Chicago: Rand McNally College Publishing.

O'Donnell, J. (1985). *The origins of behaviorism: American psychology, 1870–1920*. New York: New York University Press.

Popkewitz, T. S. (1984). *Paradigms of educational research: The social functions of the intellectual*. London: Falmer Press.

Popkewitz, T. S., Pitman, A., & Barry, A. (1986). Educational reform and its millennial quality: The 1980s. *Journal of Curriculum Studies, 18*(3), 267–284.

Schwartz, J. (1984). *The sexual politics of Jean-Jaques Rousseau*. Chicago: University of Chicago Press.

Selden, S. (1989). The use of biology to legitimate inequity: The eugenics movement within the high school biology textbook, 1914–1949. In W. Secada (Ed.), *Equity in education* (pp. 118–145). London: Falmer Press.

Smith, W. (1983). Plan and graded programme of instruction in drawing for the public schools of Massachusetts. In F. Wygant (Ed.), *Art in American schools in the nineteenth century* (pp. 226–238). Cincinnati, OH: Interwood Press. (Original work published 1879)

Sully, J. (1895). *Studies of childhood*. New York: D. Appleton.

Thorndike, E. L. (1913, November). The measurement of achievement in drawing. *Teachers College Record, 14,* 345–382.

PART II

Aesthetic Context

Prevailing modernist views of art and aesthetics have been dramatically altered by postmodernist thought during recent decades. The universals of individual expression and structuralism in art, art history, aesthetics, and criticism have been radically transformed through audience interpretations and historical and social contexts of postmodernist perspectives. Meanings of art have become intertwined with contextual considerations. Less dependent on expert pronouncements, meanings change and fluctuate, bouncing about in postmodernist space. The matrices of postmodern aesthetics, interacting with contextual spaces, are explored in this part, ranging from Greene's more traditional humanistic approaches to Wolff's discussion of the limits of sociological context, and Neperud and Krug's study of aesthetics from the "ground up."

Against the background of major aesthetic theories that Efland presented in Chapter 1, an in-depth view of contemporary directions is examined as the context within which art teaching functions. Included are nontraditional views that increasingly figure into art teaching. Although the three chapters in this part differ in focus, art and aesthetic experience in human activity represent a thread of continuity.

Maxine Greene poetically argues for the importance of aesthetic experience in Chapter 5, "Texts and Margins." Drawing upon all of the arts, Greene urges consideration of them as a way of opening new awareness, possibilities, and encounters. She also argues for an integration of an aesthetic education within art education, not in analytic or relativist fashion, but as empowerment in human experience.

In Chapter 6, "Against Sociological Imperialism: The Limits of Sociology in the Aesthetic Sphere," Janet Wolff critically examines the sociology of art from a perspective that does not deny the specificity of art. The chapter contains a very useful outline of sociology's critical examination of aesthetics against which she argues that the aesthetic cannot be reduced to sociological categories without being imperialistic. She develops intriguing views of sociology, postmodernism, and aesthetics that are very important to understanding the transitions outlined in this volume; these views are integral to the debates on art education value orientation.

Underlying the broader meaning and definition of contemporary artistic activity is an intriguing question regarding artistic and aesthetic merit of things created by nonacademically educated "makers." In Chapter 7, "People Who Make Things: Aesthetics from the Ground Up," Neperud and Krug interview several makers who are self-motivated and informally educated. It is argued that, although working outside mainstream categories of art and aesthetics, these self-educated individuals nonetheless are important to the aesthetic experiencing in art education today.

CHAPTER 5

Texts and Margins

Maxine Greene

We are reminded by the critic Denis Donoghue of how many people still consider the arts to be mere entertainments, without practical use. "It is true enough that the arts will not cure a toothache," he says, "nor help very much in surmounting the pressures placed on us by the material world." He goes on:

> But in another way, they are really momentous, because they provide for spaces in which we can live in total freedom. Think of it as a page. The main text is central, it is the text of need, of food and shelter, of daily preoccupations and jobs, keeping things going. This text is negotiated mostly by convention, routine, habit, duty, we have very little choice in it. So long as we are in this text, we merely coincide with our ordinary selves. If the entire page were taken up with the text, we would have to live according to its non-conventional rhythms, even in our leisure hours; because they too are subjected to conventions. (1983, p. 129)

The arts are on the margins, he concludes, and "the margin is the place for those feelings and intuitions which daily life doesn't have a place for and mostly seems to suppress." And finally: "With the arts, people can make a space for themselves and fill it with intimations of freedom and presence" (p. 129). The idea of making spaces for ourselves, experiencing ourselves in our connectedness and taking initiatives to move through those spaces, seems to me to be of the first importance. Some of what this signifies is suggested by Martin Heidegger (1971) when he writes about how things happen now and then "beyond what is" when an open place appears: "There is a clearing," he said, "a lighting" (p. 53) reaching beyond what we are sure we know.

This chapter is intended to open perspectives on art education and on the lives we share in this culture. Hoping to challenge empty formalism, didacticism, and elitism, we believe that shocks of awareness to which encounters with the arts give rise leave persons (*should* leave persons) less immersed in the everyday, more impelled to wonder and to question. It is not uncommon for the arts to leave us somehow ill at ease, or for them to prod us beyond acquiescence. They may, now and then, move us into spaces where we can create visions of other ways of being and ponder what it might signify to realize them. To say "we" in this fashion is to suggest the existence of a community of educators committed to emancipatory pedagogy, now in the domain of the arts. Such a community would have to include in its dialogue women and men of all classes, backgrounds, colors, and religious faiths, each one free to speak from a distinctive perspective, each one reaching from that distinctive perspective toward the making of some common world. And it would have to be a community *sharing* unabashed love for the arts.

To move into those spaces or clearings requires a willingness to resist the forces that press people into passivity and bland acquiescence. It requires a refusal of what Michel Foucault (1984) called "normalization," the power of which imposes homogeneity, allows people "to determine levels, to fix specialties, and to render the differences useful by fitting them one to another" (p. 197). To resist such tendencies is to become aware of the ways in which certain dominant social practices enclose us in molds or frames, define us in accord with extrinsic demands, discourage us from going beyond ourselves, from acting on possibility. In truth, I do not see how we can educate young persons if we do not enable them on some level to open spaces for themselves — spaces for communicating across the boundaries, for choosing, for becoming different in the midst of intersubjective relationships. That is one of the reasons I would argue for aware engagements with the arts for everyone, so that — in this democracy — human beings will be less likely to confine themselves to the main text, to coincide forever with what they are. The "main text" may be conceived of as the ordinary, the everyday. It may refer to what Foucault describes as "normalization," or to what is worthy or respectable. Most commonly, what is worthy or respectable is identified with the white, middle-class values so long taken for granted as "American." Because they have been taken for granted, they seldom have been named; therefore they have not been subject to examination or critique. The effect on the minorities, those made to feel like outsiders, is to make them feel "invisible" in the sense that Ralph Ellison uses the term in *Invisible Man* (1952): "That invisibility to which I refer occurs because of a peculiar disposition of the eyes of those with whom I come in contact" (p. 7). When Herbert Marcuse speaks of the qualities of art that allow it to indict established reality and evoke images of liberation, he may be suggesting the relevance of art when it comes to overcoming invisibility.

When I ponder such engagements with works of art, I have in mind those works considered to belong to the "artworld"; it is important to take heed of

Arthur Danto's (1981) reminder that "there cannot be an artworld without theory, for the artworld is logically dependent upon theory." An art theory can, he says, detach objects from the real world and make them "part of a different world, an *art*world, a world of *interpreted* things" (p. 135). It is a constructed world, therefore, to be viewed as provisional, contingent, and always open to critique. It is also to be regarded as one always open to expansion and revision. The canon, defined by a certain number of men in time past, must always be skeptically conceived and kept open to what for generations has been ignored. My concern, however, is not solely with enabling persons to engage authentically and adventurously with a range of work. I also have explorations of media in mind: paint, pastels, clay, engraving stone. I have written and spoken language in mind: the stuff out of which poems are made and stories and riddles, the material through which dreams can be told, fictions invented, novels given form. I think of musical sounds as well: the melody, the dissonance, the pulse of sounds that compose the audible. And I think of dance: the body in motion with its almost infinite capacity for making shapes, exerting effort, articulating visions, moving in space and time.

Pluralities of persons can be helped to go in search of their own images, their own visions of things through carving, painting, dancing, singing, writing. They can be enabled to realize that one way of finding out what they are seeing, feeling, and imagining is to transmute it into some kind of content and to give that content form. Doing so, they may experience all sorts of sensuous openings. They may unexpectedly perceive patterns and structures they never knew existed in the surrounding world. They may discover all sorts of new perspectives as the curtains of inattentiveness pull apart. They may recognize some of the ways in which consciousnesses touch and refract and engage with one another, the ways in which particular consciousnesses reach out to grasp the appearances of things.

When this happens to people, even very young people, they are clearly more attuned than they would otherwise be to grasping Alvin Ailey's reaching for a celebration at a riverside, Eva Luna's weaving of tales in Isabel Allende's novel, *Eva Luna* (1989), Stravinsky's rendering the dash and shimmer of a firebird, Toni Morrison's searing exploration in *Beloved* (1987) of what it might be like to be a mother and to sacrifice and to stand over the abyss, Keith Haring's stark shapes, or the related works of graffiti artists on city doors and walls. Learning the language of Ailey's dance by moving as Ailey dancers move, entering the symbol system of novel writing and story weaving by composing one's own narrative out of words, working with glass sounds or drums to find out what it signifies to shape the medium of sound: All these lead to a participant kind of knowing and a participant sort of engagement with art forms themselves. Aesthetic education includes adventures like these, as it involves intentional efforts to foster increasingly informed and ardent encounters with art works. Not incidentally, it involves the posing of the kinds of questions — aesthetic questions — that arise in the course of art experiences (Why do I feel spoken to by this work, excluded by that? In what sense does this song actually embody Mahler's grief? What is it about the "Ode to Joy" that makes me feel as if I am coming in touch with some transcendent reality? In what way does Marques's novel reflect, refract, explain, interpret Colombian history? In what sense is Jamaica Kincaid's West Indian island "real"?). To pose such questions is to make the experiences themselves more reflective, more critical, more resonant; and, if anything, art education as it is usually understood is deepened and expanded by what occurs.

The point of both undertakings is to release persons to be more fully present to an Edward Hopper city painting, a Cézanne landscape, a jazz piece, a Bela Bartók folk song, a Joyce novel. This, in part, is what leads me to propose that art education be infused with efforts to do aesthetic education. By art education I mean, of course, the spectrum that includes dance education, music education, the teaching of painting and the other graphic arts, and (I would hope) the teaching of some kinds of writing. By aesthetic education I mean the deliberate efforts to foster increasingly informed and involved encounters with art works that often free people to be fully present to a Cézanne, an Ailey, a Stravinsky, a Joyce. To be fully present depends on understanding what is there to be noticed in the work at hand, releasing imagination to create orders in the field of what is perceived, allowing feeling to inform and illuminate what is there to be realized, to be achieved. I should like to see one pedagogy feeding into the other: the pedagogy that empowers students to "create," the pedagogy that empowers them to attend and, perhaps, to appreciate. I should like to see both carried on with a sense of both learner and teacher as seeker, questioner, someone "condemned to meaning" (Merleau-Ponty, 1967, p. xix), and reflecting on the choosing process, turning toward the clearing that might (or might not) lie ahead. The ends in view are multiple, but they surely include the stimulation of imagination and perception, a sensitivity to various modes of seeing and sense-making, a grounding in the situations of lived life.

Most agree today that we are unlikely to come upon a fixed definition of "art" or a theory that accounts for all the art forms that have been and all that have yet to be. Most would support Herbert Marcuse (1977), however, in his claim that art "breaks open a dimension inaccessible to other experience, a dimension in which human beings, nature, and things no longer stand under the law of the established reality principle." The languages and images in works of art, when persons are released to attend and let their energies go out to them, "make perceptible, visible, and audible that which is no longer, or not yet, perceived, said, and heard in everyday life" (p. 72).

We can all recall experiences that validate what Marcuse wrote. I remember, for example, the subversion of traditional orders of reality accomplished by Braque and Picasso when they enabled so many to realize the significance of looking at the lived world through multiple perspectives. I remember the astonishing disclosures offered through the showing of 10 or so serial visions of Rouen Cathedral rendered by Monet over 3 months, now viewed all together. Like the poplar trees or the grain stacks also painted serially by Monet, the cathedral paintings reveal the changing shapes and even the changing meanings of the structure as the times of day change, the play of shadows, the slants of light. In the case of the grain stacks, we may feel a kind of shifting rhythm of relationship, an expressive rhythm, a play between a small and modest grain stack and a looming, protective one, between the shadow cast by the stacks and the glow of the sky beyond. It is not only seeing something in the visible world that we could not have suspected were it not for Monet (and, perhaps, never have tried to render for ourselves); it is also recognizing that the vision — and the meaning and the pulsation — are functions of a certain way of attending on our part. Monet did not, after all, provide for us a window on a series of landscapes that were objectively out there and objectively "Impressionist" in appearance. Just as in the case of poetry, meanings are ways of relating to things. The meanings of those Monet landscapes (like Velasquez's *Pope Innocent* or Edward Hopper's lonely city streets or Goya's *Disasters of War*) do not reside in the subject matter, in the canvas on the wall, or in our subjectivities when we come to them. Meaning *happens* in and by means of an encounter with a painting, with a text, with a dance performance. The more informed the encounter — by some acquaintance with the medium at hand, and by some use of critical lenses, some consciousness of an "art world" (Danto, 1981, p. 5) — the more we are likely to notice, the more the work is likely to mean. If the questions beat inside us, questions about whether or not something is to be called good art or bad art, what context has to do with it, what constitute good reasons, we are likely to wonder and to perceive even more.

None of this could happen, however, without the release of imagination, the capacity to look *through* the windows of the actual, to bring "as ifs" into being in experience. Imagination creates new orders as it brings, according to Virginia Woolf, "the severed parts together" (1976, p. 72): Imagination connects human consciousness and works of visual art, literature, music, dance. Imagination may be the primary means of forming an understanding of what goes on under the heading of "reality"; imagination may be responsible for the very texture of experience. Once we do away with habitual separations of the subjective from the objective, the inside from the outside, appearances from reality, we might be able to give imagination its proper importance and grasp what it means to place imagination at the core of understanding. Hart Crane (1926), the American poet, spoke of imagination as "a reasonable connective agent toward fresh concepts, more inclusive evaluations" (p. 35). In his turn, the poet Wallace Stevens (1965) talked about the way imagination enhanced the sense of reality, about it being "the power of the mind over the possibilities of things" (p. 31). Mary Warnock (1978) writes of how imagination is connected with feelings or emotions, and how necessary it is "for the application of thoughts or concepts to things" (p. 202). She writes of the need to acknowledge that imagination and the emotions, including taste and sensibility, can be, and ought to be, educated. My argument here is that a powerful way of educating them is through initiation into the artistic-aesthetic domains.

Without imagination, and for all his scientific intentions with respect to the effects of light on appearances, Monet could not conceivably have seen the facade of Rouen Cathedral in so many ways: as a stern embodiment of a dark faith; as a dancing radiant screen of promise; as a delicate lacy veil. Nor could we, without some capacity to transform those strokes of paint, those whites and golds and dark blues into (what?) a rendering of a cathedral, realize that distinctive vision within our consciousness. By doing so, we are very likely to change some dimension of our perceiving, some dimension of our lives.

Wallace Stevens's poetry exemplifies this with peculiar acuity, perhaps especially to those who themselves have tried to write poems. The children Judith Steinbergh writes about, especially Jenny Lusk-Yablick, are discovering dimensions of their own experience even as they are learning to engage with poetry. It is interesting to find this child summoning memories and heirlooms as she (like Stevens) makes a poem of a "lord of sound." Steinbergh stresses "respect for craft," and that summons up V. A. Howard's complex concern for "practising" and "practice." When Stevens (1964) compares imagination to a "blue guitar" that (to the despair of certain listeners) does not "play things as they are" (p. 165), he cannot but evoke a resonance in those who know what it is to look at things as if they could be otherwise and can attend at once to the oddity of a guitar colored blue with strings that can sound an infinity of songs. When Stevens writes of "six significant landscapes" and, letting his imagination play, realizes unexpected possibilities in blue and white larkspur at the edge of a shadow, or in a pool shining "like a bracelet/Shaken in a dance," or in the moon folded in a white gown "Filled with yellow light . . . Its hair filled/with certain blue crystallizations/From stars/Not far off" (pp. 73–74), he creates new connections between selves and things. He maps even readers' landscapes anew. There follow two even more remarkable verses, reminding readers of shaping, sculpting in a space behind grape leaves, reminding us in climax of what it can signify to look beyond.

> Not all the knives of lamp-posts,
> Nor the chisels of the long streets,
> Nor the mallets of the domes
> And high towers
> Can carve
> Shining through grape-leaves.
> (pp. 74–75)

It is not necessary to be a sculptor to share the feeling of discovering by entering a new space — now bringing together knives, chisels, and mallets so that
the star itself can become a carver, a sculptor, shining through leaves. It is
not only the starlight glimmering and outlining the grape leaves that may be
changed through such figurative work. So may the idea or the image of the
sculptor, the one who makes unpredictable forms. In the last stanza of the
poem, Stevens lets meaning like this culminate somehow and explode.

> Rationalists, wearing square hats,
> Think, in square rooms,
> Looking at the floor,
> Looking at the ceiling.
> They confine themselves
> To right-angled triangles.
> If they tried rhomboids,
> Cones, waving lines, ellipses —
> As, for example, the ellipse of the half-moon —
> Rationalists would wear sombreros.
> (p. 75)

All this, too, is wrought by means of metaphor and through the kind of
disclosure of unexpected relationships that brings something new into a reader's world. Experiencing it either from outside or within, the reader cannot
but feel released from confinement and from a type of one-dimensionality,
both of which depend on the rationalists' gaze. When they are challenged to
try rhomboids and cones, they are being lured to allow the lines and squares
to move through a spectrum of shapes to the ellipse of the half-moon. They
may exchange their mortarboards for sombreros, at least now and then, but
they are not being asked to give up thinking or attending to their texts. They
are being challenged to do those things with a greater sense of play and of
panache, of the dialectic of moon and square room, margin and text.

Explorers of the "Arts as Epistemology," like Karen Gallas and her students, are doing just that. Juan's praying mantis and the children's discovery
of the life cycle of the tree are illumined by the imaginative. They are thinking,

they are coming to know. And the coming to know is fed by their glimpses of the half-moon.

Most people can summon up kindred examples if we allow ourselves occasional adventures on the margins, if we let ourselves cut free from anchorage through choice and action, through "belonging to the world" (Merleau-Ponty, 1967, p. 456). I am not suggesting that engagements with the arts ought to lead to denials or distractions from the work that has to be done. Nor am I suggesting that the margins are places for giving way to indulgence, to sensuous extremes. As I view them, the arts offer opportunities for perspective, for perceiving alternative ways of transcending and of being in the world, for refusing the automatism that overwhelms choice.

The alternatives may be grim and, at first glimpse, ugly. They may be like the images in Elizabeth Bishop's "Night City."

> No foot could endure it,
> shoes are too thin.
> Broken glass, broken bottles,
> heaps of them burn . . . .
> (1983, p. 167)

And where the tears and guilt are burning, there is a tycoon who "wept by himself" and "a blackened moon." But this is a view from a plane, we are reminded, through a dead sky; and the poem ends hauntingly and with a parenthesis: "(Still, there are creatures,/careful ones, overhead./They set down their feet, they walk/green, red; green, red.)" (p. 168).

Like the violated children in Charles Dickens's novels, the battered women in Charlotte Perkins Gilman's works, the little ones tormented in Dostoyevsky's world (where, as Ivan Karamasov tells his brother, "It is a peculiar characteristic of many people, this love of torturing children and children only" [1945, p. 286]), like the guerrilla fighters being executed in *The Disasters of War*, like the photographs of scenes from the Holocaust, there are images and figures that speak directly to our indignation, to some dimension of ourselves where we connect with others. They open our eyes, they stir our flesh, they may even move us to try to repair.

I recently saw a painting of the German terrorist, Ulrike Meinhof, fallen on her back after what seems to have been her hanging. Her dim pallid profile and her wounded neck appear in an airless setting where there is neither clarity nor breathing space. The painter is Gerhard Richter, who worked from photographs in his rendering of the *Red Battalion* — all of whom are now dead. "Art," he wrote, "is always to a large extent about need, despair, and hopelessness . . . and we often neglect this content by placing too much importance on the formal, aesthetic side alone" (quoted in Kuspit, 1990, p.

129). Donald Kuspit comments that the "dialectic of concreteness and hazy suggestiveness" in this dim depiction of photographed reality

> emphatically articulates the major fact about the deaths: their incomprehensibility, the suspicion that surrounds them. . . . This is what makes them catalytic of "infinite," morbid speculation, including pessimistic observation of how seemingly "open" images of events can in effect be used to rewrite history by closing it down. This incomprehensibility issues in the slippery, hidden mood of the paintings. (pp. 131–132)

Richter himself apparently sees all ideologies and many beliefs as life-threatening, and he regarded the Baader-Meinhof gang as victimized by ideological behavior per se. We look, we wonder, and the questions come and batter us. We might think of Walter Benjamin (1978) writing of the mangled body as object, of the age of "mechanical reproduction" (pp. 217–251) and the self-alienation to which it leads. He spoke of our inability to incorporate technology, of war being a rebellion of technology collecting "in the form of 'human material,' the claims to which society has denied its natural material. Instead of draining rivers, society turns a human stream into a bed of trenches; instead of dropping seeds from airplanes, it drops incendiary bombs" (p. 242). Images like Richter's may perhaps evoke that kind of outrage; that may be what ideology and terror finally ask of us — along with a fundamental doubt, responsiveness to pallid pointless death.

I am trying to say that one of the functions of the arts is not only to make us see (as Joseph Conrad wrote) "according to our deserts" (1897/1960, p. 30), not only to change our everyday lives in some fashion, but to subvert our thoughtlessness and complacencies, our certainties even about art itself. Prone as we are to oppose aesthetic experience to the controls and limitations imposed by technicism, we may be too likely to find occasions for shelter in the arts, mere fulfillment of unmediated desire. Because so many of our faces are turned toward children whose spontaneity we want so badly to preserve, we choose too frequently to find purity and radiance in domains that touch the depths as well as the heights of being human in the world.

It is because I believe it so important for those of us who teach to be reminded of this that I value encounters with artists like Joseph Beuys so much, and with Robert Wilson, and Philip Glass, and William Balcon, and Toni Morrison, and Martha Clarke, and John Quare. Their association with the avant-garde or the postmodern is not the important thing. Apart from the complex quality and, often, the eerie beauty of their works, there is the problematic each embodies, the restiveness with limits, the peculiar sense of some approximation of "the ellipse of the half-moon." I think, for example, of Jenny Holzer and her mobile neon messages sculpting the spirals of the

Guggenheim Museum not long ago—red, white, like electric signs, with the phrases and the words colliding, overlapping, the meanings rising and falling. There are truisms spelled out by the electric bulbs and inscribed on marble stools, truisms sometimes as vague as Richter's images, sometimes startlingly and embarrassingly clear. There are one-liners: "The Family Is Living on Borrowed Time," "Abuse of Power Comes as No Surprise," parodies and simplifications, once on the walls of buildings and bus stops, now in distinguished museums (Waldman, 1989). Most recently, her work has been at the Venice Biennale, where it won a first prize. There are what she calls "Laments," introspective in the first person: "With only my mind to protect me I go into Days"; "What I fear is in a box with fur to muffle it. Every day I do nothing important because I am scared blank and lazy" (Waldman, 1989, p. 18).

I watch them move by, become cliché, become collage, become conceptual art, minimal art. I watch a language of signs rendering the visible world invisible at a moment when I am celebrating the slow emergence of my world into visibility. "I try not," Holzer says, "to make it completely random or sloppy, but there still has to be a wild part in it. In the writing you have to go off into the stratosphere and then come back down. That's what I like, when things spin out of control but then are pulled back so that they're available to you. I want them to be accessible, but not so easy that you throw them away after a second or two" (Waldman, 1989, p. 15). Appreciative as I am of her moving between randomness and control, of her using language to move beyond the tangible, I am caught in questions again about meaning and reference, and I find the questions almost as important as the moments of disclosure. Some of the same questions arise, I realize, when I try to penetrate the mythic, the secret, parts of Toni Morrison's *Beloved* or go back to William Faulkner's "The Bear," or try to discover (at this late date) what Herman Melville really intended by "the whiteness of the whale," or what "confidence" and "trust" actually signified in his strange story called "The Confidence Man."

Of course we need to use criticism, if only to help us elucidate, to help us notice what is there to be noticed, but we also have to find out what the critics individually assume, as we have to look from various critical vantage points at works we are trying to make clear. We have at once to resist the pull of expertise, and to be conscious of "hype" and fetishization and the ways in which the market determines value and choice. Today we who are teachers have an obligation to be aware of and wary of efforts to determine from above (or from some apocryphal center) what is acceptable in the world of art and what has to be branded unacceptable because it is charged with being pornographic, impious, homosexual, unpatriotic, or obscene. To issue edicts like the ones we recently have read, to utter proscriptions and prescriptions may be within the law. If, however, we stand by the view that experience always holds more than can be predicted, and that imagination creates openings to the unpredictable, we cannot but be chilled by what the recent prohibitions imply. Realizing, too, that creative and appreciative encounters in the domains of the arts depend on imaginative energies, we can only anticipate a lulling and a limiting consequence—miseducative in the deepest sense. We are bound to ponder as authentically and critically as we can what a Robert Mapplethorpe exhibition means to us as persons and what its banning means. The same is true with regard to Andres Serrano and Karen Finley and those who burn the flag. And it might well have been true when *Marat/Sade* and the musical *Hair* presented frontal nudity on the stage. We do not necessarily want to expose children to Mapplethorpe or Finley, although there may well be ways of doing so. We do, however, want to learn ourselves—and enable them to learn—what it is to make judgments on the grounds of lived experience and, at once, in relation to community norms. Trying to open persons to the new and the multiple, we want ourselves to break through some of the crusts of convention, the distortions of fetishism, the sour tastes of narrow faiths.

This requires us to be in continuing quest of ourselves, even as it requires that we do what we can to enable as many of the young as possible to crack the codes that prevent so many of them from engaging with works of art. Paintings, novels, works of music are not likely to be realized by untutored consciousness if they are made to appear in enclaves, out of reach, in an esoteric or somehow timeless realm. John Dewey (1934) said that works of art are too frequently presented as if they have no roots in cultural life, as if they are specimens of fine art and nothing else. Art objects are made to seem remote to ordinary people, as are many fine fictions and music that reaches beyond the accustomed horizons of sound. Set on pedestals, actual or figurative, art forms are removed "from the scope of common or community life" (p. 6). Because they are deliberately set apart from ordinary experience, they serve largely as "insignia of taste and certitude" (p. 9). They confirm people in their elitism; they serve the interests of social power. Walter Benjamin (1978), with somewhat the same idea in mind, wrote of concepts like eternal value and mystery, and used the word "aura" (pp. 222–223) to signify a distance, a uniqueness, as well as an embeddedness in tradition that made art works inaccessible to the mass of people. John Berger (1984) writes about the ways in which works of art are "enveloped in an atmosphere of entirely bogus religiosity. Works of art are discussed and presented as though they were holy relics: relics which are first and foremost evidence of their own survival" (p. 21). Later, he makes the point that the visual arts have always existed in a preserve, magical or sacred or physical, and that later "the preserve of art became a social one. It entered the culture of the ruling class, while physically it was set apart and isolated in their palaces and houses. During all this history, the authority of art was inseparable from the particular authority of the preserve" (p. 33).

There is not only the distance established by those locating art forms in a "preserve" of some kind; there is the distance created by commodification, by esotericism, by false claims of "realism," by mystifications having to do with women, people of color, the poor, and the excluded. There is also the separation caused by innocence, by lack of knowing, by a reliance on the uninformed, the innocent, or those conditioned by the media. Nor are the arts likely to open themselves naturally to young people who have been systematically demeaned, excluded from what others think to be the "goods" of their own world. John Berger (1984) argues strongly against the view that the arts can be understood spontaneously. He writes:

> The idea of innocence faces two ways. By refusing to enter a conspiracy, one remains innocent of that conspiracy. But to remain innocent may also be to remain ignorant. The issue is not between innocence and knowledge (or between the natural and the cultural) but between a total approach to art which attempts to relate it to every aspect of experience and the esoteric approach of a few specialized experts who are the clerks of the nostalgia of a ruling class in decline. (In decline not before the proletariat, but before the new power of the corporation and the state.) The real question is: to whom does the meaning of the art of the past properly belong? To those who can apply it to their own lives, or to a cultural hierarchy of relic specialists? (p. 32)

This leads back to my argument for a pedagogy that integrates art education and aesthetic education. Yes, it should be education for more informed and imaginative awareness, but it also should be education in the kinds of critical transactions that empower persons to resist both elitism and objectivism, that allow them to read and to name, to write and to rewrite their own lived worlds.

It is clear enough, of course, that there can be great enjoyment of pieces of music, paintings, film, dance performances, and (to a lesser extent) literary works grasped in moments of immediacy, without the interaction of outer and inner visions so essential if works of art are to be brought fully alive. It is clear enough, as well, that there is always a danger of imposing alienating standards, of suggesting a single "right" way of looking at a Monet poplar painting, of discerning the mirrored king and queen behind the artist in Velasquez's always problematic *Las Meninas,* of making sense of the "madwoman" in *Jane Eyre,* of interpreting the film *The Third Man* in one particular way. To take an opposing view and teach with the suggestion that it is, in any case, all subjective, "a matter of taste," would be equivalent to the kind of permissivism that leads to a mindless relativism. To assume, for instance, that nothing is missed if we attend the ballet *Giselle* and wait simply for the "story" to unfold, for Giselle to go mad and be abandoned, is to lose the possibility of an aesthetic experience with the dance called "Giselle." To judge the worth of *War and Peace* by its fidelity to the Napoleonic Wars or of *A Streetcar Named Desire* by its fidelity to New Orleans or the "truth" it tells about some kinds of pathology, is again to avoid the aesthetic potentialities in each work, to refuse the illusion, to treat it as just another window on the world.

Dewey reminded his readers of how necessary it was for their imaginative and perceptual energies to reach toward a painting or a poem if it was to be transmuted into an aesthetic object *for* the one perceiving it. He continued to insist that the aesthetic is not an intruder from without, not an affair "for odd moments" (1934, p. 54). Like many others, he used the example of a crowd being conducted rapidly through a gallery by a guide. Donoghue (1983) has similar images in mind when he speaks of the "cherishing bureaucracy" (p. 71) and the temptation to assimilate, manage, or domesticate the arts. As he sees it, the "State" (p. 74) or those in control seem to be saying that artists can do what they like, because nothing they do makes any difference to anyone. And, indeed, they will not make any real difference if people rush by paintings, go into reveries in concert halls, skim through works of fiction, come in contact with art forms only from the outside, as if the works in the various domains were indeed commodities. Dewey wrote about how important it always is to *attend* actively, to pay heed, to order the details and particulars that gradually become visible the more we look into integral patterns — what he called "experienced wholes." Dewey (1934) said:

> There is work done on the part of the percipient as there is on the part of the artist. The one who is too lazy, idle, or indurated in convention to perform this work will not see or hear. His "appreciation" will be a mixture of scraps of learning with conformity to norms of conventional admiration and with a confused, even if genuine, emotional excitation. (p. 54)

There might be recognition, he said, an attaching of correct labels, but there would not be the energizing encounter that counteracts passivity. There would not be the launching of persons into the making of meanings, the grounded interpretations or "readings" that make for wide-awakeness. Most of us recognize the delicate balance that must be achieved between the spontaneity of the initial response (perhaps the "careless rapture" of that response) and the "work" that is so necessary if the painting, dance, or fiction is to be realized. What we as teachers can communicate about that work and the energies to be released are the crucial issues, not necessarily the importance of cultural literacy or an adeptness at identifying great artists and works of art. Learning to overcome passivity and induration, learning to notice what is to be noticed, may lead on and on to new disclosures. I think of Jean-Paul Sartre (1963) saying this so clearly with regard to literature: If the reader, he wrote, "is inattentive, tired, stupid, or thoughtless, most of the relations will escape him. He will never manage to 'catch on' to the object . . . . He will draw some phrases out of the shadow but they will seem to appear as random strokes" (p. 43). When we read at our best, he suggested, we project beyond the words a theme, a subject, or a meaning. We realize through the language something that is never given *in* the language, whether it is an Emily Dickinson poem or a Sartre play. And, later, we are helped to see that the artist tries to oblige the reader or the percipient to create what he/she (the artist) discloses, to become an accomplice in freedom with the artist, an accomplice in releasing possibilities. It is this sort of action that is at the core of aesthetic education, this sort of action that may (it seems to me) save our human lives.

V. A. Howard's (1982) cautionary voice and reminders of the importance of "initiating into a trading by aspiration, demonstration, and precept" may be another way of saying this. He is talking about the discipline of growing *into* our traditions and the freedom of moving beyond them. In his essay, too, there is a sense of predicament, of a dialectic, and — through hard work — a possibility of breaking free.

If we can enable more young persons to arouse themselves in this way, to notice, to make sense of what they see and hear, to attend to works in their particularity, they may begin to experience art as a way of understanding. If we distinguish between the analytic, abstract rationality we often associate with knowing and the peculiar relational activity that brings us personally in touch with works of art, we might even call art — as Karen Gallas does, although from a different vantage point (that of the maker or creator) — a way of knowing. The experience-knowledge gained by this way of knowing means opening new modalities for us in the lived world; it brings us in touch with what Merleau-Ponty (1964) called our "primordial landscapes," where we were present at the moment "when things, truths, values" came into being for us, when we were present at the "birth of knowledge" and recovered the "consciousness of rationality" (p. 25).

Since encounters with the arts can never be end points, they may challenge us to new encounters in experience. We may have the experience Merleau-Ponty (1964) described when he talked about "a route" being given to us, "an experience which gradually clarifies itself, which gradually rectifies itself and proceeds by dialogue with itself and with others" (p. 21). It is hard for me to conceive of a better argument for the relevance of the arts in schools — if it is indeed the case, as so many people believe, that boredom and a sense of futility are among the worst obstacles to learning. To feel oneself en route, to feel oneself in a place where there are always the possibilities of clearings, of new openings: This is what we hope to communicate to the young, if we want to awaken them to their lived situations, enable them to make sense, to name their worlds.

The philosopher Charles Taylor finds a way of saying this with regard to realist painting in his book *Sources of the Self* (1989). Such painting, he writes, brings to the fore

> patterns, lines of force, whole aspects of things, which are certainly there in our visual field, but overshadowed, made recessive, by our normal ways of attending to and apprehending things. There is a vast latent content to our awareness of things and indefinite multiplicity of patterns only tacitly there, unthematized relations in what is called our pre-objective world. (p. 468)

He is talking about a retrieval, a recovery of lived experience and the meaningful forms and relationships that undergird our ordinary perception and are so often simply ignored. Painters like Cézanne and Frida Kahlo were able to convert into visible objects that which would have, without them, remained walled up in the separate life of each consciousness. Writers like Virginia Woolf (1976) can make us "see" in such a fashion that—as she herself put it—we are no longer "embedded in a kind of nondescript cotton wool" (p. 70), but are enabled to experience "moments of being" that might have been impossible were it not for the arts. Toni Morrison, at a different moment and in another space, enables us to achieve as meaningful, against our own lived experience, the tragedy of Pecola Breedlove in *The Bluest Eye* (1972) when she writes: "A little black girl yearns for the blue eyes of a little white girl, and the horror at the heart of her yearning is exceeded only by the evil of fulfillment" (p. 158). Once again, things hidden are revealed, at least to those willing to break with "induration" and try to "catch on." Again, that is one of the concerns of aesthetic education: to enable people to uncover for the sake of an intensified life and cognition. It also becomes an argument for opening the self to other ways of seeing, other ways of speaking—to the art forms of other cultures, and the stories, and the sounds. Victor Cockburn's use of folk music and songwriting suggests openings for understanding diverse and distinctive ways of being in the world.

At the heart of what I am asking for in the domains of art teaching and aesthetic education is a sense of agency, even of power. Cockburn's notion of the power of folk music "as a means of individual expression and a tool for social change" suggests possibilities in the many domains of the arts. Painting, literature, theatre, film: All can open doors and move persons to transform. We want to enable all sorts of young people to realize that they have the right to achieve works of art as meaningful against their own lived lives. Because the world that the arts illumine is a shared world, finally, and because the realities to which they give rise emerge through acts of communication, the encounters being sought are never wholly autonomous or private. Moving from our own explorations of pictorial space to a conscious encounter with a Braque painting, looking up from our own effort to make a poem to a Robert Frost or a Muriel Rukeyser poem—we can always enter into dialogue with those around. The languages can be explored; the reasons given; the moments of epiphany celebrated; the differing vantage points articulated. Communities of the wide-awake may take shape, even in the corridors of schools.

If we are indeed to make the margins visible and accessible, if we are to encourage dialectic movements from margin to text and back, we ought to open larger and larger meeting places in schools. We ought to reach out to establish ateliers, studios, places where music can be composed and rehearsed, where poems and stories can be read. There might be new collaborations among questioners, as teachers and students both engage in perceptual journeys, grasp works and words as events in contexts of meaning, undertake common searches for their place and significance in a history to which they too belong and that they invent and interpret as they live.

What we are about must be, can be, life-enhancing, as more and more living beings discover what it is to make a shape or an image, to devise a metaphor, to tell a tale—for the sake of finding their own openings into the realms of the arts. No matter how alienating, how shocking some of the images and affirmations they confront (and are urged to confront), they must learn that they can never be equated with actualities like war-wounded children, young men left broken on the side of the road, bodies scarred by torturers, the eyes of people behind bars. These are horrors too often evaded, denied, or taken for granted by those willing to remain passive, to coincide forever with themselves. So I end with a heralding of more shocks of awareness as time goes on, more explorations, more adventures into meaning, more active and uneasy participation in the human community's unending quest.

REFERENCES

Allende, I. (1989). *Eva Luna*. New York: Bantam Books.

Benjamin, W. (1978). *Illuminations*. New York: Schocken Books.

Berger, J. (1984). *Ways of seeing*. London: Penguin Books.

Bishop, E. (1983). *Collected poems*. New York: Farrar, Straus & Giroux.

Conrad, J. (1960). Preface to "The nigger of the Narcissus." In J. E. Miller, Jr., *Myth and method*. Omaha: University of Nebraska Press. (Original work published 1897)

Crane, H. (1926, October). *Poetry*, p. xxix.

Danto, A. C. (1981). *The transfiguration of the commonplace*. Cambridge, MA: Harvard University Press.

Dewey, J. (1934). *Art as experience*. New York: Minton Balch.

Donoghue, D. (1983). *The arts without mystery.* Boston: Little, Brown.

Dostoyevsky, F. (1945). *The brothers Karamasov.* New York: Modern Library.

Ellison, R. (1952). *Invisible man.* New York: Signet Books.

Foucault, M. (1984). The means of correct training. In P. Rabinow (Ed.), *The Foucault reader.* NewYork: Pantheon Press.

Heidegger, M. (1971). *Poetry, language, and thought.* New York: Harper & Row.

Howard, V. A. (1982). *Artistry, the work of artists.* Indianapolis, IN: Hackett.

Kuspit, D. (1990, April). All our yesterdays. *Artforum,* pp. 129–132.

Marcuse, H. (1977). *The aesthetic dimension.* Boston: Beacon Press.

Merleau-Ponty, M. (1964). *The primacy of perception.* Evanston, IL: Northwestern University Press.

Merleau-Ponty, M. (1967). *Phenomenology of perception.* New York: Humanities Press.

Morrison, T. (1972). *The bluest eye.* New York: Pocket Books.

Morrison, T. (1987). *Beloved.* New York: Knopf.

Sartre, J-P. (1963). *Literature and existentialism.* New York: Citadel Press.

Stevens, W. (1964). *Collected poems.* New York: Knopf.

Stevens, W. (1965). *The necessary angel.* New York: Vintage Books.

Taylor, C. (1989). *Sources of the self.* Cambridge, MA: Harvard University Press.

Waldman, D. (1989). *Jenny Holzer.* New York: Harry N. Abrams.

Warnock, M. (1978). *Imagination.* Berkeley: University of California Press.

Woolf, V. (1976). *Moments of being.* New York: Harcourt, Brace, Jovanovich.

CHAPTER 6

Against Sociological Imperialism: The Limits of Sociology in the Aesthetic Sphere

Janet Wolff

With regard to aesthetics, the two main errors of the sociology of art are agnosticism and imperialism. The more "scientifically" oriented sociology, including a good deal of the so-called production-of-culture approach, avoids questions of aesthetic judgment, or simply treats them as subject matter, on the traditional grounds of a sociology anxious about its status as science—that we can study values but cannot participate in making them. Critical sociologies, on the other hand, too often reduce the aesthetic to the political and the ideological, on the assumption that exposing the social bases of aesthetic judgments amounts to discrediting them. Neither of these approaches does justice to the aesthetic, and neither of them is good sociology. In this chapter I will review some of the issues involved in the relationship between sociology and aesthetics, arguing in particular against a reduction of the aesthetic to the sociological. My intention is to open the way for the exploration of a sociology of art that engages critically with the aesthetic, without in the process denying the specificity of art, the autonomy of the aesthetic sphere, and the complexity of the grounds (including non-sociological grounds) of aesthetic judgment.

Some time ago, I concluded an analysis of the impact of sociology on aesthetics with the words, "If the debate is between sociology and aesthetics, sociology has the last word" (Wolff, 1983, p. 108). This followed a discussion of, first, the many ways in which traditional aesthetics found itself under at-

An earlier version of this chapter was presented to the session on the Sociology of Aesthetics at the American Sociological Association meeting in San Francisco in August 1989.

tack by sociology; and second, the reasons why sociology has to recognize the autonomy and specificity of the aesthetic. More recently, it has occurred to me that my own "last word" gives support to the very sociological imperialism I want to avoid. In the late twentieth century, in a context in which aesthetic relativism is promoted for all the wrong reasons (as well as for some perfectly good ones), it is even more pressing to assess the bases of aesthetic judgment and to defend, where appropriate, a non-reductionist theory of art.

AGNOSTICISM AND THE MYTH OF AESTHETIC OBJECTIVITY

Elizabeth Bird (1979) has shown that the sociological commitment to objectivity and the refusal to engage in, or even with, aesthetic judgments can paralyze the sociological project itself. In a study of the Glasgow school of painters in the period 1880–1930, researchers found themselves obliged to make procedural decisions that were implicitly based on aesthetic evaluation. The very identification of the artists depended on the (non-sociological) classification of styles, and perhaps also standards, of work. In refusing to make such judgments themselves, the researchers could only resort to reinforcing existing judgments (for example, in taking their selection of artists from the exhibition catalogs of the Glasgow Institute).

In much the same way, any sociological study of the arts that abstains from an investigation of the aesthetic is bound to reinforce existing aesthetic categories and classifications. One of the most important successes of the sociology of art and of the social history of art has been to show that those categories and classifications are the product of social relations, ideological battles, and power inequalities. The apparent autonomy and transcendence of art operate to obscure those social facts, and this illusion is maintained and reinforced by those academic disciplines (art history, art and literary criticism, aesthetics) that are premised on the notion of art as independent of the social and political. It is clear that any sociology of art that takes over uncritically the subject matter of these other disciplines thereby colludes in the process of confirming both the autonomy of art and the hierarchies of aesthetic judgment. It is ironic that a project whose intention has been to demystify Art, by investigating the actual social processes of cultural production and consumption, should persist in leaving unchallenged the pre-sociological conceptions of its material.

Rather than listing numerous examples of this problem in recent work in the sociology of art, I will simply mention one influential text that seems to me to perpetuate this fault, namely, Diana Crane's *The Transformation of the Avant-Garde* (1987). This study of the New York art world from 1940 to 1985, which provides important and fascinating material on the operations of

dealers, critics, museums, patrons, and a variety of arts institutions, is entirely
dependent on a pre-existing classification of artists into "seven major styles"
(p. 2), from Abstract Expressionism, via Pop and Minimalism, to Neo-
Expressionism. Under these headings, she looks at more than 400 artists. As
she tells us in an Appendix, her identification and classification of these artists
were based on sources from the art world itself—major exhibitions and texts
of art criticism. But this means that the exclusion of some artists cannot be
explained—indeed, it cannot even be discussed. And yet the fact that her list
of Abstract Expressionists contains no women, for example, is in need of explanation—precisely by sociology. Feminist art history, a crucial contribution
to and revision of the sociology of art, has raised questions about the writing
out of women from the history of art and has something to say about the
omission of Lee Krasner (who was married to Jackson Pollock and whose
work has only recently been widely shown and accredited). The "seven major
styles" are the product of institutional processes, ideological preferences, and
vested interests, as well as aesthetic judgments.[1] The sociology of art has a
commitment to the critical investigation of this construction.

THE SOCIOLOGY OF AESTHETICS

It is easy enough to record the numerous ways in which sociology has challenged traditional aesthetics.
      1. Sociology exposes the myth of Art as the asocial product of the Cre-
ative Genius, by demonstrating the social processes and institutions in which
people become artists, art styles become accepted, and works of art are accredited and received by critics and audiences. This involves examining the specific
(and historically variable) circumstances in which training in the arts is acquired (guilds, academies, conservatories, art schools, writing programs, and
so on), as well as the professional and aesthetic ideologies that inform the
selection and teaching involved in these institutions. It also means insisting
on the crucial role of "mediators" or "gatekeepers" in cultural production—
those categories of art workers who are essential to the making and dissemina-
tion of the arts (see Becker, 1982). Included here would be museum directors,
curators, gallery owners, publishers, critics, journal editors, arts administrators, and many others. Most important, the sociological revision of art history
makes clear the relatively recent development of the very notions of art and
artist, both originating in the Renaissance in Western Europe, and replacing
the conception of the painter as artisan or craftsperson. The arts began to be
perceived as the inspired expression of individual personalities (see Wolff,
1993).
      2. Sociology and social history also make clear the specific historical and

social circumstances in which aesthetic hierarchies emerge. Lawrence Levine's (1988) book on the development of cultural hierarchies in the United States is an example of this work, which helps us to realize that what became "high art" in the late nineteenth century (before which time the category did not exist) was largely a product of the formation of social groups and the exclusionary practices that they came to operate. Paul DiMaggio's (1982) work on Boston more explicitly identifies the class basis of these social and cultural processes. He shows that the development of high cultural forms (he looks in detail at the formation of the Museum of Fine Arts and the Boston Symphony Orchestra) and the increasing separation of high culture from popular culture in the second half of the nineteenth century were closely bound up with the social and economic consolidation of the Boston Brahmins. The "sacralization" of art was the product of a *social* process, through which a particular urban elite achieved a cultural identity and a clear axis of distinction and superiority in relation to the lower social classes.

Feminist historians of art have examined the social and institutional conditions in which women have been systematically excluded from cultural production and the critical practices that have defined work by women as second-rate, or lesser arts (Parker & Pollock, 1981). Embroidery, once a high-prestige activity undertaken by men, became increasingly associated with women and domesticity by the eighteenth century and accordingly became separated from the other arts and downgraded to an amateur pastime (see Parker, 1984). Literary genres predominantly associated with women as writers and readers (notably romance novels) are excluded from the literary canon and are taken less seriously than other popular literary forms (like detective novels or science fiction), which now do have a place, if a marginal one, in the curriculum and in the pages of literary reviews. Aesthetic hierarchies, once again, turn out to be socially based — in this case, with respect to gender.

3. The sociology of taste, notably in the work of Pierre Bourdieu (1984) and his followers (DiMaggio & Useem, 1982), has shown that aesthetic judgment still functions in a class-related manner, and that art operates as "cultural capital" in late-twentieth-century Western societies. Sectors of the dominant groups (and usually this means the professional and managerial classes rather than the financiers and capitalists) use culture and the arts as part of the crucial process of social differentiation, by excluding other social groups that do not possess the cultural capital of taste and education. As DiMaggio (1982) shows in the case of nineteenth-century Boston, the social divisions of class continue to structure the cultural preferences and aesthetic judgments of our own society.

4. The social history of taste throws into question any straightforward notion of objective aesthetic judgment. For example, the relatively recent reassessment of Victorian art, after 60 or 70 years of consignment to the base-

ments of museums, raises questions about what appeared to be the definitive (modernist) critique and dismissal of that work. Of course, the art market plays a large part in the (re)discovery of artists and movements, as do dealers, critics, and gallery owners who promote "new" categories of work to would-be collectors. The point is, again, that there are explanations for the transformation of taste in the cultural sphere.

5. The sociology of reception (including reception theory, hermeneutic approaches, and semiotics) demonstrates the situated nature of cultural consumption and the instability of interpretation and, hence, of evaluation. We do not need to adopt the more radical versions of reader theories, which announce and welcome the death of the author, to recognize that the meaning of a cultural product depends on who is looking at it or reading it. Meanings and interpretations change with social position (class, gender, age, ethnicity, and so on), and they necessarily change from one period to another. It is impossible to read an eighteenth-century text *as if* one were a contemporary reader. The hermeneutic principle makes clear that we always read (view, hear, interpret) from our own social position and from our own experience. It follows from the fact that there is no fixed meaning of a text, that there is no fixed vantage point of evaluation.

6. The sociology of art history (and of art criticism) shows the social and political location of its practitioners, the specific institutional bases of its practice, and the ideological and political orientation of its pronouncements. Art historians (like artists) are recruited and trained in specific social circumstances and in relation to specific processes of exclusion (including aspects of class, race, and gender). They are socialized into an already existing discourse of cultural criticism (and as a result will tend to ignore or reject alternative ways of discussing cultural work). They operate in institutional contexts that have their own logic, professional ideologies, and aesthetic and other assumptions—journals, universities, galleries, and museums. In the same way, the social history of aesthetics undermines its pretense of objectivity. The development of aesthetics as a discrete area of inquiry with its own unique subject matter was premised on the socially based emergence of the aesthetic sphere as detached from other areas of the social world (see Wolff, 1983).

7. Ideology-critique has provided increasingly sophisticated tools and methods for the decoding of paintings, novels, films, and other texts, in which the political and ideological meanings available for specific spectators and audiences in representation can be analyzed. Structuralist and semiotic approaches provide access to the layers of meaning, connotation, and reference contained in any cultural work. These aspects of representation can be shown to be systematically (if complexly) related to the social and political conditions of production of the work. Rejecting earlier, and cruder, models of reflection, these approaches enable us to investigate the ways in which the visual, the

literary, the filmic, and even the musical encode *extra*-aesthetic facts. The innocence of ostensibly apolitical art is thus put into question.

8. Feminist and black criticism enables us to address the question asked by Linda Nochlin (1973) more than 20 years ago: "Why have there been no great women [or black] artists?" The question, which takes issue with every dominant artistic tradition, is answered by sociology and social history, and not by aesthetics. We now know many of the ways in which the social organization of cultural production has operated to exclude women across the centuries (although the specific obstacles faced by women varied from one period to another and from one society to another). We have also seen how literary and art criticism has colluded in the process of ignoring and undermining work that is produced by women (see Pollock, 1979; Showalter, 1971). Finally, we can understand — and therefore challenge — the operation of art history itself as a selective (and patriarchal) process, which had more or less successfully obliterated most women artists from the record and from the canon until the advent of the contemporary women's movement and its associated development of a feminist art history. Different but parallel processes of exclusion have operated to produce a tradition and a canon that consist almost entirely of the work of white artists and authors.

The sociology of art and the social history of art are bound to challenge aesthetics on all of these grounds. From the point of view of traditional aesthetics and art criticism, such a critique represents unwarranted interference by one discipline in the domain of another. But we must distinguish illegitimate from legitimate complaints of sociological imperialism.

THE AUTONOMY OF ART

In some important ways, we must grant the autonomy of the aesthetic sphere, even from the point of view of a sociology of art.

1. Historically, it is clearly the case that there did emerge a level (a set of institutions, ideologies, practices, and so on) of "the aesthetic." As Peter Burger (1984) says, "The autonomy of art is a category of bourgeois society that both reveals and obscures an actual historical development" (p. 36). Art came to be seen as independent of function and as separate from other practical, intellectual, and social activities. The process, begun in the Renaissance, was accelerated and confirmed during the eighteenth and nineteenth centuries. The new disciplines of art criticism, art history, and aesthetics reinforced this separation.

2. Culture and the arts are not reducible to the social, the economic, and the political (as successive developments in Marxist aesthetics have insisted), but are relatively autonomous with respect to those factors that ultimately

enable their existence. This relative autonomy, it is now understood, extends to the active role of culture and representation in constructing and maintaining social relations. That is, visual and literary texts are themselves an arena for the discursive production of meanings and values in society.

3. As structuralist and semiotic analyses have made clear, the autonomy of the arts consists in the operation of the codes and conventions of representation (literary narrative, musical language, filmic codes, and so on). This is one important reason why reflection theory has always been wrong. Art cannot reflect social life because it is not like a mirror or a piece of plain glass. Rather, social life, if it is somehow present in culture, is complexly mediated through aesthetic conventions of representation, which have the potential to construct their own range of meanings and connections.

4. Literature, painting, music, and the other arts all have their own institutions and practices that constitute them as distinct activities. (This is related to the point made earlier about the historical emergence of art as an autonomous sphere of operation.) So, what Terry Eagleton (1976) has called "the literary mode of production" (p. 45), although it is clearly located in a particular set of wider social relations (capitalism, patriarchy, industrialism), is relatively autonomous. Publishing houses, schools of art, museums, opera companies, and so on, are identifiable institutions, with their own histories, internal social hierarchies and relations, and ways of operating.

Of course, it is the very autonomy of artistic institutions and practices that has enabled and encouraged the kind of ultimately unsociological studies I have already discussed, which are content to take as their object an arts institution, in isolation from the wider society and in abstraction from history. Insisting on this broader perspective, however, should not blind us to the important acknowledgment of the relative autonomy of arts institutions.

SOCIOLOGICAL IMPERIALISM

"The pleasure felt by the spectator on viewing a picture, and the correspondence of his aesthetic ideology to the picture's visual ideology, are one and the same thing." This comment by Nicos Hadjinicolaou (1978, p. 180) is an example of the kind of overstatement of the sociological case that was more common in critical studies in the 1970s, but still persists. Terry Eagleton (1976) formulated a similar view of the aesthetic in the mid–1970s (in the Althusserian language that he then employed): "The value of a text . . . is determined by its double mode of insertion into an ideological formation and into the available lineages of literary discourse" (p. 186). Indeed, it is easy to conclude from the comprehensive sociological critique of the aesthetic, which I have briefly summarized above, that the aesthetic is reducible to the social and that aesthetic judgments are ultimately nothing more than political values, dressed in another language. What follows from this is that there are *no* purely aesthetic criteria for assessing culture. (The more radical move, based on the recognition of the relationship among art, ideology, and power, is the commitment to a *populist aesthetic:* Here, the aesthetic preferences of the general population are to be substituted for the minority tastes of the powerful, imposed as Art on the whole of society.)

By *sociological imperialism* I mean a critique of aesthetics that claims to explain aesthetic appreciation and aesthetic evaluation entirely in sociological terms — whether of class (or gender) ideology, of cultural capital, or of institutional values. The consequence of such a position, clearly, is a total relativism, in which there is no way of comparing cultural products, of arguing (to take examples from Bourdieu's, 1984, class-based cultural analysis) that *The Well-Tempered Clavier* is in any sense better than *The Blue Danube,* or that Jane Austen's novels are better than Harlequin romances. The "better" in each case consists, in this view, in a socially located, politically motivated strategy to differentiate social groups and to introduce the most effective practices of exclusion.

I think we can — indeed, we must — acknowledge the importance of the sociological critique of art and aesthetics, and at the same time refuse the radical reductionism of such a position. We can assess and compare cultural works (including *within* a category). And this evaluation is not (or not only) achieved in terms of sociological analysis and ideology-critique. Sociology, in other words, has not achieved the abolition of the category of the aesthetic.

POSTMODERN RELATIVISM

The progress of a sociological aesthetic has been accompanied by developments within the arts that produce a parallel argument for aesthetic relativism. The crisis in modernism, the revival of traditional forms of culture (for example, figurative and representational painting), and the celebration of postmodern eclecticism have appeared to some commentators to amount to a collapse of aesthetic values and an exposure of the myth of such evaluation. This in turn parallels the "demise of the master-narratives" announced by philosophers of postmodernism, most notably Jean-François Lyotard. Jim Collins (1989) has argued that postmodernism, on the one hand, and popular culture, on the other, have together totally demolished the high art/mass culture divide, and at the same time undermined the notion of a unified Grand Hotel of culture. Instead, he says, we confront a proliferation of disconnected, competing cultures and cultural forms. This is a vision of a fragmented, democratic, if somewhat chaotic culture, shared by a number of writers on the postmodern.

In my opinion, such theories of the postmodern are fundamentally wrong. Their perception of increased eclecticism, of the plundering of mass culture by Art, and of the quoting of Art by mass culture, leads them to the false conclusion that there is no organizing principle behind this confusion and that culture no longer serves certain clear social interests (of class, or gender, or anything else). Collins supports this conclusion with the more interesting observation, based on recent work on cultural studies and reception theory, that texts are plurivocal — that is, they speak to different audiences/readers in different ways. This is further evidence against the concept of a monolithic culture, serving key sectional and ideological interests. But this logic too is flawed. For hardly anyone now would argue for a conspiracy theory of culture, and it is clear to most sociologists of the arts that the ways in which culture negotiates ideology and meaning are extremely complex and contradictory. This complexity, again, does not mean that culture is no longer centrally part of the inequalities of power that persist in late-twentieth-century Western societies.

Postmodern theories, in other words, would benefit from a more sociological theory of culture. At the same time, they sometimes share with sociological imperialism an enthusiasm for the renunciation of the aesthetic, in the sense of an identifiable set of criteria for assessing cultural products. And it is clear that we cannot attempt to reinstate the metanarratives of truth, value, and objectivity. Postmodern theory and poststructuralist analysis have definitively exposed the situated nature of all thought and the relativity of truth to specific discourses or narratives. For some writers on the postmodern, the abandonment of values (aesthetic or any other) is more problematic than for others (see Fekete, 1988; Ross, 1988). John Fekete, for example, takes the positive view that "with the shift toward what looks like an emerging postmodern cultural framework, the prospects for the renewal of value discourses are compelling and stimulating" (p. xiv).

In the final section of this chapter, I will argue for the defense of such value discourses (and specifically discourses of *aesthetic* value) against the claims of both postmodern scepticism and sociological imperialism.

SOCIOLOGY, POSTMODERNISM, AND AESTHETICS

To point out that the aesthetic sphere is itself socially and historically constituted does not mean that aesthetic judgments can be translated into social or political judgments. We can accept the argument of the critical sociologies of art that very often the evaluation of art, ostensibly founded on purely aes-

thetic grounds, is in fact based on ideological compatibility of text and reader/
viewer. What I am interested in here, however, is the *remainder* — the grounds
of aesthetic judgment that cannot be explained in this way. Philosophers of
art have devoted many pages to disentangling the various ways in which the
terms *art, aesthetic, value,* and *beauty* are used, as well as to the relationship
among these terms. "Good" art need not be "beautiful" (although it can be).
"Good" art (in the sense of technically competent) need not be "aesthetically
valuable." Enjoyment, or pleasure, may be totally unconnected to either
beauty or skill. It is clear that there is a multiplicity of bases for aesthetic
evaluation. What they have in common, though, is a relative autonomy from
the social. And it is precisely the (social, historical) separation of the aesthetic
from other areas of social life that has guaranteed the existence of an aesthetic
discourse. My argument, then, is that the sociology of art may explore the
origins and operations of the aesthetic domain (critical institutions, social
background of critics, and so on), but that *it must acknowledge the autonomy of
the aesthetic discourse.* For aesthetic judgments are made on the basis of the
languages operative in this arena.
    Aesthetic judgments are thus often made on the basis of *skill.* A work may
be assessed in terms of its technical excellence, in accordance with a known
and accepted set of rules about what constitutes skill and excellence. They
often are made also on the basis of a notion of *originality* and/or *complexity,*
where the positive evaluation of a work depends on a recognition of that
work as breaking new ground and offering the possibility of constantly new
and challenging readings. (This criterion, incidentally, is usually the basis of
the defense of Art over mass culture or kitsch, whose attractions are thought
to be clichéd, superficial, and based on formulas.) And they are sometimes
made on the basis of *pleasure.* (Here I am thinking particularly of feminist
work, for the most part using psychoanalytic theory, on the appeal, to men
and to women, of specific types of cultural products [see Kaplan, 1986;
Modleski, 1986; Mulvey, 1989].) It is not my intention here to adjudicate
between the various grounds of aesthetic judgment, but rather, in identifying
some of these, to insist on their irreducibility to the social.
    It is true, of course, that the analysis of the bases of aesthetic judgment
may involve reference to the social. The psychoanalytic analysis of pleasure is
bound to reveal the social context of family relations in which the infantile
psychic dramas with which it is concerned take place. The question of the
originality and complexity of texts is necessarily connected to the question of
audiences, since these characteristics do not inhere in the texts, but in their
readings. But the discourse(s) of sociology cannot address the issues involved.
Sociology can locate the reception, interpretation, and enjoyment of cultural
works, but it cannot take over or replace the aesthetic discourse itself.
    In case it now appears that I have come full circle, and that my argument

in fact endorses what I earlier called the agnosticism of production-of-culture sociology, I should emphasize that sociological respect for the autonomy of the aesthetic does *not* amount to sociological blindness to the social construction of the aesthetic sphere. Rather, my argument has been as follows:

1. Art and the aesthetic sphere have been historically constructed in specific social conditions and in relation to particular social processes and interests. The practice of aesthetic judgment is undertaken by people whose own social situation and interests need to be understood, since non-aesthetic values intrude into what are claimed to be purely aesthetic judgments. Therefore part of the task of a sociology of art must be to analyze the historical construction of art, arts establishments, and aesthetic hierarchies.

2. However, the social history of the arts also reveals the emergence of a relatively autonomous aesthetic sphere in modern bourgeois society. This sphere consists of arts institutions, artists and other arts personnel, critical discourses that support and protect this domain, and so on. Crucial among these discourses is the language of aesthetic evaluation (which, however, can take a variety of forms). This particular discourse, although itself a social-historical construct, now operates relatively independently. This means that sociological analysis, which is well-equipped to expose the ideological moments in aesthetic judgments, must moderate its claims to explanation and refrain from subsuming the aesthetic in its entirety into the discourse of sociology.

A sociological aesthetics that eschews imperialism will be able to explore the social history and the social coordinates *of* the aesthetic, without invading the specific discourses of the aesthetic (whether textual, technical, or experiential). The implication of this is that a crudely sociological relativism (art seen as representing the interests of particular groups) appears to be replaced by another kind of relativism. Aesthetic judgments make sense only within specific discourses, and they do not offer the possibility of assessing competing discourses. With regard to the relativism engendered by postmodern theory, Barbara Herrnstein Smith (1988) has argued against what she calls the Egalitarian Fallacy.

> While the radical contingency of all value certainly does imply that no value judgment can be more "valid" than another *in the sense of* an objectively truer statement of the objective value of an object . . ., it does not follow that all value judgments are equally valid. (p. 6)

It remains to be seen whether, in a proper engagement between the sociological and the aesthetic, these questions of value and relativism can be addressed in the postmodern age.

NOTE

1. For entirely different assessments of Abstract Expressionism, see (in Frascina, 1985) Max Kozloff's "American Painting During the Cold War"; Eva Cockcroft's "Abstract Expressionism, Weapon of the Cold War"; Serge Guilbaut's "The New Adventures of the Avant-Garde in America"; and Fred Orton and Griselda Pollock's "Avant-Gardes and Partisans Reviewed."

REFERENCES

Becker, H. (1982). *Art worlds.* Berkeley: University of California Press.

Bird, E. (1979). Aesthetic neutrality and the sociology of art. In M. Barrett et al. (Eds.), *Ideology and cultural production* (pp. 25–48). London: Croom Helm.

Bourdieu, P. (1984). *Distinction: A social critique of the judgement of taste.* London: Routledge & Kegan Paul.

Burger, P. (1984). *Theory of the avant-garde.* Minneapolis: University of Minnesota Press.

Collins, J. (1989). *Uncommon cultures: Popular culture and postmodernism.* New York: Routledge.

Crane, D. (1987). *The transformation of the avant-garde: The New York art world, 1940–1985.* Chicago: University of Chicago Press.

DiMaggio, P. (1982). Cultural entrepreneurship in nineteenth-century Boston: The creation of an organizational base for high culture in America. *Media, Culture, & Society, 4*(1), 33–50.

DiMaggio, P., & Useem, M. (1982). The arts in class reproduction. In M. W. Apple (Ed.), *Cultural and economic reproduction in education: Essays on class, ideology and the State.* London: Routledge & Kegan Paul.

Eagleton, T. (1976). *Criticism and ideology.* London: New Left Books.

Eagleton, T. (1983). *Literary theory: An introduction.* Oxford: Blackwell.

Fekete, J. (1988). Introductory notes for a postmodern value agenda. In J. Fekete (Ed.), *Life after postmodernism: Essays on value and culture* (pp. i–xix). London: Macmillan.

Frascina, F. (Ed.). (1985). *Pollock and after: The critical debate.* New York: Harper & Row.

Hadjinicolaou, N. (1978). *Art history and class struggle.* London: Pluto Press.

Kaplan, C. (1986). Wild nights: Pleasure/sexuality/feminism. In *Sea changes: Essays on culture and feminism* (pp. 31–56). London: Verso.

Levine, L. W. (1988). *Highbrow/lowbrow: The emergence of cultural hierarchy in America.* Cambridge, MA: Harvard University Press.

Modleski, T. (1986). The terror of pleasure: The contemporary horror film and postmodern theory. In T. Modleski (Ed.), *Studies in entertainment: Critical approaches to mass culture* (pp. 155–166). Bloomington: Indiana University Press.

Mulvey, L. (1989). *Visual and other pleasures.* Bloomington: Indiana University Press.

Nochlin, L. (1973). Why have there been no great women artists? In T. B. Hess & E. C. Baker (Eds.), *Art and sexual politics* (pp. 1–39). Collier-Macmillan.

Parker, R. (1984). *The subversive stitch: Embroidery and the making of the feminine.* London: Women's Press.

Parker, R., & Pollock, G. (1981). *Old mistresses: Women, art, and ideology.* London: Routledge & Kegan Paul.

Pollock, G. (1979). Feminism, femininity and the Hayward Annual Exhibition 1978. *Feminist Review, 2,* 33–55.

Ross, A. (Ed.). (1988). *Universal abandon? The politics of postmodernism.* Minneapolis: University of Minnesota Press.

Showalter, E. (1971). Women writers and the double standard. In V. Gornick & B. K. Moran (Eds.), *Women in sexist society* (pp. 452–479). New York: Basic Books.

Smith, B. H. (1988). Value without truth-value. In J. Fekete (Ed.), *Life after postmodernism: Essays on value and culture* (pp. 1–21). London: Macmillan.

Wolff, J. (1983). *Aesthetics and the sociology of art.* London: Allen & Unwin.

Wolff, J. (1993). *The social production of art* (2nd ed.). New York: New York University Press.

CHAPTER 7

People Who Make Things: Aesthetics from the Ground Up

Ronald W. Neperud and Don H. Krug

Historically, art education has focused on the creation and study of art either from views in the prevailing art worlds or from children's developmental sequences. However, in recent decades these views have changed. Expanded conceptions of art and a questioning of the source and nature of aesthetic experience have led to a re-examination of long accepted assumptions and beliefs about what constitutes art and aesthetic experience. In this chapter, conceptions of making and valuing objects among individuals called outsider, folk, naive, and vernacular artists will be examined. Usually, these "artists" have not been educated in an academic setting, but have acquired their art skills, values, and visions through a variety of informal means. This broader conception of people who make things will form the basis for an expansion of the art, processes, and values upon which art education is developed.

One characteristic of being human is the ability to create things in a thoughtful and innovative manner. The making of things usually has been differentiated along lines of object or art, with the former representing a functional role, and the latter, inherent aesthetic qualities. The process of making useful objects has been described as work, while the process of making art has been characterized by creativity and genius. But, these dichotomies are changing with a blurring, if not outright elimination, of such demarcations.

Several situations, conditions, and events have led to a questioning of how the objects and processes of making things are categorized. The valuing of cultural diversity has led to a recognition of diverse objects not always considered as traditional arts. Artists and museum directors began to elevate functional and ceremonial objects or artifacts of various societies to aesthetic and artistic status. Changes in the arts during the transition from modernism to postmodernism further shifted lines between art and non-art as postmodern artists borrowed from diverse sources, changing forever existing art and aesthetic boundaries. In a broader sense, the body of literature critical of existing categories and structures underlying contemporary life also has contributed significantly to how we view what people make and value.

As attention is focused on the all-encompassing category of things or objects that people make, there is ample evidence that people enjoy and seem to have a need to create concrete and visible phenomena. Dissanayake has argued for recognition that the need to "make special" is a human universal (1988) and for a "homo aestheticus" (1992). Crafts, whittling, basketry, decoy making, fishing lures, and various textiles created in the home—what previously was called folk art—are all evidence of making things. Other people shape large-scale creations such as the planning and embellishment of yards and gardens. And who can say that farmers working the land, shaping it as they make decisions about what and where to plant or preserve, are not in a sense involved with making things?

Several questions arise about the diverse things that people make and value who usually are not formally educated in artistic ways. What relationships exist among traditional aesthetic and art values and the creations of untrained individuals? Do their creations differ categorically from formally recognized art? Are the experiences provided by what people make of a different order than the creation of accepted art by artists? How do these creators of objects value their creations, and does this differ from that of formally educated artists? Finally, how should art educators regard the diverse material that people make relative to traditionally recognized art?

In this chapter, studies of people who make things, including details of the makers' interests, satisfactions, practices, and values, will be reported (Krug, 1992/93). The processes of making and valuing will be examined in the context of social, artistic, and aesthetic categories in an attempt to situate them in the broad context of human activity (Neperud, 1990). Based on this material, meanings for art education practice and curriculum development will be suggested. Conceptions of aesthetics and theoretical perspectives of making things will be developed as a basis for interpreting and reflecting upon the meanings of the case studies reported here.

In art education and in the formation of American cultures, the dawn of modernity was a decisive time when the meanings and values associated with the visual arts were highlighted with social distinctions. In the process, workers were alienated from their ways of life as craftspeople and skilled workers, from traditions they had grown accustomed to and from which they had derived a great deal of satisfaction and personal self-esteem. "Brow" dichotomies formed between acceptable (high) and unacceptable (low) visual cultural practices and products, between official and unofficial forms of artistic endeavor, and between the values associated with the things people made. These brow dichotomies over distinctions of taste are still prevalent in the inclusion and exclusion of particular forms of educational practices and in the selection of institutionally legitimate forms of knowledge.

The selection and circulation of legitimate and nonlegitimate, valued and nonvalued forms of knowledge are related to particular visual cultural products or art making. These different types of knowledge are associated with art's many forms and conditions of use, production, and consumption. Art, culture, and aesthetics are interconnected concepts entangled in a web of political discourse and social relations. Things people make are deeply implicated in this web of politics, in the selection and circulation of legitimate and nonlegitimate forms of production by makers of art. People in everyday life who make things are subject to the meanings and values circulated in society, but usually these are nominated by the experts in particular art worlds, whose job has been to name and construct reputations, values, and practices as significant forms of art and to define their social and cultural interpretation.

CONCEPTIONS OF PEOPLE WHO MAKE THINGS

In the United States, distinctions between self-taught making and "authentic" institutionally trained artistic practices are well-entrenched in society's notion of "what art is." Most recently, a "new aesthetic" connected to contemporary folk artistry categorizes some makers as "outsiders." Michael Hall (1991) attributes the formation of the new aesthetic discourse to an American fascination for collecting objects and things, associated with people in everyday life, that are "home-grown," such as weather vanes, folk portraits, whirligigs, walking sticks, and quilts. He refers to this behavioral fetishness as domestic otherness and points out that some of the first collectors of folk art objects were the artists themselves.

It wasn't long before private collectors, dealers, and museum and gallery directors became interested and began to incorporate the work into the ever-expanding art market. A show of folk art was coordinated in 1924 and held at the Whitney Studio Club, where approximately 45 objects were exhibited. In 1934, another folk art exhibit took place, at the Museum of Modern Art. This show established the "place" of folk art and/or "domestic outsider" art in art world institutions. Folk and outsider arts were identified and recognized, and soon afterwards aesthetic discourses started to be circulated and distributed by art critics, gallery owners, and museum curators. Art collectors were wrapped up in "folk art fever" and were eager to accumulate the new found wealth of the maker who made things outside the mainstream (Vlach, 1991, p. 22).

In 1972, a professor of visual and literary studies, Roger Cardinal, wrote

Outsider Art, in which he proposed that the things people make as outsider artists are not distinctly different from other forms of artistic practices he had studied. Nevertheless, he asserted that the work didn't seem to have anything to do with *folk art,* because it wasn't passed on or down in a regional, ethnic, religious, or occupational tradition. It wasn't *fine art* because it wasn't learned in an academic setting, and it wasn't *commercial* because it wasn't made to sell. Cardinal (1972) wrote, "The 'alternative' art to which the present book is addressed is to be sought not in cultures different from our own, since these do not break away from cultural norms and set figurations, but in true artistic heresies *within* the boundaries of our immediate system" (p. 39; emphasis in original). Cardinal's book was instrumental in the naming of a selected group of makers as "outsider," even though the term outsider is rarely used in the text.

MAKERS OF ART AND THE ART WORLDS

The different art worlds in the past 20 years have accepted more regularly the visual cultural practices of people "outside" the mainstream, such as the working laborer, the folk artist, or the self-taught maker of art. Quite recently, internationally recognized art critics Roger Manley and John Maizel, and dealers such as Phyllis Kind, Roger Ricco, and Frank Maresca, have speculated that the public is tired of art that is meaningless, especially the type of abstract and conceptual art that doesn't seem to mean anything. Collectors of art, they propose, are eager for more than the intellectualization of visual representation and culture. People want to know something about the stories and narratives of the makers of visual cultural products. People who collect art want to feel connected to the stories associated with the makers who produce the art work, but they do not necessarily want to feel connected to the life-style difference and diversity of community heritage of these makers of art. Nevertheless, because the work of the *self-taught* people who make things tells stories eagerly, sometimes with the words painted right on the image, a "new aesthetic" is beginning to emerge.

The outsider artist is identified as being alone, outside the cultural mainstream. Materially and semiotically, the outsider artist's reputation is connected to the long held assumption about the autonomous individual and the isolation of an artist's life separated or distanced from people in society. It is a (mis)conception circulated by influential members of the art worlds.

Therefore, it is critical to participate in the social struggle over how things people make and the makers themselves are named and ascribed with meaning. "Unless [we as] art educators recognize the importance of understanding the cultural and political dimensions of visual arts education, classroom instruction will do nothing more than promote traditional conceptions of art and the technology of artistic practices" (Hicks, 1989, p. 57). As transitions in curriculum restructuring take shape, it is critical to remember that "culture is something people make for themselves; an active process which is lived, not fixed, and not consumed. Culture is something which happens in human relations as a result of human agency" (Thompson, quoted in Duncum, 1989, p. 19). The stories people tell about their own practices as self-taught makers of art are very different from what is written about them as "outsiders" in scholarly journals or in the popular periodical press (Ardery, 1991; Hall, 1991; Lippard, 1990; Manley, 1991). Therefore, it is appropriate that we turn to the makers of art and listen to what they have to say about the things that they make.

SOME PEOPLE WHO MAKE THINGS

Several Wisconsin artists were identified and interviewed, and their work was photographed in an attempt to discern how they went about making things, what kept them going, and how they and their work related to the broader spheres of art and aesthetics. Also, of particular interest was how these individuals got started in making things, considering that they were self-taught or learned their art-making skills outside of formal educational situations. Artists who were interviewed demonstrated a continued effort to create and an innovative interest as opposed to working from patterns and kits, made things to which they had a personal interest or attachment, and were self-initiated and not prompted by others. The study began with artists with whom we were familiar, but once started, there seemed to be a network of people throughout the region who met the criteria. The following case studies were chosen to indicate the diversity of different details associated with the specific creative practices of self-taught artists. The interviews focused on questions such as how they got their start, how they went about making things in terms of materials and techniques, sources of ideas, values (aesthetics), and how they were affected by change, including directions they would like to investigate.

Ellis Nelson

Ellis is a retired auto mechanic and machinist turned sculptor. In taking the backroads from Frank Lloyd Wright's Taliesin East at Spring Green to the Wisconsin River town of Muscoda, one goes by Ellis's old repair shop turned sculptor's studio. Dominating the surroundings is a large metal dinosaur among a variety of works ranging from nicely balanced abstract pieces gently moving in the breeze, to bat shapes floating over the shop, cut from sheet metal, with wings curved by pounding, and embellished with details torched into the metal. Ellis is friendly, an outgoing person always willing to show people around his collection of creations. He is very proud of his ingenious machines, most of which he invented and built to facilitate his work.

Getting a Start. In response to our question about how he got his start in making things, Ellis gave this lengthy reply:

Well, how I actually got started was in the winter, middle of February. Somewhere I got some sheet metal. I'd never done any artwork before. And, it was on a Saturday, and I said to my son, "Why don't you help me bring in that big piece of metal in here and I'll make a sign out of it; it'll look like a dinosaur." So my son told me, "If I were you I wouldn't do it; you don't know anything." He discouraged me right off. He did help me bring it in though, so I did make a fairly nice looking dinosaur. I made the body of the largest piece, with three-dimensional legs on the side. So I set it out here for 2 or 3 days, and the Boscobel paper did an article on me and had pictures in it. A week later, I got a call from the *Telegraph Herald* in Iowa, and they wanted pictures of it.

Curious about who might have influenced him, we asked Ellis, "Is there anyone in your family who is an artist? And, do you think of yourself as an artist?" Ellis replied, "Well, I never thought of myself as an artist. Not really, none of the family, my mother, father, sister, or brother. They knew less about art than I did when I started, and that was nothing. I was an automobile mechanic for 27 years." We asked, "How did they respond to your new interests?" Ellis said, "They liked it real well." "What about the community?" He continued, "Pretty well, but you will find that in a smaller community, people have a different view of art. To them art is a good crop of corn. If you don't have a good crop of corn it's a different thing."

Sources of Ideas. Since the range of Ellis's subject matter indicated a considerable diversity of interest, we asked, "How do you come up with your ideas? Do they sit for a long time or do you get inspired when you awake in the morning, after a dream, or when?" Ellis replied:

Well, usually a few are thought out ahead, like a drawing of the crucifix. I did think about that for about 10 days before. But mostly, I think about it during the night. That is true that when a person wakes up in the morning or just before you wake up, a person's mind is the clearest, and that's

A dinosaur and assorted figures guard Ellis Nelson's shop

when a lot of these things come to mind. I have a vision of it [the object]; I think anyone can understand that.

We wondered, "Is there a point at which the material and the process take over, for example, when you start to see the shape of the form coming out of the process? Is there a time when you're putting something together when it changes the initial vision?" To this, Ellis responded:

Yes, that happens quite regularly. When you start to build something you don't tie yourself down to the certain idea entirely; you kind of add to it to get it to a certain point and then stand back and look at it and maybe add a few things here or there. When you get to a point when you can't make another move, you just sit down in a chair for about half an hour and it will become clear.

In further probing the source of Ellis's ideas, we repeated an earlier question, "Do you always have a finished form in mind, or do you shape it as you go along?" Ellis elaborated:

A lot of time I form it as I go along. The reason I like the free-form art is I gather up different shapes of metal, and I will add them to see what

I like, like these. Let's look at these pieces. Now this is a free-form, that turns in the wind. It's all scrap metal. I get it from the salvage yard. Well, I get these bodies [bird forms] from a local industry that hones cylinders.

"Do you ever do commissions?" we asked.

Well, I try to avoid that; although once in a while I do something a person wants. One lady from Madison said that she wanted something that was 12 feet high and wondered if I would build something. I asked what she liked. She liked a metal free-form, but she also liked birds. So I said I would build something that she might like. I built a thing like this with about a 6-foot wheel. It was quite striking, the shape and all. I called her a few days later and told her I had something I was sure she would be interested in. She came down the next day and she liked it. It was exactly what she wanted, so she bought it and took it home. Once I found out what she liked, I knew I couldn't go much wrong.

We saw a work that suggested a bird's nest. "Yes, that's a bird's nest. That was the last hatch. There were three of them." We said, "The heads turn freely; is that because of the type of materials you use, or did you have another reason?" Ellis replied, "It was probably the type of material." Turning to another piece, he said, "This I call fall. The wheat sags in the fall and the bird's sitting. That's my ideas. That's a free-form. It doesn't mean anything," which contradicted his initial description. In probing Ellis's sources of ideas further, we asked, "Were you ever inspired by other artists?" Ellis replied, "Well, not really. Let's put it this way: When you go to the junkyard you're not going to find a Picasso. They've probably got a little different kind of material to work with than I do." Ellis said he still used scrap metal as well as some sheet metal. We asked, "Do you ever do anything you don't like?" Ellis quipped, "I don't like making six redbirds in a day, but I do it."

In looking about Ellis's shop, one notices many clippings from papers and magazines of small images that evidently are a source of some of his ideas. For example, it was evident that an image of a dinosaur didn't just pop out of his head. For years he had been familiar with the dinosaur on the Sinclair oil sign in his service station. From this he made the connection to the large piece of sheet metal out of which he crafted his first piece. Also, once a shape enters his visual vocabulary, such as a bat-form, he continues to draw upon it, changing it slightly in the process of making.

Ellis's Values. Some of Ellis's values about what he likes have been suggested in his comments about making forms, but he also commented quite directly about what he liked. Ellis began, "What is it about them that I like one over another? Well, some of them are more of a challenge than others, and I do like a challenge. So, I am liable to build a sculpture that will balance and turn in the wind." We asked, "Does it make any difference to you whether you build a fox or an abstract?" Ellis suggested, "I like abstract more than I do figurative. Abstract is real interesting. I've got one here that I don't think you'll like, but the Frank Lloyd Wright organization has two of them. They bought another one for Arizona" (Taliesin West).

There are a variety of bats suspended from Ellis's shop front. To our inquiry about liking bats, Ellis said, "Yes, I do like bats. As a matter of fact someone brought me a sprayer to fix so that he could kill bats in his building, and I still haven't fixed it." In continuing our tour to see his work, Ellis said, "This is a different bird. Here is one of my more recent creations. The head is offset a little to get a little more motion in the creature." It was interesting that he was beginning to add slight variations to his sculpture to obtain more subtle expressions. In continuing his talk about bats, Ellis noted that bats are one of his most interesting sculptures to make. "I never make two alike. I never get tired of making bats. It's always interesting what they're going to be like."

The Future. When we interviewed Ellis, he had been working full time at making things for several years. "I work from about 7:30 in the morning until about 5:30 at night. Maybe, I might come out after supper, if something real interesting is going on." When asked about the future in making things, Ellis replied:

Well, what keeps me going is I can go out to the shop and say, well today I can build something entirely different. Nothing compared to what I did before. A lot of time it works out that way. Enjoy a hobby. It's very enjoyable working with metal. I don't think it's for everyone. It's great though if you like to work with metal.

Ellis indicated that he was very dedicated to his job. His philosophy and work habits certainly support this. He continues to attend to ever more subtle visual distinctions, as noted in comments such as, "Yes, it does change the shape of the sculpture if it turns at all. And I have noticed at times when it turns and shines, it will cast a shadow across the yard too."

Ellis is beginning to receive some attention in news and artistic circles, which we can tell he enjoys. Since the first article on his work, he has filled a scrapbook with articles and photos that have appeared in a variety of regional newspapers. Some of his work is now invited into regional exhibits; this he apparently values, but he also is very appreciative of whoever wants to stop by and look at his collection of creations. We believe that he values the social process of talking to others about what he does more than any recognition he is beginning to receive. Ellis still creates for himself, as attested to by his work habits and enjoyment of the making process, although he is beginning to appreciate the validation of his efforts through visitors' comments, sales, and the occasional exhibit. He really didn't regard what he made as art until others convinced him.

Simon Sparrow

Simon Sparrow lives in Madison, Wisconsin, where he makes drawings and large, heavy, complex collages on boards. The collages are made from beads, sequins, glitter, costume jewelry, and a vast array of tiny found objects that he sometimes buys and sometimes receives from his friends and admirers. Simon was born in West Africa. His father was African and his mother was Cherokee from North Carolina. Simon's parents met in the United States, but traveled to Africa. Simon is the youngest of several children born to his parents in Africa. His parents moved to the United States when Simon was an infant. He was 5 when his parents separated; he speaks fondly of the Seminole man his mother later married. Simon grew up in North Carolina and from his accounts led something of a charmed life.

Getting Started. As a very young boy Simon drew pictures in the sand, made clay figures, and eventually began to draw on scraps of cardboard. When he was 7, a stranger on the street offered him $10 for his first drawing, a large sum of money at that time. Simon talked about the experience.

Well, the time I started drawing . . . I was only 7 years old at the time. It was the first picture that I drawed on something. I used to draw on the ground . . . I used to make houses and buildings out of dirt and clay. We would make clay houses, clay animals, and little stuff. And it wasn't what you'd call great, you know. Nothin' like that. You could tell . . . that they was houses and buildings and things like that.

The first picture I ever drawed on a piece of big cardboard, it was about this big. I drawed some different animals, and he gave me $10. I ran in the house and I told my mother. I told her he gave me $10 and she said, "What? You got $10 for that thing?" (Laughs) That man gave me $10. She said, "Ah—he's crazy." No, Ma, he's not crazy. He knowed a good drawing when he seed it. She said, "Yeah, I know." And . . . that picture built my inside for drawing pictures. I used to set and do peoples. Draw animals . . . I'd draw anything. Anything. Mountains, hills, valleys (heavy sigh). That was like 1930s.

These experiences, along with his many other special attributes, led his mother to call Simon her *mystery child*. Still, Simon ventured away from home at an early age. At 12, he set out by train on his own to Philadelphia.

Through a series of fortunate happenstances, Simon found a place to live with a friendly couple who ran a restaurant. He worked in the restaurant and drew portraits of the customers in his spare time. During this period, Simon's work mirrored what he saw — buildings, people, and animals. Simon joined the Army with a group of his friends and moved to Nashville, Tennessee in 1943, at the age of 16. He continued to draw during his military duty. He drilled the troops during the day, a job for which he showed considerable aptitude. Simon said that he was never sent into combat during World War II because of his skill in drilling.

Simon's Values. After the military, Simon moved to New York City. At this time, he made things constantly and maintained a large studio where he also lived. Simon's work continued to explore realistic subjects, until an event changed his life. One day, Simon was walking home and came upon his apartment building engulfed in flames. When the terrible fire cooled the next day, all that was left in his apartment was a single painting standing upright, totally undamaged, amid the charred remains of his studio. Simon interpreted this as a *sign,* and from that time forward his life and art changed. Simon tells the story.

In New York, I had a place there, a big studio, I had all kinds of pictures drawed. And uh . . . I don't know, and I can't say, but I know that uh, it was evil or Lucifer burned it down. That was in 1973? Yeah. When it burned down, I had everything. I had statues. I had the crucifixion of Jesus Christ, all in one — all twelve of the apostles were in one and Jesus was in the center and all the rest were around, about Him. And, yeah, . . . after that uh, this got burnt down. I think 5 years, 4 or 5 years, something like, before I could get back into it. And all my work had changed. I wouldn't sell. You couldn't buy a piece from me for a million dollars. I can't know, just the Spirit, I think, allowed me just to make them. Couldn't sell 'em.

So, I did drawings . . . and that changed . . . when I was in New York City. The spirit rise. When I come to be spiritualized, ya know. I been a preacher. I just preach the Holy Scriptures from the Bible. The Holy Words, of God. When uh . . . the Holy Spirit leads me to speak. I can set and listen at a lot of things . . . and I cannot cut in, no kind, no way. See . . . because the Holy Spirit don't allow that. Uh . . . now if I'm speakin' for Christ, and of the Father and uh . . . if I'm speakin' at that time. I cannot speak anything else because it's the Holy Spirit do the speakin'.

It's like we . . . is a led; it's like we have a child, and take that child's hand, and lead that child to follow others. That's the way that the Holy Spirit leads me to the Father.

I have a feeling . . . my art work that I make follows in His same footsteps. I can't draw, I can't do anything without the Spirit leading me to do it. Not anything! I can look at it, but I can't touch it! It's just the Spirit guides me into the knowledge, and guides my hands, not my mind, not my thoughts — it didn't work like that.

Simon's sense of value, which was reflected in his art work, changed. He began to hear a strong spiritual voice. The spirit began to direct him as he created art. He became unable to create unless the spirit directed him. He also began to preach from the Bible on the street and developed a group of followers. The preaching and spirit directed his art making and it became the mainstay of his life. Simon stated, "My art work and preaching are together, they are the same. . . . During the time that I am preaching, the Spirit brings me many ideas for my pictures" (Cubbs, 1991, p. 5). According to Simon, the Spirit comes and works within him. He responds to a spiritual force that compels him to make things, sometimes by creating art and at other times by preaching. Throughout this time he worked on his art by drawing and painting. His spiritual life continued to direct the bulk of his daily activities.

Simon continued to make art, and the work features faces, bodies, and mysterious figures in fanciful landscapes of abstract designs. Currently, his large collages are covered with brightly colored patterns and geometric shapes. Some work is done simply in graphite pencil and some is done with oil pastels, drawn and smeared with Simon's fingers. Simon has made hundreds of drawings and claims he does not understand the stories, symbols, and shapes that appear. He is simply a conduit for the Spirit. On some days, he works feverishly all day and on others, he cannot work at all.

When talking about his expressive cultural practices Simon said, "All my work comes from the Holy Ghost." He insisted, "When I start a work, I never have any idea what it is going to be. The art flows from my hand like the river flows. When a piece is done, I'm sometimes shocked myself at what came out" (Jensen, 1985, p. 16). Simon's work has been warmly received into the different art worlds since it was recognized as something special by a guidance counselor at a local high school.

Simon has never felt comfortable with the art system and now prefers that his agent handle selling his art work as this is unpleasant for him. The sales of his art have helped to ease a lifelong struggle with financial instability. Simon operates a gallery and studio space: to supplement his income, to show his art work, and as a place where he can welcome frequent guests, admirers, and his spiritual followers. He is a superb storyteller and a kind, gentle, and

Simon Sparrow and collage

spiritual man. It is difficult, while in the studio space, to find separations between Simon's storytelling, art, and spirituality as they are so intertwined. Simon seems pleased by the publicity that his work has brought, but seems to view it all as a sideshow to his greater, more significant relationship with the spiritual world. He stated, "The Spirit of God enters and moves through my body. Most people can't see that. They can't see that it's the Spirit that uses the body if you belong to God . . . . My pictures are made not by myself, but by the Spirit of life itself" (Cubbs, 1991, p. 5).

Much has been said about the interconnectedness of Simon Sparrow's art making and his spiritual beliefs, expressive cultural practices, and African-American heritage. While Simon has stated that there is no direct connection between his work and African symbolism, some metaphors associated with African-American and African practices seem to sustain his work. Included among these is *spirit possession*.

During an inspirational sermon, characterized by call and response between preacher and audience, one "may get the spirit" which means that one experiences an emotional high attributed to spirits. Although the contemporary sophisticate may question such explanation, it is common to religious ceremonies among some Africans and also is associated with black and other religious practices in this country. The spirit seems to take over and direct the body, rather than behavior being directed by rational thought. Sparrow seems moved to create in a spiritual sense. What and how he creates is motivated by spiritual qualities that seem to direct rather than follow a step-by-step logical sequence of activities. In effect, spiritual qualities serve as his source of inspiration in making things just as in his preaching.

Another metaphor associated with Sparrow's work is *minkisi,* which is the Kikongo term for traditional medicines made by the fetish priest (Thompson, 1981, 1983). One must know the correct ingredients in order to make the medicines, which include earth, vegetable matter, and human-made objects such as nails, glass, buttons, and cloth. These medicines are enclosed in a pouch, which is fastened to the exterior of an object. The *minkisi* includes earth as embodying a medicine spirit, a living spirit captured within the medicines producing a life force that can be used to do one's bidding. In a sense, Simon's collages, fashioned out of colored sequins and other found objects, are his version of *minkisi,* representing a life force within his work.

There is a spiritual *flash* and *shine* in Simon's work made manifest through his use of a colorful array of glitter and similar materials. Just as an interaction between Simon and spirit serves as a motivating force in his work, so too does the use of glitter serve to heighten the visual/emotional call and response between his art and audiences.

Creating. Simon's art is an accumulation of objects in which form is created through the process of putting together collected objects. Simon's art is created through this process of accumulating various collected materials in which spirit forces are involved. When asked various questions about making art, he always went back to the spirit as a motivating force in the creation of work, a process that he did not understand or care to understand, but rather accepted on faith.

Simon uses a great variety of glitter in his works, which he regards as a human-made type of earth. In addition, beads, glass balls, old jewelry, Christmas ornaments, sunglasses, shells, and other objects small enough to be glued to a board are used. This accumulation of objects, which can be likened to *minkisi,* has various meanings within his work, meanings that may have a visual or spiritual rather than rational basis for inclusion. Shells are used, for example, as an element in religious objects throughout the world, including Africa. The shine and glitter can associated with the flash of spirit.

Representational elements in Simon's work are relatively simple, such as a face or a division or spaces. It seems that attention is directed more toward the qualities of an accumulation of materials rather than to the association of symbolic elements. At least, the symbolic aspects are closely associated with material accumulations and with spiritual forces that direct as well as are reflected in his work. While Simon Sparrow's expressive cultural practices may seem relatively simple at first, they are immensely subtle and complex in their motivation and association with symbolic meanings that seem to have ties to his African-American heritage.

Loretta Sylke

Loretta loves to paint pictures of childhood experiences. She represents the world with playful strokes from an untutored hand. She is a memory painter and has been called by art critics a folk artist who is wonderfully naive and an outsider. Loretta lives with her husband, Arthur Sylke, in a small ranch style house outside the city limits of Princeton, Wisconsin. Adjacent to her home is a small two-room gallery her husband built so she would have a place to exhibit her paintings. The gallery houses Loretta's large collection of personal paintings executed in oil and watercolor. The subject matter is mixed and reflects a time past or Loretta's personal experiences with family, friends, neighbors, and loved ones. As we sat talking about her painting and artistic practices, she discussed getting started and how she became interested in painting memory pictures.

Getting Started. Loretta is a sturdily built woman, whose stature reflects her independence and ability to meet a challenge. She raised six children mostly on her own. Her first husband she characterized as part gypsy or as a wanderer. She stated, "Well, I had been working in the supper club for 12 years, because my children were growing up and I was trying to, you know, I was a single parent for a long time. But we moved out here, after my son was killed in 1967." Loretta's son, Charles, died in an automobile accident. Her desire to paint was aroused after she lost her son. It was a way to help heal the memory of the tragic episode. She stated, "When you paint you forget about everything else. I think that what we need sometimes is just to escape from reality and you can forget everything about all the hardships that you have had."

Loretta was a painter before her son's auto accident. Upon moving to Princeton from Chamberlain, South Dakota, as a single mother, Loretta worked extremely hard to achieve financial stability. She moved several times before settling in Princeton, but it wasn't until after she married Arthur Sylke that she was able to stay at home and paint. Her choice not to work was also related to her son's death. Loretta said, "After my son was killed, it was a real blow. So, I gave up my work . . . I really felt I wanted to stay home, but after working so long, I wanted to occupy myself and so that's when I really started in."

Loretta did not paint alone or in the solitude of her own home. "I had some people around me that were painting and we used to go down to a place near the lake." Later, she joined a local chapter of the Wisconsin Rural

Artists but found its tight organization unappealing. Loretta had been painting landscapes, still lives, and wildlife pictures. She really enjoyed painting her immediate environment. "I did sort of still lives. I liked to plant and paint pussy willows. That's really what I started out doing. I would get a pallet knife full of paint and put it on really heavy." Loretta continued, reflecting back on why her style changed, "Someone had the idea my husband was helping me with my work. It really ticked me, you know . . . . Yeah, like I don't have the ability to paint or anything because I'm a woman! So I thought, well nobody's going to say that my husband painted my memories because he don't know what my memories are. So that's really how I got into it." Loretta used her memories as a source of ideas. It was her way to take ownership of her work and substantiate its authenticity to other people who had questioned her artistic abilities.

Source of Ideas. Loretta's childhood is her prime source of ideas. She grew up in South Dakota in the early 1930s. Her mother and father were immigrants from Germany and Russia, respectively, and made their living by working the land. "We had cattle and they grew grain. We used to have to go and stack the grain, you know, how they did years ago . . . you would make the grain in bundles . . . we'd have to go out and stack 'em. I had three brothers and one sister and we lived on a farm and it was during the depression. Times were really hard, but we never went hungry. But we knew what it was like to go without a lot of things."

The memories of Loretta's childhood are vividly recalled in her artwork. We asked her how they serve as a source of ideas. "Well," she replied, "I paint what I can associate with. Like my childhood memories. They're mine, you know, and nobody can say that they belong to anybody else. They're my memories and that's why they're special to me." Some of her most deeply felt recollections were about the farm, work, and her relationship with family. Loretta also talked about the land, school, and the depression. She told us how she chooses which memories to paint: "The things I really remember are like the sandstorms or the dust storms of the depression. Those really stick in my mind because I can still almost smell it. You'd come home from school and it would blow so hard. There would be little drifts inside the windowpanes. Inside. It would come right into the house. Even though you had your house closed tight . . . . The sand looked like snow drifts against the fence. Things like that are really etched into my mind." Other memories Loretta discussed were of her father making sausage, her first train ride, and an experience with caring for mother duck eggs. Recent paintings are of immediate family remembrances, of her six children, or her 11 grandchildren.

Loretta's Values. Loretta values her time to paint. We asked her specifically what she finds valuable about painting. She responded, "I think that painting — that it is relaxing. You can get lost in your work. When I paint I forget about my trials and tribulations." This refers to why she got started back in 1967, and its relationship to her son's auto accident. In the front room of the Sylke residence are pictures of all of Loretta's children and grandchildren. The portrait of her oldest son, Charles, still occupies a central location among the family grouping. Family values are an important part of Loretta's life style and belief system. Family values are represented in the personal experience narratives of Loretta's oil and watercolor paintings. They are part of the stories depicted by the chosen scenes and selected people. Birthdays, anniversaries, work, and daily events illustrate family values that are significant in her way of life.

Loretta's painting ability has been recognized by regional art critics. She has been invited to exhibit her work in many shows over the past 25 years (e.g., Wisconsin Women in the Arts, Art League of Beloit, and the Wisconsin Grassroots Exhibition). In 1993, Loretta was invited to submit three paintings to "The State of the Arts 93 Exhibition," sponsored by the Fine Arts Institute of Boston University. This was the latest of her shows, all of which are kept neatly ordered in her scrapbook.

Loretta showed us the scrapbook and commented about the various exhibits that she participated in. One of the articles we noticed was written by art critic James Auer from the *Milwaukee Journal*. Auer (1975) in his piece referred to Loretta's artwork as "wonderfully primitive." When asked about the name given her work, Loretta stated, "That don't bother me as much as outsider (laughs). I don't especially care for the term outsider." She indicated she was aware of the term currently circulating about self-taught artists through an antiques magazine she reads. She continued, "If people enjoy my work — that's enough, you know. If they come and say 'Gee, I like that,' I don't really care if they call me primitive — I don't care about being called an outsider, too much. Really I get too much satisfaction from painting to be bothered by that." Loretta continues to paint, but her time is split between painting, quilting, and caring for her 11 grandchildren. Her health has been poor the past 5 years, and it has deterred her from painting regularly.

The Future. Loretta Sylke still occupies much of her time painting and making quilts. In her family there is a long tradition of quilting, and she uses her past acquired skills to make story quilts for her grandchildren. We asked about her future plans. She stated, "I think I'm going to slow down a lot, I want to do other things too — enjoy life. We are winding down a little now. I will continue to paint, but I've decided I better finish the quilts. Because I'm one that if I don't complete something that I've started and put it aside, it's very hard for me to get back to it. I have to keep with it." Loretta's most productive period of painting was between 1972 and 1977. Painting is not central to her life anymore. It has been replaced with another creative activity—quilting. But painting is and will continue to always be her first love. Loretta loves to work with her hands. She has all her life, and it is what motivates her to be productive.

Carter Todd

Carter can often be seen in the Student Union Rathskeller, seated at a table with his drawing materials or visiting a fellow artist, Simon Sparrow. Carter was interviewed not because of achievements he attained in spite of several disabilities, but simply because he consistently pursues and achieves a high level of artistic production and finds art to be an element central to his way of life.[1]

Getting a Start. Carter is in his forties and has been drawing for over 13 years. Getting started with art has been inseparable from the physical and mental disabilities that have made Carter's daily routine more difficult. Carter's life has been shaped by a rather complicated personal history.

Carter was born and raised in Indianapolis. His parents were sensitive to his mild cognitive and physical disabilities. Carter's upbringing was very similar to that of his sisters and brothers, and the family encouraged social awareness, adjustment, and adaptation. However, Carter's immediate special needs were not attended to in his youth. When Carter was in his early twenties, a series of unfortunate events greatly affected his life. Carter's father died when he was twenty-three. Shortly thereafter, he began to have epileptic seizures. In his confusion and frustration, Carter struggled to understand who he was and why he had several physical and emotional obstacles in his life. According to those around him, Carter needed to integrate the various self-images and identities into a stable, coherent personality. His problems were further compounded by an alcohol addiction, which he has successfully combatted during his years as an artist. Carter's lack of emotional and physical stability made it very difficult for him to live at home with his mother. Carter was invited to live in Madison with his sister Sally and her husband Ernie Johnson, a social worker.

Carter used to live with his sister and brother-in-law, Sally and Ernie. They had an artistically gifted son whom they encouraged to draw. Carter expressed a wish that he could draw like their son. Later, when Carter was hospitalized with a severe case of hepatitis, Sally brought him colored pencils and adult coloring books. Carter enjoyed the way drawing and coloring occupied his mind, and this new pastime was especially welcome because he neither read nor cared to watch television. After this initial contact with art materials, Carter's drawing lapsed until he later returned to it as a form of therapy during treatment for his alcohol addiction. His work was encouraged by Sally

Carter Todd drawing, approx. 9 × 12″

and by staff members and other patients during this period of treatment. Carter's drawings were exhibited in the hospital hallways and were later assembled, along with an essay describing his warm personality, into an album entitled "The Carter Todd Collection."

The supportive environment and positive reinforcing values and attention associated with Carter's drawing experiences influenced him to continue his art. Carter's art enabled him to interact with other people in a very positive manner. It also helped provide a more integrated identity and a focus that helped in dealing with alcohol addiction. Supported by his sister and family, along with a broad circle of friends, Carter received encouragement in maintaining a constructive disposition. This support and artistic work provide Carter with the security and reinforcement that he needs to carry on. Thus, in a very personal way and through a complex process, Carter has become a productive artist today.

Artistic Values. Carter's drawings are about places, both local and imagined. They are about houses, trees, driveways, and sidewalks. Carter often tells a story or narrative to go with his drawings as he seeks to make contact with others. The desire to interact with others, both mentally and physically, is many times fulfilled through his drawings. We talked with Carter as he drew, and this is one of the stories he shared with us. Carter started, "I never know what I'm going to do until I go do it." Carter drew a house on a blue sheet of construction paper. "This was the Meyer's home until they sold it to the Joneses. There are some bushes next to the tree." Carter colored the apple tree red and outlined it with a green border. "When I draw I try to make everyone happy. That's what life is about. . . . Now these people are fussy about their sidewalk too. I have to straighten everything out." Carter had pointed to the Jones house. He retraced the lines he had previously drawn. As he drew, Carter moved back and forth between personal stories about his own life and short descriptive narratives associated with the drawing. He looked up from the kitchen table where his drawing was placed in front of him and kept on, "I used to work at Henries Restaurant, . . . Burger King, . . . and an ice cream shop. I used to do a lot of yard work until my heart condition went bad. Then the doctor told me I couldn't do that anymore. I had two heart attacks, just recently, in the last year. . . . Then I quit and I have been drawing ever since." Carter returned to the picture he was working on, talking as he drew. "The gardeners are coming to take care of the gardens. Mrs. Jones has to decide what color she wants the house. Mr. Jones is in Texas. . . . He will return tomorrow. She told the painter she wants a blue house with green window wells. . . . She changed her mind. She wants them violet. She is pretty happy because her house is almost done." Carter stopped, smiled broadly and added, "This is my imagination." Sometimes Carter supplies an imaginative narrative as he sits, works, and visits with friends.

A recurrent theme in Carter's work reflects his desire to give things to and interact with other people. Carter's drawing provides a vehicle for him to resolve a part of his life he feels is incomplete. The stories at least partially fulfill that need and are a personal way for him to reconcile his strong sense to establish community with others. Carter showed us a mug that had one of his drawings printed on it. The text on the mug read, "Belonging to the Community: Celebrating Ten Years." Carter is a member of several social groups and organizations. In a sense through his drawings and stories Carter can give people what they want. His stories may come from his past memories, from experiences, or from an active imagination. Carter's drawings have no specific titles. However, they most often incorporate a narrative that he usually keeps to himself but is willing to share with his friends when asked.

The subject matter of Carter's drawings are of his familiar environments: houses, other buildings, gardens, walkways, yards, and streets. Through these themes, Carter has direct contact with everyday familiar places. Carter is very prolific. When asked about his drawing practices he said, "I do like to draw all the time. . . . When I get tired and I go out and ride my bike. . . . I draw about two pictures a day. Some of the large houses and scenes take two days or more." The drawings are solidly colored right up to the edge of the paper. The colors are chosen rather arbitrarily and are not always of a true-to appearance. Carter is sometimes so motivated that once started he continues to draw until the early hours of the morning in one of his favorite hangouts. He seems to have an incredible drive to create that provides him with a strong sense of accomplishment and satisfaction.

The Future. Carter only recently started to consider himself an artist. He accepted this name because people kept referring to him as an artist and repeatedly told him that his drawings were good. This has been reinforced by his artistic acceptance by a midwestern gallery that handles his work. Carter's work is recognized and valued as that of an "outsider artist" because his art is relatively free from conventions and clichés so often characteristic of formally trained artists and from the constraints associated with work by other artists. There is a certain drive to create houses, driveways, and sidewalks. Most of his work is of familiar places minus humans. One might say that he has established a "style," characterized by repetitive subject interpretations and use of the medium of colored pencils. This approach does seem to give Carter control over an environment and, together with the recognition of his work, to enable him to control situations that might otherwise be considered hostile.

Some art people have suggested that Carter should work larger or use media other than colored pencils or markers on block pads of paper (usually about letter size). However, Carter agrees with those who suggest that his mobility would be severely limited, and it is his mobility that allows close contact with a network of supportive friends. It is these social dimensions of his life that sustain him, more than any further recognition that he might gain by expanding his repertoire as an "outsider" artist. As it is, Carter is highly mobile and he moves quite readily between his favorite hangouts. The Union Rathskeller is one place where he visits friends and draws. Carter shares his living quarters with a friend who also enjoys drawing. He spends his hours at home and away with friends and acquaintances. Carter loves to converse, make jokes, and express a kind word. He gets satisfaction from helping other people. He said, "I was thinking about teaching children how to draw. . . . I had a lot of kids come up and watch me draw when I was down at the Union. . . . They would draw with me." His drawings serve as the medium through which he exhibits his warm feelings for others. Thus, while Carter's drawing process may serve as a form of therapy, his works possess qualities that are recognized and admired, and they enable the important social contact with other people.

CONCLUSION

In one sense, it is extremely difficult, and perhaps misleading, to draw conclusions in the form of generalizations recognizing the uniqueness of individuals and the processes through which they make things. But, having said that, there are some patterns of characteristics that may enable us to recognize and value the unique contributions of people who make things.

An Interpretation

First, it is amazing how many people make things, a great variety of things, usually for their own needs. However, as soon as one begins to apply qualitative criteria to the products, such as galleries and collectors have done in recognizing the distinctiveness and expressiveness of "outsider art," the more traditional focus on objects supersedes the individual/process orientation. Yet even those who make things from patterns may derive some personal and social satisfaction from putting together craft kits and the like, which are usually considered to result in visually inferior products. Perhaps such activities may be the beginnings of a process of growth and change that is certainly discernible among those who make things valued for their uniqueness or other qualities. Generalizations are drawn and applied with caution.

From this study of people who make things it is apparent that there are almost as many ways of "getting a start" as there are individuals. Some have a fascination with materials and processes. Others get a start in making something that is closely related to some professional activity in which they previously engaged, such as Ellis Nelson whose work with machinery, metal, and mechanics continued into his art. The object is not to identify some generalization as the basis for an active art education, but rather to recognize and value the human propensity to make.

Once started in creating an object, and after attaining a certain degree of skill in the process, these people still have a strong desire to engage in working with materials and tools. They acquired or even invented tools to refine a process or an object as a manifestation of an idea. Many of the people interviewed, as well as many others who have been observed, indicated that they had changed their tools, changed techniques, and acquired new materials in order to get closer to an idea or form they had in mind.

What individuals create does not necessarily stand alone in an art for art's sake sense. *Narrative* is widely used to accompany the objects, sometimes in parallel, sometimes in explanation, and sometimes in amplification of suggested meanings. Loretta's work was specifically connected to stories about her youth and family experiences. Ellis Nelson gave detailed accounts of how he came to create particular pieces. Carter Todd developed elaborate explanatory stories, while others commented about their social contacts in making or selling objects. With only a few exceptions, most of the people interviewed were willing to sell what they made. Although a few individuals took commissions on a regular basis, most began to sell on a rather informal basis — a friend liked or wanted some particular piece, or a visitor strongly admired a piece already created. Through these informal circumstances, people who make things begin to receive recognition and come to acquire that status of artist as so named by visitors. Eventually, their work may find its way into collections, galleries, and even museums. In effect, this is an informal process of socialization as an artist, in contrast to a more formal route by those educated in professional institutions.

Most individuals are willing to talk about what they do, granting interviews readily and willingly. This re-emphasizes the social dimensions in making things; the process of socializing seems to be of almost equal importance to the making of things. It is a very human interactive process that through a network connects them to others. In this sense, the process has meaning for them as does the object that they make.

Do the values, aesthetic and otherwise, of people who make things change? The answer is most certainly yes. This question was partially answered in the observation that they sought to improve upon the process of creating through acquisition of new skills, processes, and materials. This was more than skill acquisition, for in many instances it enabled them to come closer to an ideal, to express an idea better, or to make something "nicer." In fact, these tangible and intangible characteristics seem to differentiate the person who feels compelled to continue the process in contrast to those who are willing to continue replication of prefabricated models or other objects in which the dimensions of change are not involved. In these ways, a social conception of aesthetics, such as that espoused by Wolff (1983), seems to fit their situation more readily than a more formalistic conception.

New Meanings for the Study of Art in Education

In recent years, Ellsworth (1989a, b), Gablik (1991), hooks (1992), Wolff (1981, 1983), and others have cautioned researchers against using dogmatic forms of cultural analysis and have suggested that research should deconstruct the erected lines of division that separate theories, practices, and cultures. It is our opinion that research in the field of art education should take an interdisciplinary and culturally responsive approach to the study of art and art making. People interested in knowing more about different cultural groups and their artistic practices should conduct inquiry that moves back and forth between the details of the makers' actual lived experiences, the social structures that influence and affect their lives, and the broad theoretical explanations of culture. In art education, theories need to be reconnected to the specificity of art and the practices of people who make things. Cultural inquiries should be situated within particular social, political, economic, and historical conditions.

If art educators are going to conduct cultural studies in local communities and make connections between theories and practices, it is critical to understand the social, cultural, and historical context and multiple perspectives out of which these theories and practices derive their specific pertinence. Research about people who make things needs to be reconnected to the culture of the people involved, and not imposed on the people of a particular culture from the outside (Congdon, 1991; Gablik, 1991; Krug, 1993; Neperud, 1988; Wasson, Stuhr, & Petrovich-Mwaniki, 1990). The specificity of art, as connected to visual expressive cultural practices, must be presented as generated from actual life situations, from cultural and historical experiences, as are cultural interpretations and other socially produced practices. Culture, practice, and theory interact and need to be re-presented as mutually constructed. This is the underlying assertion of a culturally responsive approach to pedagogy.

A Culturally Responsive Approach to Pedagogy

A culturally responsive approach to education advocates a community orientation, recognizes diversity as a force in the lives of people, and investigates the formation of interests, satisfaction, practices, and values in the construction of the maker's cultural identity. Beginning at a local and community level, a culturally responsive approach to inquiry considers not only the product (object) and the producer (artist), but also the viewer, the practice, and the cultural context at a particular time and place. It is necessary for people to engage in a dialogic process. Several authors in art education and other fields of study have already made significant contributions to this aspect of curriculum design (Blandy & Congdon, 1987, 1988; Bowers, 1974; Congdon, 1986; Duncum, 1989; Hicks, 1989; Johnson, 1993; Krug, 1993; May, 1989; Neperud, 1988; Wasson et al., 1990). The following six guidelines are a synthesis of perspectives. They are suggested as a way to conduct inquiry about the interconnectedness of art, aesthetics, and culture. The purpose of the inquiry is to foster respect and understanding of differing points of view through the investigation of art forms, artists' perspectives, and artistic practices. To that end, students, teachers, and researchers should use a culturally responsive approach to:

1. Seek ways to understand how the things people make and their expressive cultural practices mark a time, place, and event in the formation of their cultural identity
2. Look for ways to expand their knowledge and understanging about the interconnectedness of art, aesthetics, and culture in the everyday lives of people and how this knowledge relates to the formation of the makers' self-identity and sense of place in the community and society

3. Conduct inquiry that minimizes and eliminates negative and pejorative stereotypes and prejudices against people and the things they make
4. Use an interdisciplinary approach that links the field of art with other areas of inquiry, e.g., art, art history, anthropology, communication arts, cultural studies, education, folklife, folklore, and sociology
5. Conduct inquiry to understand how the things that people make are associated with meanings and values that are relationally situated within social, economic, religious, technological, political, historical, and cultural contexts
6. Strive to expand the notion of visual material culture and expressive cultural practices to include a broad representation of makers of art and include their narratives and art forms in cultural studies programs and art education curriculum

We believe that it is in the everyday expressive cultural practices of makers of art, that research and inquiry need to understand better the formation of Self-identity, social identity, and social relations in the lived experiences of the everyday—in the lives of people in society.

The study of culture in art education circulates as forms of knowledge through language, communicative practices, and other types of discourse. The most pervasive and prominent discourse in art education occurs in the selection and teaching of official art modeled after a universal or single aesthetic. The single aesthetic is a form of knowledge that has been chosen as the *selective tradition*. It embraces the notion of aesthetic individualism and a perspective that is derived from the many different art worlds centered in the great Western traditions of European civilizations. Since the single aesthetic perspective excludes a wide and diverse selection of knowledge, which encompasses cultures from non-Western traditions and nonmainstream makers, its latent and manifest function in the curriculum has recently been called into question by some socially and culturally conscious art educators.

We should look specifically at making and valuing in the contexts of social, artistic, and aesthetic forces that are active in people's lives. Four areas of inquiry—interests, satisfaction, practices, and values—are interconnected with the formation of the maker's cultural identity. How can these areas of inquiry be brought together to study contexts, communitym, and artists? We propose that a culturally responsive pedagogy is a way to minimize certain limits and open up possibilities for active, imaginative, and participatory inquiry. The curriculum maker is not unlike the working artist. Each is engaged in a passion of labor that is about "disclosure, reconstruction, and generation" (Greene, 1971, p. 240).

Art education practices have commonly assumed that art means the official arts as circulated in museums, art centers, and galleries, and as presented by a hierarchy of experts. As revealed in this and preceding chapters, views of what constitutes art, aesthetics, society, and culture have changed dramatically in recent decades. Nowhere has this been more apparent than in what constitutes art and valuing of art, and who we consider to be artists. This investigation of people who make things, and contextual circumstances surrounding their creative processes, suggests real changes for the meaning of art education.

We cannot simply add "outsider art," non-Western art, folk art, indigenous art, or the diverse forms created by the "other" to the bottom of a pedagogical hierarchy with fine arts at its apex. Rather, the field of art from which teachers may choose has been leveled, thus reflecting their multicultural teaching situations.

Art education should be open to emerging forms of visual communication circulating in the day-to-day lives of people in the lived culture. This means that an art teacher's curricular practices cannot begin and end with predetermined means and ends. Rather, there needs to be ongoing dialogue with students in which they reveal the visual culture that has meanings for them, so that they do not become disaffected. Initiation of dialogue through questioning strategies or provocative imagery may elicit reactions from students; without dialogic inquiry and action research, education reverts to monologic didacticism. Local cultural art forms are readily available in comunity contexts for this initial interactive process to begin in which one seeks to know more about aesthetics from the ground up. Perhaps it is time for inquiry in art education to begin with people who make things in their own community and from the details of their everyday lived experiences and personal environment.

NOTE

1. The authors wish to recognize the contribution of Lisa Toppleman in calling their attention to the art of Carter Todd. In a graduate seminar taught by Professor Neperud, Lisa interviewed and wrote about Carter. Several subsequent interviews by the authors provided the basis for Carter Todd's inclusion in this chapter.

REFERENCES

Ardery, J. (1991). The designation of difference. *New Art Examiner, 9*, 29–32.
Auer, J. (1975). *Review of rural Wisconsin Rembrandts*. Milwaukee, WI: Charles Allis Art Library.

Blandy, D., & Congdon, K. G. (Eds.). (1987). *Art in a democracy.* New York: Teachers College Press.

Blandy, D., & Congdon, K. (1988). Community based aesthetics as an exhibition catalyst and a foundation for community involvement in art education. *Studies in Art Education, 29*(4), 243–249.

Bowers, C. (1974). *Cultural literacy for freedom: An existential perspective on teaching, curriculum, and school policy.* Eugene, OR: Elan.

Cardinal, R. (1972). *Outsider art.* New York: Praeger.

Congdon, K. (1986). The meaning and use of folk speech in art criticism. *Studies in Art Education, 27*(3), 140–148.

Congdon, K. (1991). Art worlds, environmental images, and art education: A folk art focus. *Journal of Multicultural and Cross-cultural Research in Art Education, 9*(1), 65–72.

Cubbs, J. (1991). *Religious visionaries.* Sheboygan, WI: John Michael Kohler Arts Center.

Dissanayake, E. (1988). *What is art for?* Seattle: University of Washington Press.

Dissanayake, E. (1992). *Homo aestheticus: Where art comes from and why.* New York: Free Press.

Duncum, P. (1989). Toward foundations for a socially critical art education. *Journal of Social Theory in Art Education, 9,* 12–25.

Ellsworth, L. (1989a). Why doesn't this feel empowering? Working through the repressive myths of critical pedagogy. *Harvard Educational Review, 59*(3), 297–324.

Ellsworth, L. (1989b). Educational media, ideology, and the presentation of knowledge through popular culture. In H. Giroux & R. Simon (Eds.), *Popular culture: School and everyday life* (pp. 47–66). New York: Bergin & Garvey.

Gablik, S. (1991). *The reenchantment of art.* New York: Thames & Hudson.

Greene, M. (1971). Curriculum and consciousness. *Teachers College Record, 73*(2), 237–253.

Hall, M. (1991). The mythic outsider: Handmaiden to the modern muse. *New Art Examiner, 9,* 16–21.

Hicks, L. (1989). Cultural literacy as social empowerment. *Journal of Social Theory in Art Education, 9,* 58–63.

hooks, b. (1992). *Black looks: Race and representation.* Boston: South End Press.

Jensen, D. (1985, July). Art from the outsider. *Airwaves,* pp. 14–17. Madison, WI: Wisconsin Public Television.

Johnson, K. (1993). Significant others. *Art in America, 81*(6), 84–91.

Krug, D. (1992/93). The expressive cultural practices of a nonacademically educated artist, Ellis Nelson, in the micro and macro environment. *Journal of Multicultural and Cross-cultural Research in Art Education, 10/11*(1), 20–48.

Krug, D.(1993). An interpretation of the expressive cultural practices of nonacademically art educated makers of art in Wisconsin (Doctoral dissertation, University of Wisconsin-Madison). *Dissertation Abstracts International, 93*–30823.

Lippard, L. (1990). *Mixed blessings: New art in a multicultural America.* New York: Pantheon.

Manley, R. (1991). Separating the folk from their art. *New Art Examiner, 9,* 25–28.

May, W. (1989). Teachers, teaching, and the workplace: Omissions in curriculum reform. *Studies in Art Education, 30*(3), 142–156.

Neperud, R. W. (1988). Conceptions of art in the service of art and aesthetic education: A critical view. *Arts and Learning Research, 6*(1), 95–106.

Neperud, R. (1990). *A photographic documentation and analysis of outsider artists*. Report submitted to the Graduate School, University of Wisconsin-Madison. Research funded by summer salary grant from the Graduate School.

Thompson, R., with Cornet, P. (1981). *Four moments of the sun: Kongo art in two worlds*. Washington, DC: The National Gallery of Art.

Thompson, R. (1983). *Flash of the spirit: African and Afro-American art and philosophy*. New York: Random House.

Vlach, J. (1991). *By the work of their hands: Studies in Afro-American folk life*. Charlottesville: University Press of Virginia.

Wasson, R., Stuhr, P., & Petrovich-Mwaniki, L. (1990). Teaching art in the multicultural classroom: Six position statements. *Studies in Art Education, 31*(4), 234–246.

Wolff, J. (1981). *The social production of art*. New York: New York University Press.

Wolff, J. (1983). *Aesthetics and the sociology of art*. London: Allen & Unwin.

PART III

Culture and Community: Context of Art Teaching

The fundamental transformations occurring in the practice of art and aesthetics in recent decades have prepared a basis for art education within the particulars of community context. Just as the meaning of art depends on and interacts with the context of society, so too does contemporary art education. The aesthetic, structural, and language codes and conventions operating within particular social and historical frames, whether representing Native Americans, Hispanics, other racial and ethnic groups, or groups defined by class and gender issues, must be reckoned with in art education practices. Meaning in a postmodern sense depends on how particular historical, social, and cultural matrices intersect and change to define the circumstances to which art education must be accountable.

After the myths of modernism and universal meanings have been deconstructed, this section suggests a growing optimism that educators can respond in a reconstructive sense to their cultural and community circumstances. June King McFee, long recognized for introducing the importance of cultural content to art education, reminds us of those traditions in Chapter 8, "Change and the Cultural Dimensions of Art Education." Culture refers not to a cultural elitism, but to the beliefs, values, and attitudes of particular groups. McFee provides a view of culture and art education against which particular suggestions for change are recognized, implying that art education changes are based on cultural views. She also outlines some practices in art education that follow changes, thus providing a basis for understanding and curriculum development within the particulars of a culture, such as that of the Wisconsin Indians discussed in the next chapter.

In Chapter 9, "Social Reconstructionist Multicultural Art Curriculum Design: Using the Powwow as an Example," Patricia Stuhr discusses Native American approaches to multicultural art education based on a reconstructionist approach. To the question of whose knowledge, Stuhr answers, "the cultural specificity of a community's resources and aesthetic values." Based on her extensive ethnographic studies of the Wisconsin Indians, Stuhr selected the powwow, the greatest display of

Wisconsin Indian cultural aesthetic production and performance, as the basis for curriculum development. Rather than treating the powwow as an historical artifact, Stuhr argues from a reconstructionist position that students, teachers, and community members should be involved and challenged by local activity, in this case the powwow, in decision making and community action. Curriculum development is not a passive, bookish enterprise, but rather a total community engagement and commitment. What Stuhr demonstrates in this chapter is a reliance on contextual particulars to get at content through democratic participation, which from a traditional content focus would have been achieved by studying *about* rather than *participation in* an activity.

Neperud's Chapter 10, "Texture of Community: An Environmental Design Education," also takes a reconstructionist approach to involving students, teachers, and community in environmental education. Active engagement with the community becomes the basis for integrating design with other curricular activities in this increasingly important part of art educators' presence in a community. This view demonstrates how contemporary environmental design education is allied to multicultural education.

A thesis of this volume is that art education practices shift in response to social and cultural content and context. Art education at any point in time reflects an intersection of both historical and contemporary context. Art education today has a particularly strong contextual component, including social, political, cultural, and environmental conditions, the understanding of which is central to the meaning of ideas and practices.

CHAPTER 8

Change and the Cultural Dimensions of Art Education

June King McFee

The education of art teachers for multicultural classrooms during periods of rapid and extensive change requires critical reanalysis of the whole art education system, starting with preparation of higher education faculty. Culturally sensitive teachers need to be aware of the meaning of culture, its impact on how students' learn, what they already know, and how they are being affected by forces of change. But today we have more diversity of cultures and more change and reaction to change than ever before — in our schools, in our society, and in the characteristics of our national identity. In this chapter selected materials from cultural anthropology, anthropology and education, cross-cultural and cognitive psychology, sociology and the social foundations of art education are used to elucidate these factors. Implications are then drawn to help teachers address cultural diversity and change in the art classroom.

THE CONCEPT OF CULTURE

To begin we must clarify the two uses of the concept of culture in art education. One comes from a tradition of nineteenth-century elitists in Western societies, who identified culture and the state of being cultured as belonging to those people who shared their attitudes about what was an acceptable life style and what was good art. They assumed that others who had values at variance with theirs had less culture and in many cases no culture at all (Goodenough, 1981). The assumption that the values and symbols of Western civilization, as people like Hirsch interpret and select from them, should dominate education, is clearly a narrow nineteenth-century elitist view of culture (Hirsch, 1987). Some cultures may dominate, have more political and economic power, and even have more complex cultures, but these do not become criteria for placing the values of one cultural group over another in a democratic society. Nor is a subculture necessarily inferior to a dominant culture.

The assumption of cultural elitism reinforces the concept that culture is a particular body of knowledge and not, as anthropologists and other social scientists identify, systems of beliefs, values, and attitudes that have developed within the group maintaining them. All people are recognized as having a cultural belief and value system. The concept of culture, as used by anthropologists, has itself evolved over time. Part of this change is due to political changes in the world, as colonialism decreased and as the autonomy of cultural groups fluctuated (Clifford, 1988). Sometimes the boundaries of cultural groups and political boundaries were the same. At other times multiple cultures were bound within one governing political system. In today's world the migrations of peoples and changes in boundaries are greater than ever before. But we still have examples of some large nations that remain more homogeneous, even though their culture is changing internally. Japan is such a nation. Australia, Canada, and the United States, by contrast, are experiencing more diverse immigration from more parts of the world than ever before in the in histories of immigration.

Cultural studies based on fieldwork have been done largely in smaller, more remote areas where clear boundaries made research more describable. Concepts from these studies have been useful in trying to understand more complex societies. Also, in the last decade of the twentieth century the studies of remote peoples are relevant because children who are carriers of their culture now sit in our classrooms.

In 1951, the anthropologist Clyde Kluckhohn published his survey of the definitions of culture and identified three points of agreement:

1. Individuals in a cultural group learn a somewhat similar pattern for thinking, classifying, organizing, and relating information.
2. They invent or borrow symbols to use in learning and communicating cultural meanings and documenting them in the creation of artifacts.
3. The core of their culture carries on their traditional values and ideas.

Three decades later, Geertz (1983) referred to the diverse social science theories of how different people think. He cautioned, though, that often the emphasis is on how others differ from us (the culture of Western anthropologists). He posited that if we assume this we will look for ways they are inferior and miss ways they may excel. But if we assume we are all equal, we may look for likenesses and miss differences.

Geertz would add to Kluckhohn's list the ways people in different cultures define themselves as persons. These vary from a strong sense of individuality as separate from the group to the individual immersed in the social milieu, acting as a group member more than as an individual (Geertz, 1983). He further stresses that we are trying to find out how others, "across the sea or down the corridor organize their significant world" (p. 151). It can be added that in this process we gain insight into ways we organize what we have learned that has significance in our group's culturally perceived world.

Hofstede (1984), a Dutch cross-cultural psychologist, speaks of "the collective programming" of the minds of a cultural group, which distinguishes it from the ways other groups have learned to think with their own program. He identifies three levels of programmed thinking: Universal, used by most humans; collective, that learned in a cultural group; and individual, what individuals structure from their experience with universal, collective, and their own patterns of thought.

Triandis (1983), another cross-cultural psychologist, divides culture into two aspects, objective and subjective. Objective elements include ways a people use space, the objects (including art) they invent, and the tools they develop. Subjective elements include what they consider as the norm — their values and their hierarchy of values.

Brislin (1983), from the same discipline, shows the importance of symbols in a culture. We use them to express values, and then the symbols themselves take on value. We become culturally centric about them and value them more highly than other people's symbols.

Further, we learn symbols as children and accept the patterns in which they are presented; then we use these symbolic patterns to try to understand our later experiences. For this reason we see culture, as represented through symbols, as prepatterned and representational as well as emergent (Dougherty & Fernandez, 1981).

By contrast, another study by Hofstede (1984) focuses on cultural diversity among Western cultural traditions. He questioned whether there were differences in motivation that could be identified. One aspect of motivation is related to how one sees oneself in relation to the group, and how one behaves as a result of this culturally learned way of achieving. His findings suggest that in Spain, Portugal, Yugoslavia, and France there is a strong pattern of need for security and group solidarity. In Greece and German-speaking countries it is for individual security, while in Great Britain and its dominions and former colonies (including Canada and the United States) the most powerful force for motivation is personal, individual success. In northern European countries, including the Netherlands, it is for collective success of belonging and for the living environment.

This suggests an extension of Geertz's definition of culture as the way people see themselves as individuals. It suggests that the culture is also a pattern of how people are motivated to act: for themselves, for the group, for security, or for something called success.

Anthropologist Pierre Bourdieu (1984) analyzed relationships between the social and economic conditions and the cultural patterns of people living at different socioeconomic levels in France. It is assumed that there is an overall culture that differentiates French people from other political groups, but the study shows how in complex cultures, subcultures develop variations according to social class. This pattern of culture within each class is used to reinforce the solidarity of each class and separate it from the others. It is possible to ask if this trait is reinforced in France because of the emphasis on group solidarity, which Hofstede found. We will refer to Bourdieu's study in relation to our study of cultural studies of art because he found that acquisition of surroundings and art is a key factor in the differentiation and identification of class.

In a comparative study of images and social realities in Great Britain, France, and the United States since 1930, Marwick (1980) illustrates that there are "fuzzy" distinctions of "social class" or status in these countries based on variations in opportunity, equality, life styles, acceptable possessions, and living and working situations. Based on Bourdieu's study and the wealth of evidence of different cultures, we are forced to recognize that there are different concepts about what art forms express a given social class' identity and what children growing up in these classes tend to learn about what is acceptable as art.

Finally, an analysis of cultural anthropology by historian James Clifford (1988) is included in this brief review of concepts of culture. His is an attempt to identify functions of culture as the contemporary world changes so drastically. He cites increased individual mobility, and a wider range of at-home mobility due to mass transit, planes, and motor vehicles, and worldwide migration to large cities by people from different ethnic and cultural backgrounds. At the same time almost no place in the world is not touched by modernization, with its products and its media-projected images. Many societies in the world are more multicultural than ever before. The cultural differences one finds in one's neighborhood may be as great as those encountered on a trip to a remote country on another continent.

Clifford (1988) provides us with more insights into thinking about culture. It is never static. It may appear to die out, but may spring up in new forms. It is often contested politically, but survives. Observers of other cultures are themselves part of a culture. We see other cultures through our own cultural screen. In the present world of increasing interconnectedness, individuals are less culturally authentic, particularly if we no longer conceive of culture as a static state.

Even in more cohesive cultures some people are more at the core of the culture, others more peripheral. Some try to change the culture, others to resist change (McFee & Degge, 1992).

Clifford (1988) points out that ethnographers need to document how a culture is holding together and how it is being negotiated now. He suggests that cultural aspects are sometimes lost, sometimes adapted, and that new cultural characteristics are invented. He indicates that the thoughts of dominant societies about others can no longer be as stable as before and that a cultural group's concepts of themselves as contrasted with others are not as clear-cut as was once believed. In other words, our stereotypic knowledge of other cultures is even more inadequate to work with individuals or groups that appear to represent a given culture. Malcolm McFee (1969) used the metaphor of the 150% man to identify individual Blackfoot Indians who had not given up their traditional culture in learning to cope in the dominant rural Montana farming culture. Our assumption that some of the old must be lost to learn the new is questioned. Acculturation, the learning of a new culture, does not necessarily mean unlearning old cultural patterns (M. McFee, 1969). For some people culture change may not be so much change as it is cultural extension, that is, individuals becoming more multicultural.

One also has to look at *reification,* the persistence of cultural groups in maintaining their identity. Culture change is not one-directional. Some aspects may be subject to change, others not. A cultural group may refuse to change in some ways but be flexible in others. New immigrants from a given culture often seek out members who arrived earlier. Often these earlier residents have begun to develop some kind of adaptation to the dominant and other subcultures, but in many cases the efforts to maintain culture are intense. For example, two children from the same southeast Asian village may have had different experiences on arriving here. One may have settled in an adaptive community, and the other in a reifying community. They will carry their culture differently when they arrive in school because of their experiences in the transition and settling experience. One may be deeply entrenched in his or her background culture and may be rewarded at home for resisting the new cultural surroundings. The other may be openly seeking to learn and select from the new, and may be rewarded for it. Different generations or individuals in the same family may be moving in different directions.

CULTURE CHANGE

We will look briefly at the history of ideas concerning culture change. One of the most comprehensive analyses was done by John Berry (1980), whose specialization is behavioral development of peoples in different sociocultural settings. As a cross-cultural psychologist, he has studied cultural groups in arctic and central Canada, Africa, Australia, and New Guinea; he is also a critic of cross-cultural theory and research.

Berry found that there was much research on states of change but little evidence on how the change took place. Change was conceptualized mainly in terms of Western civilization and defined in terms of peoples becoming more Western. Race and ethnic relations were studied as separate entities and not in terms of learning other cultures. We may add that exposure to the artifacts of other cultures needs more study as a factor in culture change as these objects transmit values about ways of thinking, knowing, and obtaining information. Most studies of change focus on how minorities are changing and less on how whole societies or majorities are changing.

Berry (1980) reviewed research on the effects of imposed education. Mainly, he referred to studies where a Western educational system had been imposed on a non-Western people. Berry does not refute that change may take place, but asserts that the assumptions underlying the research do not allow us to come to definitive conclusions about the effects of education in changing perception and cognition or even personality. In Berry's own study of nine Amer-Indian groups, he found that people with more education tended to identify with the dominant culture (which fosters the educational system). But he still found people who were more educated that were strong in the reification of their ethnic identity.

Berry (1980) also worked with Witkin in some of his cross-cultural studies of perception. They found that field-independent individuals, those who were least affected by their visual environment or could easily separate themselves from their environment, were most able to retain their cultural sense of identity in new cultural situations. They also had much less stress in the acculturation process.

Handler (1984) identifies the shift in use of the concept "culture change" by some anthropologists to thinking of culture as a cultural system. The older concept implies moving from one static condition to a somewhat different static state. The second conceives of culture as a system in which all parts or elements and events are constantly changing, yet persist over time. Much of what cross-cultural psychologists have discussed has been change as it affects individuals. Both change among groups as studied by anthropologists and changes in individuals need consideration in education.

Comprehensive studies of culture change in systems as complex as America, with all its changing subcultures, are most difficult. But certain demographic and technical changes are clearly affecting the whole. An Associated Press release (March 15, 1989) highlighted the diversity of Los Angeles and its suburbs, which presaged current national trends of increasing population diversity in urban areas. There were 160,000 pupils who each spoke one of 80 primary languages. In Orange County 40% of the students were from minority families. The rate of immigration to the area from around the world has tripled since 1985 and continues to increase. Cities are passing laws that require at least 50% of commercial signs be in English. The mayor of one suburban city said the law was necessary because the city was looking more like Hong Kong than itself. Business, while still conducted mainly in English, is also taking place in other languages. Schools, the visual environmental, government regulations, business, and the courts are all having to adapt to culture change as evidenced by varieties in language. But when change lags, the consequences can be serious. It was reported that in a skyscraper fire at night the emergency instructions were in English, but most of the janitors in the building could not read them.

There are many other factors that are changing culture. For example, the complex systemic dynamics of change from the local to the international and from the international to the local, and the effects of one change affecting other changes, increasingly influence the content and context of culture. As the numbers of subcultures represented in our society increase; as changes in family structure, working patterns, and child rearing practices affect each other; as world economy fluctuations impinge on the workplace and the schools; and as communication and computer technologies affect knowledge, social organization, and the nature of work, no aspect of education and few aspects of art can remain isolated and untouched.

Education is at the heart of culture change. It is a central point where the children of many cultures share the same learning space, where conflicts of values between dominant and minority cultures arise where conflicts of identity and social recognition emerge, and where the institution of education with its lines of authority and structure of acceptable practices and procedures tries to superimpose a kind of order. Each cultural group has sets of values about what is art and its significance in human experience, and each child has his or her own cultural and adaptive sense of it.

A description of a cross-cultural study of adaptations to culture change in preschool education should make these analyses more concrete. Each culture uses a system of educational control to help children learn the accepted dominant culture in some specific way. Tobin, Wu, and Davidson (1989), specialists in human development, cultural anthropology, and the family, respectively, studied a sample of preschools in China, Japan, and Hawaii. They identified the social changes in each country that needed to be compensated for, causing particular values to be stressed in preschools, to help children enter the mainstream society.

In China, where the birth rate is limited to one child, it is expected that the child will be spoiled by four grandparents and two parents, so preschool is used to foster discipline, doing things in groups in quiet, orderly ways and at specific times and places. According to teachers, preschool also is designed to help children become more self-reliant.

In Japan family size is decreasing and extended families are more remote, so preschool serves to foster socialization—getting along in larger groups. Teachers supervise more remotely and let children solve their own interpersonal problems. They are allowed to be spontaneous, playful, and argumentative and use space freely.

In the American preschools children tend to come from families where divorced, single parent, or working parent families are predominant. Teacher–pupil relations are more personal. Children are picked up and comforted. Activities allow for choices. Children socialize with other children to some degree. But the stronger socialization skills of Japan and group-belonging skills of China are not as evident in the American preschools, where independence is stressed (Tobin, Wu, & Davidson, 1989). Some of the culture change in these three societies comes from pressures of overpopulation in relation to resources in China; increased isolation of families caused by centralized industry and business opportunities in urban areas in Japan; and changes in family structure and inflation in America. These changes affect child rearing and preschools, which in turn affect the ways children are prepared to enter the larger society.

These researchers felt that these early socializing institutions were used to conserve culture in the face of other forces that would tend to change it. The use of preschools to conserve culture probably means that each society is trying to maintain some values and to counteract forces of change by reeducating children to the old values. The study also indicates that culture change is not necessarily linear but is probably more systemic—that is, as focuses of change are introduced, they tend to have multiple effects.

The differences among the cultures also illustrate the problems a child might have adapting to a new culture. For example, a child from China who had not had preschool training before coming to America would probably react differently than one who had been taught self-discipline. American children learning in Japan may lack skills in working in groups and have trouble repressing their independence learned at home.

ART AND CULTURE

Art is one of the major communication systems in most cultures. Each member of a culture learns to "read" or understand the culture through the art that expresses values, patterns of organization, social structures, and belief systems. Every culture has some form of art, even though the members may not have a concept or word for it. The world is rapidly moving to international visualization of images as a means of communication. Much of this is in art forms, from adornment of the human body to computerized graphics and animation of culture-laden images. Almost 40 years ago, during a master's degree oral, a committee member asked me to define art. A visiting scholar from the University of Utrecht threw up his hands and interjected loudly, "It will take her her lifetime." I am beginning to realize how right he was.

Mainly I have relied on anthropological perspectives on the functions of art in cultures to try to achieve a more universal common denominator of the phenomenon art. This was necessary because interest in world arts has increased tremendously in the nineteenth and twentieth centuries, and is now so critical because of worldwide communication and migrations of people that require multicultural education in much of the world (McFee, 1988b).

The following is my current, tentative, pan-cultural operational definition of the making of art: *Those human activities which purposefully and qualitatively interpret, invent, extend, and imbue meaning through organized visual form or enhance the form and meaning of objects. These activities are conceptualized as processes and products of what we call art.*

Trying to comprehend aesthetic experience in other cultures is especially complex. The common denominator of aesthetic experience seems to be the making of and responding to order, which varies from culture to culture. The degrees of acceptable order or disorder include reference to visual elements, techniques, functions, traditional ordering patterns, and degree of acceptable improvisation (McFee, 1980).

It is very difficult for any one investigator to exclude him- or herself from his or her own cultural modes of aesthetic experience in order to analyze the aesthetics used in another culture. This happens when members of one value-sharing subculture of art, such as adherents and producers of fine arts, try to understand the aesthetics of another subculture, such as that of popular arts. The first group often rejects the premise that the second subculture has an aesthetic because it is different. Conversely, fine arts are often rejected because the culture and aesthetics are unfamiliar to adherents of the popular arts.

There has been a resurgence of interest in art by anthropologists since the mid–1970s and a growing recognition that art and aesthetic values provide sources for studying cultures and the ways they may be changing.

As noted before, Bourdieu (1984) found that social class and related life styles were powerful factors in the development of attitudes toward art. The need to acquire appropriate goods to signify social class is very strong. To own what was legitimized as good art within one's class is a powerful tool to identify one's social class. To be able to express one's aesthetic abilities in the choice of environmental objects and art is a factor in maintaining one's class, whatever it is (Bourdieu, 1984).

Silver (1979) made a comprehensive review of studies of art in culture up to the mid–1970s. From this he provides a useful framework for thinking about art. The term *ethno art* is used instead of *primitive, folk, Western,* or *fine art*. This encourages us to look at the culture that surrounds a given art form and respond to it in its own most used cultural context, rather than lumping art into broad categories. Silver uses the term *ethno-aesthetics* for identifying the given cultural value system of an ethnic group, that is, the structure within which aesthetic criteria are developed. He cautions that the ways we categorize aspects of art in Western society, such as form and function, fine and applied, are not universals as we have so often assumed. Of course, all members of an ethnic group do not share the same culture, so this system also has its limitations.

Earlier Herskovits (1959) had shown that Western assumptions have led us to treat what we considered to be fine art differently from primitive art. Fine artists are traced by their names and histories; primitive artists are lumped into groups and we have had little interest in the individual. For a long period primitive arts were hung only in natural history museums, not art museums. We rarely know the criteria by which primitive arts are selected.

Geertz (1983), in his analysis of the place of art in culture, stresses that art is more than a means of symbolizing and communicating meaning, it is primarily a means of knowing. *This knowing of artists in terms of their culture is what is communicated.*

But all artists are in some degree at variance with their cultures. If they are reflecting on underlying assumptions or structures beneath surface realities, they are cultural critics, separating themselves from the common perspectives in order to understand them. So we would have to extend Geertz's analysis from a means of knowing to include a means of analyzing, dissecting, and reorganizing what is known. Art can be a new synthesis of the artist's creations revealing new levels of meaning. At the same time there are artists who reflect accepted cultural ideas through their art. They are close to objectifying the cultural ideal. This also is a means of knowing.

Geertz (1983) points out that people in different cultures define themselves differently as persons. As we saw in the study of the different ways children are taught in Chinese, Japanese, and American preschools, there are different ways children learn to define themselves in relation to their groups. Geertz has studied in Java, Morocco, and Bali, and in each of these groups, he finds the self defined differently in relation to the group in philosophical, social, and personal dimensions. In a chapter entitled "From the Natives' Point of View," he discusses the difficulties of a Western man breaking out of his own cultural constructs to comprehend how people from another culture define the self; the self in relation to the continuing reality, to the group, and to what is considered to be inside or outside; and the factors that separate one from another. While he refers to the aesthetic and poetry, rather than the visual arts, much of what he describes is related to artists. The artist's sense of self affects his or her art of knowing.

This may appear remote information to a classroom teacher, but carriers of these cultural differences are sitting in classrooms trying to comprehend a structure or a sense of reality far different from their own. If we try to understand the artist's message from another culture without some comprehension of the artist as a person, and in some relation to a culture or cluster of cultures, we can hardly interpret the artist's message or respond to the cultural traditions of artistic form.

Maquet (1986), an anthropologist, inquires into cultural experience with the visual arts and aesthetics. He differentiates between phenomenological realities—mental constructs of culture-sharing people—and realities of any one individual or the objective reality of a thing. He describes art as "socially constructed reality" (p. 8). He further identifies different realities of art, such as cultural specializations, that we find in media arts, folk arts, fine arts, or among art critics, educators, and philosophers, and separates these from what he calls "everyday reality." By everyday reality he means those experiences we share no matter what subcultures we specialize in or to which we belong.

His overall work does not result in class categories or summaries of what art is or is not. He challenges our categorizing of the art experience of people and shows how culturally learned constructs affect their experience with a work of art from their own or others' culture. He explores the question of how different people separate human-made things into art and non-art, and how people use different perceptions in viewing what they culturally know as art and non-art. He asks whether there is a mode of consciousness different from cognition.

He shows how objects may be considered art in one context and not art in another. For example, a mask carved for dancers to embody culturally invented spirit images during ceremonies becomes an inert painted wood carving in a glass showcase—an artifact in a natural history museum, a work of art in a "primitive art" museum. Original instrumental forms created to be used in daily living or in rituals, when separated from their context, become visual documents about a people or works of art created by them.

Maquet (1986) rejects the idea of artists communicating with viewers, but rather believes the artist and the viewer share a degree of relationship in experience. Communication comes through cognitive and active processes, while aesthetic responses are contemplative.

Maquet's disclosure of his intellectual eclecticism, his rich multicultural experience, and his emphasis on phenomenology should be recognized when comparing his work with findings from other anthropologists inquiring into the place of art in culture and human experience. It is well to remember that Maquet subtitles his book *An Anthropologist Looks at the Visual Arts,* not an anthropology of art drawing from and building on the work of other anthropologists studying art.

Clifford (1988), whom we previously referred to in relation to contemporary forces on culture, also analyzes the functions of art institutions in changing the meaning of art. In a chapter entitled "Histories of the Tribal and the Modern," he examines 1984–85 New York exhibitions. Using penetrating historical analysis, he describes the routes and categorizing systems by which a modern dated Brancusi and an antique undated Arctic mask arrive and are hung together, both looking like modern art. Our interest here is how the institution, with its cultural value system and power to mold thought, can change the meaning of art forms, can make objects not considered art in one culture to become "art" in another, can combine cultures, or "rise" above cultures.

Clifford posits that underlying this effort is a great need by "the modern West" to collect the world, to categorize the world in its own systems. He implies that the selection process elicited similarities, for one reason, because both art forms were not bound by past Renaissance Western fine art constructs. A serious omission to the exhibit was any reference to the cultures from which the "primitive" works came. He feels that the whole presentation was based on the assumption that the less one knows of the cultural context in which a work evolved, the more pure aesthetic responses can be. But Western viewers are more or less immersed in the culture of the modern, so they tend to judge the "primitive" by how alike it is to the modern and aren't as free to make purely aesthetic assumptions as the designers of the exhibitions may have assumed.

The critical point for art educators in this is that they recognize the different value systems of art institutions, academic disciplines in art, art history, criticism, aesthetic theory, and even art education. Each of these value systems molds the content of art to fit itself. Each such institution or discipline is undergoing change: becoming more open and less categorical, more open to culture change, or reifying itself into its traditions for stability and in defense of its most valued territory. In summary, each ethnic group has internal variations in acceptable behaviors and symbolic meanings, depending on the region and on the social hierarchy of the group. But these differences may be hidden behind a facade of sameness because of mass media, mass dress, and popular culture.

ANTHROPOLOGY APPLIED TO EDUCATION

Anthropology and education specialists have particular insights into change as it affects schooling. They have applied theories and methods of anthropology to studying the school as an institution of mainstream or dominant culture, culture change as it affects school practices, cross-cultural comparisons, and the diversities of adaptation to school by children of minority or subcultural backgrounds.

The following adaptations of insights gathered over more than 30 years by George and Louise Spindler (1983) are important cautions in thinking about cultures or culture change as it relates to education. Analysis of a culture should include both the diversity of people's adaptation to it as well as the changes going on in the culture as a whole (p. 55). Diversity within an overall culture comes not only from the variations in subculture backgrounds but from the accommodations and conflicts between diverse groups (p. 66).

In a later paper reflecting on their work as ethnographers, the Spindlers (1988) provided a review of their findings, from which the following points are adapted:

- Culture change takes place within individuals as well as among groups. Some individuals choose to change.
- Children from subcultures in conflict with the dominant school culture have learned different ways, or "instrumentations," for achieving success and self-esteem. When they fail in school because their ways of achieving haven't been rewarded, they compensate in ways that may further alienate them from the school.
- Subcultures or minority cultures have many aspects. A given child or group may range from having a traditional, stable family background to, at the other extreme, having learned ways of behaving in a particular street culture.

Not knowing for sure where we are, it is hard to know how we are changing. When we look at culture change or variations in some aspect of change as it affects education and art, we need to be aware of these complex variables and areas where, really, not much is known.

Wolcott (1989), another specialist in anthropology and education, has written a new "Afterword" to his experience 25 years ago as a teacher and anthropologist in a Kwakiutl village in British Columbia. What he would look for now, after his years of research since then, is useful for us here. His original question was why so many Indian children failed in school. Now he would focus on "cultural acquisition: how each child acquires his or her particular version of what the world is about" (p. 140). Originally he was concerned with what students didn't know and how far behind they were from norms in the dominant cultures. Now he is concerned with what they know and what it is that gets their attention. What is important in their world? How do they solve problems? How do they sort things? If teachers are concerned solely with what students don't know about the teachers' culture, they can't help children from other cultures build new constructs and learn new things from their own rich cultural perspectives.

He cautions us that in teaching across cultures and in multicultural situations we need to know what individual children know as well as the collective knowledge of children from a given group. It is the teacher's attitude that he stresses, an openness and respect for cultural diversity both within and between groups. Although he doesn't state this, it also requires a more qualified involvement with one's own culture.

ART EDUCATION AND CULTURE

Art educators who study the relationship of art to the social sciences add more insight into the cultural and social aspects of art from which much change comes.

There is a growing awareness among art educators that both art and aesthetics follow cultural patterns. One area of concern is difference in culture by sex. This has led to different cultural attitudes and values of men and women, and women's art and men's art. In a detailed analysis, art educator jagodzinski (1987) traces the history in Western and some Asian and Eastern cultures showing how long the two worlds of men and women have been divided. He traces roots of such ideas, such as the dominance in Western democracies of masculine-related processes and categories over those considered feminine: the intellectual over the emotional, aesthetics over art, high arts over low arts, men's arts over women's art, the public over the private, and architectural design over interior design.

Collins and Sandell (1988) also refer to these same value systems as pervading in art history, art criticism, professional arts (fine arts), and aesthetics. They add that these disciplines have contributed to the dichotomy between fine arts and folk arts and crafts and others that have a function beyond the aesthetic. They are particularly concerned with attitudes toward the arts done by women, who usually have lived more limited, culturally constrained lives. But they posit that society as a whole is supportive of the nurturing, humanizing role of the arts in life and education. They analyze the value systems underlying the disciplines on which the Getty Foundation's discipline-based art education is based and ask for change to a more inclusive concept of art.

Chalmers (1981) looks at the interface between the methods of the anthropologist doing fieldwork and the art educator analyzing and teaching art. Fieldworkers try to recognize the cultural context of their own backgrounds through which they observe other cultures. He posits that this search for more objectivity is needed by teachers and students to be able to see the impact of their own culture on how they view art or the effects of other people's culture on their art.

Even if we can't see art in its actual context, as it is being inspired, motivated, used, and judged, and the artist rewarded, we can look to the art to reflect on the culture that produced it. We can compare field reports on the culture with art objects to seek out influences from the culture to art, and from art to the culture. Both the artist and the viewer, with art work between them, view it through a cultural screen. Our task is to try to see the art in its culture as created by the artist as part of that culture (McFee, 1980).

Chalmers (1987) also studies the social roles of art and the crucial networks between users who provide significance, artists who work within sociocultural constructs, and the social institutions that intercede between artists and users. He shows that each of these social interactions and their values affect each other. He argues that students need to comprehend art in its social context to understand others' art, and in this process become more aware of the functions of art in human experience universally. We can add that without the sociocultural understanding of art in their own culture, students miss an important avenue for understanding changes that take place in art— among the artists, the art institutions, the art disciplines, and the users, and as art reflects change or leads to change in society itself.

Neperud (1988) emphasizes experiencing in his study of aesthetics in the light of perceptual and cognitive psychology. He reviews research that indicates that stored information, the structures of verbal and visual constructs that an individual has learned, affects what an individual responds to. He concludes that while studies show little difference between people of diverse cultures in some perceptual and cognitive processes, cultural groups vary widely because of differences in what they have seen and heard and the environments in which they have learned to see. This, he suggests, is a large factor in aesthetic responses.

Hamblen (1987) has analyzed the selection processes used by art and historical museums that are imbedded in their cultural and political value systems. She sees these institutions as screens that filter the arts of the world through their culturally defined aesthetics and what they accept or reject as art.

Calvert (1988) describes a rare exhibition that stressed cultural variations and change, "Artistic Traditions of Canada's First Peoples," which treated Native Canadians' work as works of art with historical and aesthetic traditions. The exhibition pointed out differences in aesthetics between groups, changes resulting from contact with the West, the effects of users (what traders would accept for trade), the introduction of new materials, the development of collections, and finally what she calls "the rich variety of aesthetic sensibilities, materials and art forms that constitute native art history" (p. 113). Consider the impact on our knowledge of other peoples and their art if this standard of collecting and exhibiting were more generally used.

Jones (1988) analyzes historical trends of philosophical realism that have persisted over time and influenced many of our institutions and practices, specifically in education and art. She clarifies conflicting points of view about what constitutes appropriate education in a democracy by pointing to a middle ground between the extremes of objectivism, on one side, and relativism, on the other. Learning the subject matter from multiple perspectives, allowing for the differing orientations of students, and recognizing the sociocultural context of both the subject matter and the students, are necessary to educate people to practice democracy. Jones uses M. McFee's field research, which identified people who learned to function well in another culture without losing their ability to excel in their own subculture. She points to the need for educated people who understand and can function in more than one culture in multicultural democracies. By contrast, she notes the tendency of members of the dominant society in the United States to be absorbed in their own culture. She points to 150% humans as a goal for education.

Boyer (1987) posits a sequence of experiences needed in developing cultural literacy that starts with developing awarenesses in one's own culture through analyzing personal experiences, followed by exploring the social and historical influences that affect art in one's own community, and then looking at art in other cultures. The effectiveness of this system in multicultural communities needs to be explored.

Blandy and Congdon (1987) have been instrumental in focusing attention on the needs for change toward more democratic education through their anthology, *Art in a Democracy*. Blandy's major concern is children with disabilities who are left out of educational theory and practice except as members of a special class. Congdon explores the roles and functions of folk arts as a significant part of the American art scene, but one that has been neglected by many historians and critics, and some art educators.

In a paper written for a conference reviewing the place of discipline-based art education, I (McFee, 1988a) reviewed the different arts that have had an impact on our society and thus need to be addressed in more socially democratic art education programs. Each of these arts has a network of supporters, users, critics (although not in the formal sense) and a subculture of aesthetic values about what is more and what is less valued. The crafts have extensive networks of museum support groups, publications, and users. Folk arts and popular art have academic status as areas of inquiry, based more on anthropology than that in art history, which is based on historical methodologies and traditions. Each art needs to be understood in its social context and judged accordingly. The following curriculum areas can be developed to help students recognize the functions of visual art in culture and allow for diversity in democracy:

- Studying multiple cultural realities made accessible by visually communicated values, beliefs, and feelings in art.
- Clarifying the structure and relationships between people, places, things, and events in terms of the art expressed in different cultural value systems, or in one culture as it changes over time.
- Comparing the differences in quality and culturally defined roles, institutions, and events among cultures.
- Analyzing change through artists who challenge cultural patterns through expression of divergent ideas, feelings, values, structures, and relationships through visual art forms; analyzing artists who maintain culture.
- Providing cross-cultural awareness for relating to others that are changing cultures through change in their art.
- Identifying the mixing of cultures. Communicating and giving cohesion and clarity to cultural change.
- Analyzing changes in the design and organization of art for differing cultural purposes.

THE IMPLICATIONS OF CHANGE
FOR ART EDUCATION POLICY

In reviewing these positions on art we can see many points where change in cultural systems is affecting or should affect policy, remembering that change is not unidimensional and that a change in one part of a system modifies other parts to some degree. The following are a few of the possible complexities of change useful for art educators.

Culture as analyzed in this chapter includes a group's values; attitudes; belief systems; social structures; concepts of reality; cognitive styles; ways of knowing, motivating, categorizing, and making order; creating symbols, environments; technologies; and art. All of these are in the process of change and adaptation to other cultures, and are influenced by technological, political, economic, social and environmental, and demographic change. Art is a major communication system for enhancing, creating the essence of, maintaining, or changing culture.

Looking at Silver's (1979) summary of art in culture in relation to Clifford's (1988) analysis of contemporary effects of migration in creating cultural diversity and broad world art trading, we can assume that more people have more contact with more diverse arts. But this change does not tell us how people's learned categorizing systems will change, for example, from using the concept "primitive" to the less restricting term *ethno art*. Also, as cultures are mixed and art is traded, it becomes more difficult to identify the cultural context of a given art and how much it has been diluted by the influence of world trade users. The Canadian exhibition of diverse Indian artists, recording their history and aesthetics, reported by Calvert (1988) is a glimmer of culture change among institutions displaying such art and can be a model for educators.

Acceptance of Geertz's (1983) concept that art is a means of knowing, and Maquet's (1986) concept that art is a construct of reality, hopefully will change attitudes toward art by educators. Forms of art and art making represent processes of knowing and constructing meaning, and thus are a vital part of education particularly in a visual age.

We can relate this to the proposition of Neperud (1988), using cognitive psychology data, that it is the cultural aspects of experience that most affect how people see, and that their reservoir of remembered images, based on culturally motivated seeing, plays such a strong part in how people from different cultural groups respond to art and the environment. This is strongly supported by the reflection of Wolcott (1989), who today would first find out what students already know. We can ask what they know, how they see, and how they have learned to construct reality. Children in a given multicultural classroom may represent many different ways of knowing, have different realities, behave differently in relation to art, and vary widely in their concepts of what is pleasing or orderly. They could all be different from the teachers. Not only do teachers need to work as ethnographers in looking at art, as Chalmers (1987) suggests, but they need to be ethnographers in their classrooms, seeking to gain some insights into the cultures represented there.

From Bourdieu's (1984) study of French society, we find that art is one means of establishing and expressing social class. Thus the owning of certain kinds of art identifies status and affects individual attitudes toward art. This is one way value is given to art. As social class changes so might art preferences change. We can expect changes in the valuing of art even by culture-sharing people when social mobility occurs.

As Collins and Sandell (1988) show, traditional roles of male and female status are identified through images, including the kinds of art produced and valued. As sex roles change, cultural ways of knowing and valuing may change, producing differences in the kinds of art created and used to reinforce the sense of identity and social belonging. Art teachers need to be careful not to stereotype students according to sex or status, as well as by culture, in what they expect of them or how they reward them.

It is necessary to look beyond the facade of the mass-media-projected dress codes accepted by students and reinforced by peers, to find individuals. The Spindlers' (1988) caution is particularly relevant when trying to assess where students are rather than what they are trying to look like.

If we use Maquet's (1986) concepts of art as "socially constructed reality" and not as communication between artist and viewer but as a sharing of mutual experience between artist and viewer, then changes in social experience by artists and viewers could change experience with art.

The rapid increase in the numbers of cultures represented in North American society is forcing reanalysis of curriculum. Each cultural group has a somewhat unique repertoire of aesthetic values and attitudes and degree of acceptance of dominant values. Thus, there are many more culturally based art attitudes and forms to be responded to. The question, "Which culture's arts should be taught to whom, and how?" must be addressed. Representatives of all these cultures are now in our classrooms. Each child brings his or her own cultural art attitudes as they have been learned, as they have been adapted to the dominant culture and other subcultures, and as he or she has responded to the art forms in the culture of mass media. Not only children from minority cultures but all children are affected by changes in their socio-economic experience—changes in location, parental situation, access to and type of television programs, and visual environment, and changes in the dominant culture itself.

If art becomes more democratized, as some art educators stress, and as cultural pluralism requires the underlying assumptions of Western hierarchies as identified by jagodzinski (1987) to be questioned, we may ask: Must the intellectual supersede the emotional in value, the aesthetic over the art work, some cultures art over others, public over private, or one civilization's or one sex's art over another? Or is it possible for art to be more of an open vehicle, rich in historical, cultural, social and individual, intellectual and emotional, public and private meaning? If so, how would the art support systems—museums, schools, users—have to change? Could aestheticians and critics allow for more cultural diversity and become aware of their own cultural roots and limitations? Can art educators become more aware of their own cultural assumptions about value in art and be willing to seek out the art knowledge and ways of knowing about art among their students?

Teachers of art, developers of art curricula, teacher educators in art, and school administrators all need to be aware of their own cultural boundaries in and about art, before they can make wise decisions about what to teach in this changing multicultural society. They must look at their assumptions about what is or isn't art. Then they must ask how much of this categorizing of art is based on their particular cultural pool of ideas and values, and the art forms they were raised with. How did the people who influenced them judge art? What opportunities have they had to be exposed to other cultures' art forms, and to art in their own culture? Is this enough experience to make judgments about what art should be in the schools?

Art education can help students gain broader perspectives for reflecting on their own culture's art, thus giving them more latitude for their own aesthetic responses and creations. They can become more aware of their own and other cultures' impact on themselves as individuals and thus be able to change or modify that impact. A key point is that Western culture needs to be understood in its great subcultural variety, and that it is only one among world cultures, all with complex variations.

IMPLICATIONS FOR CHANGE IN PRACTICE

Teacher education must radically change if classroom teachers are to be aware of cultural diversity and the different strata of the dominant culture, as they are affected by change. Teachers experienced in only one culture are ill-prepared for teaching in multicultural classrooms, as most classrooms are today.

Complaints that undergraduates cannot deal with such complexity must be addressed. Teachers can achieve the goal of being culturally aware and sensitive if they can learn basic concepts of culture and seek out and listen for information from their real cultural informants—the children in their classrooms. Teachers need to learn to observe student art as coming from other cultures as well as their own.

People in teacher education, those coming out of our doctoral programs, require strong preparation in the cultural domain to be able to help prepare teachers with strategies for comprehending and for reaching students far different than themselves.

Faculty and curriculum directors, working with classroom teachers, must take leadership in developing curricula that allow for diversity of response according to students' background and cultural adaptations. Field study reports, films, videos, and audiotapes of cultures as they are or can be related to art need to be prepared in forms students can respond to. Strategies need to be devised to help students analyze the cultural functions of art in maintaining and changing culture. More strategies need to be developed for helping students study their own culture and the role art plays in it. This includes curricula for preservice and inservice teacher education and for elementary and secondary classes.

Finally, much research in classrooms is needed to identify strategies teachers can use to find out how students see, think, value, and structure reality, as a basis for understanding more about their modes of responding to and creating art. All these implications point to the need for education of more multicultural people to function in a multicultural society. Cross-cultural study of art can be a rich avenue for helping students enlarge their cultural perspectives, be more aware of their primary culture in relation to others, and see art as central to the sociocultural as well as aesthetic life of people.

REFERENCES

Associated Press release, March 15, 1989. "Lowering babel of languages strains: L.A."

Berry, J. W. (1980). Social and cultural change. In H. C. Triandis & R. W. Brislin (Eds.), *Handbook of cross-cultural psychology: Vol. 5. Social psychology* (pp. 82–117). Boston: Allyn & Bacon.

Blandy, D., & Congdon, K. G. (Eds.). (1987). *Art in a democracy*. New York: Teachers College Press.

Bourdieu, P. (1984). *Distinction: A social critique of the judgment of taste*. Cambridge, MA: Harvard University Press.

Boyer, B. A. (1987). Cultural literacy in art: Developing conscious aesthetic choices. In D. Blandy & K. G. Congdon (Eds.), *Art in a democracy* (pp. 91–106). New York: Teachers College Press.

Brislin, R. W. (1983). Cross-cultural research in psychology. *Annual Review of Psychology, 34*, 363–400.

Calvert, A. E. (1988). Native art history and D.B.A.E.: An analysis of key concepts. *Journal of Multicultural and Cross-Cultural Research in Art Education, 6*(1), 112–122.

Chalmers, G. (1981). Art education as ethnology. *Studies in Art Education, 23*(3), 6–14.

Chalmers, G. (1987). Culturally based versus universally based understanding of art. In D. Blandy & K. G. Congdon (Eds.), *Art in a democracy* (pp. 4–12). New York: Teachers College Press.

Clifford, J. (1988). *The predicament of culture*. Cambridge, MA: Harvard University Press.

Collins, G., & Sandell, R. (1988). Informing the promise of DBAE: Remember the women, children and other folk. *Journal of Multicultural and Cross-Cultural Research in Art Education, 6*(1), 55–63.

Dougherty, J. W., & Fernandez, J. W. (1981). Introduction to symbolism and cognition I [Special issue]. *American Ethnologist, 8*(3), 413–415.

Geertz, C. (1983). *Local knowledge*. New York: Basic Books.

Goodenough, W. H. (1981). *Culture, language, and thought* (3rd ed.). Menlo Park, CA: Benjamin/Cummings.

Hamblen, K. A. (1987). Qualifications and contradictions of art museum education in a pluralistic democracy. In D. Blandy & K. G. Congdon (Eds.), *Art in a democracy* (pp. 13–25). New York: Teachers College Press.

Handler, R. (1984). On sociocultural discontinuity: National and cultural objectification in Quebec. *Current Anthropology, 25*, 56.

Herskovits, M. (1959). Art and value. In *Aspects of primitive art* (Lec. Ser. No. 1; pp. 42–68). New York: Museum of Primitive Art.

Hirsch, E. D., Jr. (1987). *Cultural literacy: What every American needs to know*. Boston: Houghton Mifflin.

Hofstede, G. (1984). *Culture's consequences: International differences in work-related values*. Beverly Hills, CA: Sage.

jagodzinski, j. j. (1987). Toward an ecological aesthetic: Notes on a green frame of mind. In D. Blandy & K. G. Congdon (Eds.), *Art in a democracy* (pp. 138–163). New York: Teachers College Press.

Jones, B. J. (1988). Art education in context. *Journal of Multicultural and Cross-Cultural Research in Art Education, 6*(1), 38–51.

Kluckhohn, C. (1951). The study of culture. In D. Lerner & H. D. Lasswell (Eds.), *The policy sciences* (pp. 86–101). Stanford, CA: Stanford University Press.

Maquet, J. (1986). *The aesthetic experience: An anthropologist looks at the visual arts.* New Haven, CT: Yale University Press.

Marwick, A. (1980). *Class: Image and reality in Britain, France, and the U. S. A. since 1930.* New York: Oxford University Press.

McFee, J. K. (1980). Cultural influence on aesthetic experience. In J. Condus, J. Howlett, & J. Skull (Eds.), *Arts in cultural diversity: INSEA 23rd World Congress* (pp. 45–52). New York: Holt, Rinehart and Winston.

McFee, J. K. (1988a). *Art and society in issues in D.B.A.E.: Strengthening the stance, extending the horizon* (Seminar Proceedings Cincinnati 1977; pp. 104–112). Santa Monica, CA: Getty Center for Education in the Arts.

McFee, J. K. (1988b). Cultural dimensions in the teaching of art. In F. H. Farley & R. W. Neperud (Eds.), *The foundations of aesthetics, art, and art education* (pp. 252–272). New York: Praeger.

McFee, J. K., & Degge, R. M. (1992). *Art, culture, and environment: A catalyst for teaching.* Dubuque, IA: Kendall/Hunt.

McFee, M. (1969, February). The 150% man in Blackfeet acculturation. *American Anthropologist, 70,* 1096–1107.

Neperud, R. (1988). A propositional view of aesthetic experiencing for research and teaching in art education. In F. Farley & R. Neperud (Eds.), *The foundations of aesthetics, art, and art education* (pp. 273–319). New York: Praeger.

Silver, H. R. (1979). Ethno art. *Annual Review of Anthropology, 8,* 267–307.

Spindler, G., & Spindler, L. (1983). Anthropologists view American culture. *Annual Review of Anthropology, 12,* 49–78.

Spindler, G., & Spindler, L. (1988). A life with ethnography: A conversation with George and Louise Spindler. *Qualitative Studies in Education, 1*(2), 167–178.

Tobin, J. J., Wu, D. Y. H., & Davidson, D. H. (1989). How three key countries shape their children. *World Monitor, 2*(1), 36–45.

Triandis, H. (1983). Essentials of studying culture. In D. Landis & R. Brislin (Eds.), *Handbook for intercultural training. Vol. I: Issues of theory and design* (pp. 82–117). New York: Pergamon.

Wolcott, H. (1989). *A Kwakiutl village and school.* Prospect Heights, IL: Waveland Press.

CHAPTER 9

Social Reconstructionist Multicultural Art Curriculum Design: Using the Powwow as an Example

Patricia L. Stuhr

Sociocultural anthropologists, writing from the perspective of the "new anthropology" or "postmodern anthropology," present us with an innovative way to consider culture and ethnic diversity in the 1990s (Clifford, 1988; Collins, 1989; Nash, 1989). Their insights allow for the understanding and investigation of culture and ethnicity with all of the internal and external complexity of these socially constructed phenomena. The complexity recognized by these authors has implications for curriculum in general and art education specifically.

BACKGROUND OF THE PROBLEM

Many art educators, myself included, advocate using community resources and aesthetic values as a basis for teaching and study of multicultural art in schools (Barrett, 1990; Blandy & Congdon, 1988; Chalmers, 1981; Grigsby, 1977; McFee & Degge, 1980; Neperud, 1988; Stuhr, 1990). But cultural boundaries are often blurred, and interactions between cultures are constantly affecting art and aesthetics in their production, forms, viewing, and understandings (e.g., American Indian beaded baseball caps, blue jeans, and cowboy hats and boots worn as part of powwow outfits; and Wisconsin's Tourist Division advertisement of powwows as a tourist attraction). This complexity of culture must be dealt with as a reality, and the art/aesthetic production, forms, viewing, and understandings embodied in this conception should be taught in a way that reflects this phenomenon of culture. In the past, methods of teaching about the art/art worlds of diverse social groups or cultures tended to simplify, and thus to stereotype, information. This type of art education produced a proliferation of soft drink can and cardboard toilet paper roll totem poles and papier mache African masks.

In this chapter, I intend to show how investigating, understanding, and dealing with the complexity of the issues of sociocultural art/art worlds enhance multicultural learning rather than inhibit it. A discussion concerning curriculum ideology that is multicultural and social reconstructionist, the presentation of multicultural position statements, a definition of culture, and guidelines for multicultural curriculum development will be presented first to aid in the accomplishment of this goal.

In order to understand the curricular intent of this chapter, it is essential to understand the educational and social reform theory on which it is based. Education that is multicultural and social reconstructionist is both a concept, educational reform movement, and a process (Banks & McGee Banks, 1989). Social reconstructionist multiculturalism educates students to

> become analytical and critical thinkers capable of examining their life circumstances and the social stratifications that keep them and their group from fully enjoying the social and financial rewards of this country. Or, if they are members of dominant groups, it helps them become critical thinkers who are capable of examining why their group exclusively enjoys the social and financial rewards of the nation. This approach teaches students how to use social action skills to participate in shaping and controlling their destiny. (Grant & Sleeter, 1989, p. 54)

Included in this ideology is the foundation for an education that takes into account the concerns of diverse social groups based on race, class, gender, age, and handicap. A goal of multicultural and social reconstructionist education is to reform society toward a more equitable distribution of power and resources in the United States and improve academic achievement for all students. "It draws on the penetrating vision of George Bernard Shaw, who exclaimed, 'You see things, and say, "Why?" But I dream things that never were, and I say, "Why not?"'" (Grant & Sleeter, 1989, p. 54).

There are many types of multicultural education programs. The uniqueness of the multicultural and social reconstructionist approach is centered in four practices.

> [1] democracy must be actively practiced in schools . . . .[2] students learn how to analyze their own circumstances . . . .[3] students learn social action skills to increase their chances for success with the first two recommended practices . . . .[4] coalescing, or getting the poor, people of color, and White women to

work together for the common good of society. The coalescing of groups across the lines of race, class, gender, and exceptionality is important because it can energize and strengthen the fight against oppression. (Grant & Sleeter, 1989, p. 57)

Multicultural and social reconstructionist education is also "a process whose goals will never be fully realized. Educational equality, like liberty and justice, are ideals toward which human beings work but never fully attain" (Banks & McGee Banks, 1989, p. 3). The problems of prejudice and discrimination will continue to plague various social and cultural groups no matter how hard we try to eliminate them. Often, when prejudice and discrimination are eradicated in one area, they take root in another. It is precisely for this reason that we must be continually vigilant and train our students to be aware of, and fight against, this human shortcoming (Banks & McGee Banks, 1989).

Recently, Wasson, Stuhr, and Petrovich-Mwaniki (1990) developed six position statements to advance ways to construct and teach a multicultural art/aesthetic curriculum. These authors were influenced by the concepts of postmodern anthropology and sociology and theorists involved in multicultural and social reconstructionist curriculum. The six position statements address teaching about sociocultural complexity for the purpose of social reconstruction.

1. We advocate a socioanthropological basis for studying the aesthetic production and experience of cultures which means focusing on knowledge of the makers of art, as well as the sociocultural context in which art is produced.

2. We acknowledge teaching as cultural and social intervention and therefore, in any teaching endeavor, it is imperative that teachers not only confront, but also consistently be aware of their own cultural and social biases.

3. We support a student/community-centered educational process in which the teacher must access and utilize the students' sociocultural values and beliefs and those of the cultures of the community when planning art curricula.

4. We support anthropologically-based methods for identifying these sociocultural groups and their accompanying values and practices that influence aesthetic production.

5. We advocate the identification and discriminate use of culturally responsive pedagogy that more democratically represents the sociocultural and ethnic diversity existing in the classroom, the community, and the nation.

6. We want to focus on the dynamic complexity of the factors that affect all human interaction: physical and mental ability, class, gender, age, politics, religion, and ethnicity. We seek a more democratic approach where the disenfranchised are also given a voice in the art education process; and the disenfranchised, as well as the franchised are sensitized to the taken-for-granted assumptions implicit in the dominant ideology. (pp. 234–235)

Wasson, Stuhr, and Petrovich-Mwaniki (1990) synthesized a definition of culture using some ideas from historical anthropology and the postmodern anthropology perspectives.

> We define culture as a people's way of perceiving, believing, evaluating, and be-having which can be affected by the environment, the economic system, and modes of production. Culture has four characteristics: (a) it is learned through enculturation [living it] and socialization [formalized instruction], (b) it is shared by most of its members, (c) it is adaptive [to changes in both the social and physical environments], and (d) it is dynamic. Culture is . . . a transitional pro-cess. Cultures are remade through specific alliances, negotiations, and struggles. Cultural institutions are relational and political, coming and going in response to governmental policies and the surrounding ideological climate. (p. 235)

Societies in culture are always dying or surviving, assimilating or resisting (Clifford, 1988). Society refers to the organization of individuals as members of a community, which often share values and interests. Societies differ from culture in that they deal only with the human element and not the institu-tional or material production elements. There may be many societies within one culture. In fact, there usually are. Further, a particular culture may have many overlapping and interactive social factions and facets within itself. These factions and facets exist simultaneously on a continuum, aiding both cultural maintenance and change through the processes of enculturation, accultura-tion, and assimilation (Neperud & Stuhr, 1987).

Enculturation is the process of acquiring characteristics of a given society or culture through observation, participation, and/or living in it (i.e., inter-nalizing values and norms for accepted behavior in regard to eating, sleeping, kinship relations, language, etc.). The process of acculturation involves the adaptation and/or integration of specific cultural patterns, materials, and con-cepts, and the application of these in sometimes novel ways to one's own culture or society. For example, instead of using dyed porcupine quills to dec-orate moccasins as historically had been done, some Indians used trade beads obtained from the Europeans. Assimilation is the process by which subordi-nated cultural groups adopt the characteristics and values of the dominant culture, sometimes under duress; for example, obtaining advanced schooling or training outside of one's cultural norms in order to obtain employment in the dominant culture. When various cultures or societies within a culture have different values for what is considered knowledge or acceptable ideas to trans-mit, cultural conflict ensues.

Wasson, Stuhr, and Petrovich-Mwaniki's (1990) six position statements can provide the basis for planning, implementing, and evaluating a multicul-tural art education program that promotes social change and individual student emancipation. Based on these position statements, we suggest that when studying the art of various sociocultural groups, including their own, students should follow the guidelines listed.

1. Identify important social issues related to religion, ethnicity, socioeconomic class, gender, age, and mental and physical abilities;
2. gather data related to them,
3. clarify and challenge student values,
4. make reflective decisions,
5. take action to implement their decisions.

For example, students could identify current social issues, such as, (a) the lack of representation of American Indian women in art galleries across the nation, (b) depictions of violence in popular music videos, or (c) the treatment of religious art from other cultures as superstitious paraphernalia. Once the issue is identified, the class or individual groups of students can gather pertinent information related to the specific issue. With the help of the teacher, students can analyze the information, discuss their feelings and attitudes toward it, and challenge existing biases and preconceptions. Students then need to negotiate and adjust their viewpoints in order to arrive at possible decisions and modes of action regarding the original issue. This action could affect how students, teachers, and/or community look at, discuss, and produce art. (Stuhr, Petrovich-Mwaniki, & Wasson, 1992)

These guidelines were developed largely in response to the proliferation of flawed assumptions and teaching practices existing in multicultural art education. One such assumption is that teachers who present exemplars of cultural products, such as Egyptian hieroglyphics, American Indian totem poles, and Japanese prints, followed by the attempted production of some bastardized forms of these cultural aesthetic objects, are teaching about another culture in a meaningful way. Such hollow "tokenism not only trivializes the aesthetic production of all sociocultural groups, but, what is worse, it avoids confronting the real challenge of critically apprehending the meaning of the object, artist, and process in the sociocultural context" (Stuhr, Petrovich-Mwaniki, & Wasson, 1992). Art, presented in this way, becomes stereotypic and historically static. In addition, it neglects to make legitimate connections and contributions to students' lives in ways that are principled, ethical, and affective in nature.

To avoid such miseducation in planning and implementing multicultural art education curricula, a number of sources and questions can be used to collect and analyze sociocultural information. The kinds of sources most likely to give teachers/students the best data are: (1) the history of the area; (2) the cultural, social, political, religious, and economic factors that impinge upon it; (3) physical and cultural environmental influences; (4) demographic factors; (5) local values and belief systems; (6) sociocultural/ethnic groups; (7) individual differences (age, gender, sex, exceptionalities); and (8) artistic/aesthetic production and resources (Stuhr, Petrovich-Mwaniki, & Wasson, 1992).

In order to facilitate the discovery of this type of information by both teachers and students, two sets of questions have been developed. One set can be used when interviewing an artist(s) within a sociocultural context, and the other when investigating a specific art/aesthetic form(s) of sociocultural production (see Figures 9.1 and 9.2). The types of questions suggested here are helpful in revealing the seats of power and the political and economic structures used to maintain control of them. The questions make possible an investigation of who is empowered and who is disempowered within a specific sociocultural group's art world. These questions also can and should be used to investigate the art worlds of the dominant culture. The ultimate goal of this type of questioning strategy is to have students reach decisions/conclusions as a result of critically analyzing this information, and then, based on these findings, to reconstruct social situations in a positive manner.

The purpose of this chapter is to present multicultural and social reconstructionist curriculum possibilities based on comprehensive ethnographic data that I gathered during my attendance at Wisconsin Indian powwows and festivals. The data are then used to provide an extended example of the type of multicultural curriculum development that is possible through the use of the Wasson, Stuhr, and Petrovich-Mwaniki (1990) position statements and the Stuhr, Petrovich-Mwaniki, and Wasson (1992) five guidelines for curriculum implementation. Following the description of four powwows, there is a discussion of roles in curriculum construction and implementation for teachers, students, and individuals who participate in a particular sociocultural art world.

The powwow was selected as the curriculum content example in this chapter because it is the site of the greatest display of Wisconsin Indian cultural aesthetic production and performance. Native Americans acknowledge the powwow as their highest art form (Dufrene, 1990). It is also the tribal event most frequently credited with preserving Indian culture (Lurie, 1971; Parfit, 1994).

One cannot view, understand, or appreciate traditional forms of American Indian art/aesthetic production in the context of historical Western art. Indian art/aesthetic forms function in significantly different ways and are integrated with aspects of Indian theology, philosophy, and life (Stuhr, 1991).

Stuhr, Petrovich-Mwaniki, and Wasson (1992) make this recommendation.

> If teachers have difficulty choosing a multicultural issue or area of investigation, we suggest choosing an issue from that culture which is the most disenfranchised.

FIGURE 9.1 The Artist Interview

General Information . . . . Date: / /

Name . . . . Gender: M / F

Date and place of birth . . . .

Current address/ph # . . . .

Interview Questions (Note: The following questions represent areas of inquiry rather than questions that have to be asked verbatim)

Socioeconomic status/background
1. What kind of formal education have you had? (EXPLAIN—schools attended, grades completed and dates, degrees earned and dates)
2. What is/was your occupation(s)?

Artistic production
3. Describe/show the art form(s) that you produce.
4. How and when (age) did you learn to produce this form(s)?
5. Who taught/influenced you to produce this/these form(s)?
6. What is/are the function(s) of your art form(s)?
7. How is/are the art form(s) used?
8. What aspect(s) of the art form's(s') production is/are most important: process, product, or symbolic significance? WHY?

Sociocultural context
9. What is/are your ethnic affiliation(s)?
10. Has your ethnic identity influenced your form(s)? If so, HOW?
11. Has being male/female influenced your artistic production?
12. What are the values that are important to you personally?
13. What is the social significance of your art form(s)?
14. What is your artistic status in the community? Outside the community? REASONS?
15. For whom do you produce art? For what reasons?
16. What do you consider to be the major influences on your art?
17. How have these factors affected your art?
18. Which persons have influenced your art? HOW?
19. If a person wanted to see your work, where would he/she go to do so?
20. How do you think person from another sociocultural group might interpret your work? WHY?

Environmental
21. Has/have your geographical and/or physical environment influenced your art form(s)? If so, HOW?

Note: The language used in the questions suggested in Figures 9.1 and 9.2 should be adjusted by the teacher according to the cognitive level of the students.

FIGURE 9.2 Studying the Art Form(s)

1. In which culture was/were the art form(s) produced?
2. Identify and describe the geographical features of the region/place inhabited by the producer(s) of this/these object(s). In what ways have climate, landform, vegetation, and natural resources affected the art form(s) produced?
3. In what time period(s) was/were the art form(s) produced?
4. Describe the physical appearance of the art form(s).
5. How did/does/do the art form(s) function in the culture?
6. What aspect(s) of the cultural aesthetic production is/are most important: the process, the product, or the symbolic significance?
7. What is/was the social significance of the art form(s)?
8. What were/are the aesthetic values of the culture?
9. Who is/are the artist(s)? Gender(s)? Age(s)? Social status?
10. How was/were he/she/they selected to become artist(s)?
11. How was/were she/he/they trained?
12. For whom did/do he/she/they produce the art form(s)?
13. Is/are the art form(s) being produced today? Is it/are they the same or different? HOW?
14. How is/are the art form(s) being used in the culture today?

By closely examining and confronting the data collection from this culture, students, teachers, and the community will become more sensitized to cultural diversity [and sociocultural inequities] and be able to assume a powerful role in a liberating educational process. (p. 22)

The American Indians in Wisconsin constitute a disenfranchised group: The state reports unemployment figures ranging from 26% for the Oneida Reservation to 85% for the Mole Lake Chippewa Reservation (J. Gordon, Great Lakes Tribal Office in Wisconsin, personal communication, 1991). This makes them a tenable group to use for studying art and planning curricula in Wisconsin.

If one were teaching in Miami, Florida, the Hispanic/Cuban art world might be selected for study. The African-American community aesthetic/cultural production might be investigated in Detroit or Chicago. In Minneapolis the newly established Hmong community's art might be the focus of class research. However, when selecting a sociocultural group to be investigated and studied, teachers need to be sensitive to, and empathetic with, the views of the community in which they teach. For example, if one were teaching in the city noted as the birthplace of the Ku Klux Klan, one probably wouldn't investigate the African-American culture. One might study a social or cultural group that also has been or is discriminated against, and from which inferences for reducing or resolving African-American–white racial conflicts could be drawn.

Students will be empowered through their critical investigation of social conflicts that have an impact on the discussion, production, and use of art in all sociocultural groups. They will find liberation in the acknowledgment of the positive changes they can bring about through their own actions. The students will no longer believe they are powerless to implement change, after they have experiences that prove this false.

On Collecting Indian Powwow Data

In the summer of 1990, I conducted descriptive field research at Wisconsin Indian powwows. The subjects of my study were American Indian artists and their cultural/aesthetic forms, spectators, and event organizers. I relied primarily on ethnographic strategies such as interviews (both formal and informal), participant observation, photographic documentation, and review of pertinent historical and contemporary documents (posters, pamphlets, newspapers, and journal articles on the powwows from the various sites). The value of such strategies is well-documented in the work of Spradley (1979, 1980). I had attended numerous Wisconsin powwows in the 7 years prior to this research on Wisconsin Indian life. I drew on those experiences for this chapter also.

Initially I had anticipated that only artists/performers and spectators would be interviewed, but once in the field, I recognized the importance of talking to the organizers as essential to understanding the sociocultural milieux. Examples of the types of questions that were investigated/asked were: Who produced/performed/viewed these powwow art/aesthetic forms? (Male? Female? Both? Families?) What ages were they? (Young? Middle Aged? Old, All of these?) Why did they do this? Did/do other members of their families do this? How did they become involved? Where were they from? What is their tribal/ethnic affiliation? How much did they invest in this? (Time? Effort? Money?) How had their art/aesthetic forms(s) or viewing habits changed since they began producing/performing/viewing? If things have changed, how? Did any culture(s) other than the one with which they are affiliated influence their or the powwow's art/aesthetic forms? Were their children involved in the powwow's art/aesthetic forms in any capacity?

In both the six position statements for the development and teaching of multicultural art/aesthetic curriculum and the multicultural curriculum guidelines, we advocate that curriculum construction and ownership be shared with the students (Stuhr, Petrovich-Mwaniki, & Wasson, 1992; Wasson, Stuhr, &

Petrovich-Mwaniki, 1990). For practical reasons the students probably would have to limit their research to a single powwow, and then only one aspect of it, such as the construction of ceremonial dance outfits or the aesthetic and spiritual construction of the drums. The kind of investigative work that I did independently could easily have been done or shared by students in grades 4 through 12 and their teacher(s), after some training and classroom role play in the use of social and anthropological investigation techniques (interview and observation methods). Teachers and students might incorporate the production of newer media images and text into this process (i.e., photographs, videos/films, computer graphics, and computer text that document the investigation on site and in the classroom). Education in historical research methods (use of the library and historical community resources) would be helpful. This type of ethnological and critical thinking curriculum activity requires collaborative and multidisciplinary effort on the part of the teacher(s), students, and community members.

PRESENTATION OF THE POWWOW DATA

In this section a historical overview of the powwow and a description of the traditional Odanah, Wisconsin powwow and the Milwaukee, Wisconsin Indian festival, which incorporated powwows, will be presented and discussed.

Historical Background on Powwows

Victoria Gokee explained to me that freedom for Indian people to conduct powwows openly is a fairly new occurrence. She described it in this way.

> This here powwow is from an old tradition. We couldn't feel comfortable doing it until recently. The 1978 Indian Freedom of Religion Act gave us the legal right to do it. The powwow has a lot of [spirituality] connected to it. Before we couldn't even feel safe. With that Act being passed like that we could again. (V. Gokee, personal communication, 1990)

Today, most powwows in Indian communities are held annually and have a pan-Indian quality. Wax (1971) states that the common styles of dance, song, and ceremonial dress and the rapid transmission of innovation in these matters from one group to another are what makes the powwows pan-Indian. The powwow as a secular or social phenomenon grew out of the nineteenth-century Plains Indian tribes' cultures, especially the Lakota (Sioux), and has been greatly influenced by their forms of dance, song, and ceremonial dress. Previously, although many tribes had some forms of dancing, singing, and adornment that were purely social, most forms were ritual and held a place within ceremonies for healing, hunting, warfare, or other types of blessings. Now, most of the historical context for these rituals and ceremonies has vanished, and the songs and dances are performed primarily for social and entertainment purposes. Because of this change, far more borrowing and innovation are taking place within the powwow today.

Wax (1971) notes that the ceremonial clothing design, dance, and song are a trio of interconnected art forms. They can be performed by persons of any age and either sex. Women, however, do not generally drum, although they may sing to accompany the male drummers. Drumming is a privilege founded in tribal narratives (mythology) and extended only to men and boys (Johnston, 1976). Indian music is often problematic for tourists visiting a powwow and sometimes for the native participants and spectators when they are not familiar with the language or the meanings of the songs.

> Of the three arts, singing is the most subtle, sophisticated, and, being far from Western patterns, the most difficult for an outsider to comprehend and appreciate. In most local powwows or ceremonials, the singing is still done in a native Indian language, making the lyrics incomprehensible to an outsider. This barrier is doubly unfortunate, since Indian singers are judged [among other criteria] on their virtuosity in composition, and dancers in a tribal powwow are judged on their interpretation of a lyric. (Wax, 1971, p. 149)

Many Indians travel great distances to attend powwows that may last from 2 days to a week. They may register and participate in competitions for the best dancer, designed ceremonial outfit, and singing or drum group within specific categories. These art forms are subject to Indian judgments (Wax, 1971). Most powwows pay all of the registered singers and dancers a modest sum even if they win nothing in the competition. Most Indians attend powwows for the social and ethnic identification opportunities.

The Odanah Powwow

The organizers described the powwow held on the Odanah Chippewa Reservation as traditional.[1] The Odanah powwow was advertised as The 10th Annual Bad River Traditional Manomin Celebration and was held on August 17–19, 1990. *Manomin* is the Chippewa word for wild rice. It is still grown and harvested on most Chippewa reservations. This powwow has evolved out of the Chippewa's traditional celebration of thanksgiving to the Creator or Great Mystery, *Gi'-tchie Man-i-to',* for the wild rice harvest. Individual families continued to celebrate the rice harvest privately in their homes after missionaries and government agents banned the formal tribal celebration of this occa-

sion for being pagan and against the tenets of Christianity. This family celebration persisted in some homes until 1980, when the first powwow was
reinstated (Odanah Powwow Committee, personal communication, 1990).

The planning for the 1990 powwow was arranged by the same 10 people
(the Powwow Committee, five males and five females) who had been responsible for its inception and occurrence the previous 9 years. With the tribe's
permission, this Committee initiated the first powwow when they were in
their late teens and early twenties as a social event and to help mend a tribal
feud that distressed them. The members met to organize the powwow once
a month all year until spring; then they met every 2 weeks. The month before
the event, meetings became even more frequent (Odanah Powwow Committee, personal communication, 1990).

The organization of a powwow entails setting the powwow agenda; ar-
ranging for publicity and printing of posters, pamphlets, newspaper information, caps, and t-shirts; soliciting sponsors and donations from the Indian
community and local towns; inviting an emcee to preside over and narrate
the event and an elder to bless the grounds and to give the convocations;
setting up the powwow arbor and grounds with appropriate spiritual rituals;
installing electrical power and a P.A. system; asking special drum singing
groups and veterans (warriors) to attend; appointing powwow guards, but-
ton admission salespeople, and people to prepare the free meals served during
the powwow; selecting people to judge Jr. Miss and Miss contests and dance
contests; setting up and operating the tribal powwow concession stand; ar-
ranging space for food and Indian art/artifact vendors and portable rest
rooms; monitoring the powwow and camping areas; and paying dancers,
drum groups, and all bills. This last responsibility, the group said, is the most
important in order for the powwow to retain a respectable reputation (Odanah Powwow Committee, personal communication, 1990).

Admission to the Bad River powwow for persons 11 to 60 years "young"
was three dollars. Children younger than 11 and elders had free entry. No
alcohol or drugs were allowed; this was strictly monitored by patrolling powwow security guards.

The powwow grounds encompassed an area the size of a small midwestern fairgrounds. There were areas for parking and camping. These sites were
overseen by powwow guards who wore arm bands and carried walkie-talkies.
The camping area was utilized by the participants who came from distant
areas, as well as some local residents who found it convenient to camp with
recreational vehicles or tents.

An area also was designated for the use of Indian vendors who sold food,
artifacts, and arts/crafts (including tapes of Indian music). The artists/craft-
people who sold their work at the powwow said they did so for various reasons: to make money, to meet interesting people, to defray the cost of at-

tending the powwow, and to afford themselves the opportunity to trade with other artists for their ethnic work; because they enjoyed it, it is one of the few places where Indian people can market their work, it is a way to reach the Indian customer, it is something the whole family can be involved in together, and it is a way to form ethnic sociocultural connections. At this powwow there was only one non-Indian participant with a stand, the editor of a local proactive Indian newspaper. She displayed and distributed Chippewa treaty support brochures, which discussed the spearfishing rights of the Indians.

The focal point of the powwow site is the dance area. It consists of a central circular arbor, constructed with 12 wooden poles (one central pole and 11 others positioned at the perimeter of the arbor) and covered by a conical roof of cedar boughs. This is the area where most of the drummers and singers are stationed. At this powwow there were 22 drum/singing groups. A drum group, referred to simply as a drum, consists of a lead singer/drummer and between 5 and 10 other male singer/drummers of various ages. Outside of this arbor is the circular dance arena. There is no defined mode of dress for the members of the drums. A number of the groups wore shirts, caps, or jackets that identified their drum group name and locality.

Grand Entries for the powwow were set for approximately 7:00 p.m. Friday, 1:00 and 7:00 p.m. Saturday, and 1:00 p.m. Sunday. The powwow opened with an elder saying a prayer in Chippewa and giving a convocation in both Chippewa and English. He admonished everyone to pray and keep in mind the sorrow and problems of the locality and the world (e.g., spearfishing treaty rights problems and the escalating trouble in Iraq). The commencement of a song signaled the start of the powwow dancing and singing activities. A Grand Entry starts with the emcee's announcement for all to rise and of the first drum song, generally performed by the host drum, in this instance, the "Bad River Singers." A formal procession, moving in a clockwise direction, entered from the east into the circular dance arena. The procession was led by flag bearers, who were selected American armed service veterans and veterans of Indian battles within the United States (e.g., Wounded Knee, Gresham Monastery), carrying their Indian tribal/national flags (large, regal feathered staffs) and the American flag. They were followed by the head male traditional dancer and other traditional male dancers attired in their tribal ceremonial wear and usually dancing in the traditional fashion of their nation. Next appeared the fancy dancing males, in the elaborate and colorful fashions of the Plains Indians and for the most part dancing in the more spirited style of the western Indians. Traditional Indian women dancers led by a head female traditional dancer followed the men, succeeded by the fancy dancing women. Young boys and girls followed in the same order as their adult role models. The smaller children of both genders and fashions of ceremonial dress brought up the rear of the dance procession in a less organized manner.

This sequence of dancers is followed only in the Grand Entry. During most other dances the performers are interspersed, unless a specific type of dance that requires other arrangements is announced. The emcee announced all dances and told spectators when to stand out of respect, and when photographs were allowed and when they were not.

To be selected as a head dancer is an honor. Usually a powwow committee selects individuals for this honor. The committee approaches them with courtesy gifts and tobacco and requests that they accept this ceremonial distinction (A. Sullivan, personal communication, 1991).

Individuals are not allowed in the dance area without ceremonial dress or a specific purpose for being there (such as veterans in a Grand Entry), unless an intertribal dance is announced by the emcee. When a dance is designated as intertribal, all people, including non-Indians, are invited to dance, even if they are without ceremonial dress. An intertribal dance is accompanied by a generic powwow song, which is chosen by the drum whose turn it is to perform. Some specific tribal dances called were sneak-up, squaw dance, veteran or warrior song, crow hop, shawl, mission two step, feather, fish, swan, and alligator. Only the registered dancers participated in these dances. The hoop dance was performed solo by a little girl who had been taught this dance by her grandmother.

All dancing was stopped by the emcee when it was noticed that a sacred eagle feather had accidentally fallen on the ground. Warriors were solicited to do a special dance and song to retrieve the feather. A male elder came up to the emcee stand to tell a narrative, which explained the extraordinary attention given to a "downed" eagle feather, and to caution that photographs of the ritual were forbidden. One never leaves a sacred eagle feather to be trampled upon, but respectfully returns it to the owner, because in Ojibway (Chippewa) narrative (mythology), the fallen feather symbolizes a fallen warrior who has sacrificed his life to protect his people. After the feather was ceremoniously recovered from the ground, it was given away by the owner in a traditional fashion. This type of incident occurred three times at this powwow. If it had occurred once more, it would have been taken as a bad omen and the powwow would have been canceled.

The announcer's stand was set up on the left side of the dance area, but this is not a requirement. The stand resembled that of a baseball announcer and displayed a sign advertising the powwow. The home (Odanah) drum had been placed at the front foot of the booth. The emcee's stand was flanked on both sides by wooden bleachers for spectators, who would ring approximately a third of the dance area. Large speaker units were installed at various sites near the bleachers. Young people of both genders often set mini tape recorders and/or boom boxes with recorders on them to tape various powwow singers, especially the more popular drums. They use the recordings for entertainment and to help them learn the drum/songs or practice their dance steps. This practice was repeated at all powwow sites. Floodlights were affixed to the center arbor and at strategic points around the outside of the dance area to facilitate evening dancing. Good lighting is important since the colors and designs of the ceremonial clothing are essential to understanding and appreciating the festival.

Vendors had rented spaces and set up their stands beyond the bleachers. The Powwow Committee had a stand at which it sold shirts, caps, coffee, pop, and snacks to defray powwow costs. A church group had a camper-trailer set up for selling food, including the powwow staples: fry bread, which is a delicious deep fat fried, flat, round, bun-sized bread usually eaten with honey, and Indian tacos made with fry bread and ground deer meat seasoned with taco spices and garnished with tomatoes, lettuce, and cheese. There was also a large, open-air tent set up to serve feasts (free Indian meals) to the dancers, singer/drummers, and spectators. Many people in the Chippewa community donated food, time, and energy to the meals. The dishes are often prepared from traditional recipes using wild game from the area and fish from the nearby lakes, including Lake Superior. Before a feast was served, a ritual plate offering was made by a young Indian woman in full ceremonial dress to the Great Mystery at the dance arbor. A prayer of thanksgiving was said by a male spiritual leader.

Because of rain the evening of the second day, the powwow was moved indoors to the nearby Tribal Community Center. The physical format of the drum/dance and spectator portions of the powwow remained about the same, except that the dancing and the music seemed more intense. It seemed that most danced or, if male, drummed and sang at some point during the evening. Folding and lawn chairs, many supplied by the viewers themselves, were substituted for the spectator bleachers. The vendors moved to the kitchen section of the center, where many took turns relieving each other to enable participation by all in the festivities.

When Indian participants arrived at the powwow site, regardless of their participatory roles, they first greeted the elders as a sign of respect. After exchanging a few words, they moved on to their specified areas or off to their peer or family groups. There were about 500 individuals in attendance, ranging in age from infants to 103 years old. Approximately three-fifths of all persons attending the powwow wore at least some items of ceremonial apparel.

There were 259 registered dancers. Fully attired male dancers wore or carried some or all of the following ceremonial items: shirt, leggings, vest, diaper/loincloth (gym shorts or sweat pants were usually worn under this), bustle, moccasins, garters (wrist, arm, leg), headdress, roach headpiece, hair feathers, bag/pouch, pendant and/or choker, breast plate, staff, war club,

Female *(l.)* and male *(r.)* dancers at the Odanah Powwow

rattle, and fan. The female dancers' ceremonial outfits included items from the following list: dress, blouse, skirt, dance shawl, moccasins (high or low top), belt, bandolier bags, leggings, beaded pendants and/or necklaces, beaded earrings, beaded barrettes, and hair ties (beaded or appended to fur or feathers). Ceremonial dress varied for both men and women, depending on their national/tribal affiliation or the type of dances in which they specialized. The traditional outfits were more subdued and subtle in color than the bold and dynamic hues of the fancy dancers. All items included in the dance gear were custom-made and often intricately decorated with beads, ribbons, fur, jingles, and so forth.

There was some innovative ceremonial attire noted: sunglasses, beaded and nonbeaded baseball caps and sun visors, some with feathers stuck in them. A few teenagers sported punk hair styles colored with dye. One teen-aged female had on a striking black and white ceremonial outfit that incorporated elements of both traditional Indian and punk counterculture dress. T-shirts, blue jeans, and cowboy hats and boots were common. A few male youngsters wore shirts with smile faces and Simpson characters on them.

Few of the 60 or so non-Indian people in attendance participated in the dancing; they were spectators for a few hours or customers for the vendors.

Most Indian people did dance at some point in the powwow. Sustained inter-action between the Indians and non-Indians was rarely observed.

Some of the local Chippewa Indian people at this powwow displayed physical characteristics of African-American heritage. During the period be-fore the Civil War, the Underground Railroad made a stop on the Odanah Reservation before travel continued on to Canada. The people displaying the characteristics of blended racial heritage claimed only the ethnic culture of the Chippewa.

Indians, old and young alike, stayed into the evening. The Grand Exits and evening convocations took place at sunset, around 9:15 p.m., and offi-cially ended the dance activity for the day. The Grand Exits were led by the warriors, followed by the dancers in the same order as they had entered the arena. By this time some individuals were nodding off and most of the pow-wow activity ceased for the majority of the participants. An exception to this were the teens and young adults, who continued to socialize late into the night. This youthful social activity is known as snagging.

On the last day of the event, the families of last year's Odanah Jr. Miss and Miss Powwow Princesses hosted a "giveaway." The princesses are selected primarily on their dancing ability and performance. At a giveaway presents and sacred tobacco are presented to various members of the community by families (sometimes individuals) for, in this case, the privilege of having had their daughters represent the tribe in this honored way for the year. The to-bacco is used as an offering to the Creator and is placed at a sacred site near the dance arbor. The giveaway can be quite expensive for the families in-volved. Blankets, lawn chairs, plastic baskets, dish towels, school supplies, and so on, are presented to members of the community to whom they feel a spe-cial thanks is owed. A song and dance are declared in the recipients' honor.

Although all of the Indian people interviewed said they attended the powwow for the sociocultural entertainment and community aspects, some, like a member of the Odanah Powwow Committee, went on to explain a deeper level of meaning and participation.

> It's [the powwow] like a calling card to a lot of other things. There's the powwow and everything that goes along with it. It's like just one facet of our culture and our tradition. There's a lot of other things and kind of the way I notice it happening, is that the powwow, it's a big thing. There's music there. There's the heartbeat of the drum, those sounds that touch us way deep inside somewhere, they touch us. But the dancers are out there telling their stories. There's color there, and movement. There's sights and smells, and everything that goes along with it. It drives people, it pulls people together. Myself in particular, that made me interested

enough; it made me interested to learn [more]. It opened the door up to a lot of other things. When you get into the actual ceremonial, spiritual, and religious part of our culture, it's not that big [the size of the group actually participating in this realm of the culture]. Usually it's a smaller group. Usually it is pretty low key; usually it's secluded. That's how it is nowadays. It's [spiritual and philosophical aspects] some pretty deep stuff. And that's not the type of thing that a little [young] person would walk up on and find extremely attractive. But they could come to the powwow and feel those things, and get hungry for the rest, and start asking themselves questions, like: What's this all about? . . . really in-depth kinds of questions. You know, looking at what we have now. I'm real happy to be envious of the younger ones now, that are young enough to not have known a time when the drums weren't here, and that circle [powwow dance area] wasn't there. (Odanah Powwow Committee, personal communication, 1990)

For some the powwow is motivational. After developing an understanding of the powwow's cultural significance, some decide to pursue a deeper understanding of the spiritual and philosophical meanings underpinning the traditional Indian way of life. The symbolism embodied in the aesthetic/art forms and performances of the Indian people is paramount to this cultural understanding.

Milwaukee Indian Summer Festival

The Milwaukee Indian Summer Festival held September 7–10, 1991 attracted a record 43,000 individuals. Parking was available in many areas adjacent to the festival grounds for four dollars a vehicle, and tickets to the festival were available at turnstile entrances to the grounds at six dollars for adults and three for school-age children and senior citizens. Tickets purchased in advance were slightly less. People from various ethnic backgrounds of all ages were present.

Camping was not allowed on the festival grounds. Indian people participating in Indian Summer stayed with friends or relatives in the city, rented hotel/motel rooms, or camped outside of the city in designated camping areas.

The main goals of the festival were to provide the urban Milwaukee Indian population with an opportunity to gather and renew friendships and ethnic ties, to practice traditional cultural ways, and to entertain and educate both Indians and non-Indians about American Indian culture (C. Brown & J. Klumb, personal communication, 1991).

The Milwaukee Indian Summer Festival was organized and planned in

1990 by a board composed of 14 urban Indian members. Each member of the board was responsible for guiding a specific committee, for example, cultural, education, bingo, raffle, environmental, or powwow. Indian Summer is partially funded by various local civic and corporate sources such as Miller and Old Style Brewing, The DeRance Foundation, The Milwaukee Foundation, Milwaukee Gas and Electric, banks, insurance companies, and other businesses.

An annual competition is held to select a well-known Wisconsin Indian artist's work to be reproduced for promotional purposes. It is judged by the festival's board of directors. This year's designer was Nick Hocking. He is a Lac Du Flambeau Chippewa and his winning design was printed on 6,000 brochures and 2,500 posters for the event. The artists selected the previous 3 years were on site in a large tent selling their artwork, which included paintings, drawings, prints, t-shirts, and notecards. During the festival they were also available to sign prints of their past posters. Indian Summer was advertised on local radio stations, T.V. stations, and newspapers, and through letters sent out to area schools.

The powwow portion of Indian Summer was planned by a member of the board of directors and a group of five to six additional urban Indians.[2] Prizes, totaling $25,000 for the best dancers and drum groups, attracted American Indian contestants from across the nation and Canada. This is considered a great deal of prize money on the powwow circuit. Most of the Indian participants and observers could be found congregated in the powwow arena.

The last day of the festival was set aside for the local schoolchildren. Eight thousand students were bused in from different parts of Milwaukee and surrounding communities, and others from across Wisconsin and Illinois, for this occasion.

The Milwaukee Summer Festival grounds are located in downtown Milwaukee along the shore of Lake Michigan. The grounds include clean, well-maintained paved paths and manicured grassy lawn areas. Skyscrapers are visible in the background. The grounds are equipped for handicapped individuals. Announcements concerning performances were made over a P.A. system, which served the complex. The advertised schedule of events was strictly adhered to.

Space, buildings, and tents were rented to vendors of food, Indian artifacts, and souvenirs. Alcohol was forbidden on the three-fourths of the grounds devoted to the powwow and Indian performance areas. On the rest of the grounds, where many vendors and food stands were situated, the sale of beer was allowed. Indian security guards wearing navy blue baseball caps and t-shirts labeled SECURITY in white patrolled the areas on golf carts. Teepees made of canvas were provided for the Indian people demonstrating and

Spectators at the Milwaukee festival being taught Indian dances

selling their aesthetic cultural productions, such as ceremonial attire and accouterments, beadwork, basketry, blanket weaving, doll making, pottery, jewelry, and so on, to protect them from the elements.[3] The Indians demonstrating arts and crafts were invited from all areas of the United States. They were not charged rent for their spaces, but were allowed to sell only what they produced on site (J. Klumb, personal communication, 1991). They were selected on the basis of their national reputations (L. Littlewolf, personal communication, 1990). There were few Wisconsin Indians included in this group. In past years more local artists had been invited.

Corporate sponsors provided stage areas, such as the Miller Stage, where educational and entertainment performances were given, mainly by Indian men and boys, of various kinds of traditional dancing, drumming and singing, and flute playing. A highlight in this area was Nick Hocking and his wife Charlotte, Chippewa Indians from the Lac Du Flambeau Reservation, who taught Indian traditional dancing to non-Indian children and adults to help dispel misconceptions they had about the art forms and to enable them to understand the powwow music and dance in a more contextual fashion.

Hocking and members of the Lac Du Flambeau Chippewa Reservation band constructed an Ojibway (Chippewa) village where a birch bark wigwam, a birch bark canoe, totem birch bark shields, a fish drying rack, and stretched animal skins (the black bear was the biggest attraction) were exhibited on a conspicuous area of the grounds. Nick, dressed and painted in full Ojibway traditional ceremonial regalia, was available for photographs and to answer observers' questions. Other members of the Lac Du Flambeau Reservation were also present to answer spectator queries.

The theme of the 1991 Indian Summer was "Honor Mother Earth." The ascribed traditional value of the American Indians' harmonic relationship with nature/environment was aligned with the causes of other non-Indian groups. A huge tent was constructed that contained environmental displays, one of which was labeled "Living with Mother Earth." Another display provided information on the endangered timber wolf and featured a stuffed member of the species. There was an area entitled "Children Saving Our Vanishing Wild Life," where children's efforts toward this end were shown, and another area for children to color and draw the sights they'd seen and the experiences they'd had at the festival. There was also an environmental sculpture constructed from recycled materials.

The American Boy Scouts had an area set aside for display and activities. In other areas pony rides and Indian face painting were available for a price. One section was set aside for a mock settlement of white fur traders, with long hair and beards, who were decked out in frontier clothing and armed with early American weaponry. It seemed ironic that Indians dressed in ceremonial outfits were snapping pictures of these re-enactors.

Non-Indian spectators and participants reported attending the festival for entertainment, to learn about the Indians, or for sociocultural-political and/ or financial profit. Indian participants listed community contacts, entertainment, the opportunity to dance, education, and financial profits as their reasons for attending the festival. Based on the reasons non-Indians and Indians gave for participating in the powwow, one could infer that a reciprocal and advantageous relationship evolved from the event.

My personal opinion is that the alignment of the non-Indian spectators and participants with the Indian population under the guise of noble causes needs monitoring by all involved because of the treatment perpetrated by well-meaning white men and women in the past. This alignment carries with it the threat of manipulation and scapegoating. The non-Indian vendors could also be a threat to Indian sales, if they are allowed to undercut native prices.

CONCLUSIONS

The type of thick descriptive data provided by this study of the Wisconsin Indian powwow is available from site and primary source investigation. Using participant observation, interviews, and historical research methods, students could discover this same kind of information about powwows and/or other aesthetic Indian festivals. The multicultural and social reconstructionist art curriculum possibilities based on this type of cooperative investigation are endless.

The study of the powwow as curriculum content provides us with an example of internal and external data about sociocultural complexity. The boundaries between various Indian cultures and the dominant ideology of the American culture, as well as of other cultures, are often blurred. The convocation and prayer said in both Chippewa and English at the Odanah powwow's commencement is an example of this type of cultural blending. A further example is the spiritual leader's references to issues at the local level (spearfishing treaty rights problems) and the international level (Iraq/American situation) in his opening prayer. Still another instance is the recognition that a man (the spiritual leader) steeped in the traditional ways of the Chippewa people was addressing the community using a microphone, over a P.A. system, in an announcer's booth. These types of cultural interactions continually affect the powwow as an aesthetic/art form in the ways it is viewed and perceived and the understandings of it that are produced.

Cultural maintenance and change, through the example of the powwow, can be seen to have been affected by the processes of enculturation, acculturation, and assimilation. Enculturated behavior was apparent at the powwow in the demonstration of proper respect to elders, etiquette during drum/dance performances, use of the Ojibwa (Chippewa) language in the songs, and so forth. Evidence of acculturation was apparent in the design and decoration of the ceremonial dress of the dancers, the use of electronic equipment, and the type of articles sold by the Indian vendors. The process of assimilation was obvious in specific areas of the powwow, such as obtaining grants for funding of the nontraditional festivals/powwows and using the powwow as a forum for environmental and political perspectives and the education and integration of diverse cultural groups.

If the powwow was dealt with in curriculum construction only as a traditional or past historical form, much important information concerning the cultures' current social, political, and economic relations would be lost. A monocular presentation of a sociocultural aesthetic/art form deprives the students, teacher(s), and community of the opportunity to challenge their values, to make reflective decisions, and to take action to implement these decisions with regard to art curriculum and their social life both in and out of school. Past art education methods have tended to rely on the teacher or books as the experts. That teaching/learning perspective gave only one viewpoint. Through the multicultural curriculum envisioned here, multiple roles and opportunities for teaching and learning are available for the teacher(s), students, and the community. The responsibility for art education in this author's opinion should be perceived as an interdisciplinary, cooperative, and shared endeavor.

Implications for Art Education

Once the students and the teacher(s) have established the rationale for and importance of investigating the art/aesthetic components of a sociocultural form (in this example the powwow) and have compiled some or all of the ethnographic information from the community, they are ready to identify specific, important social issues as suggested by the curriculum guidelines at the beginning of this chapter. The issues should be related to religion, ethnicity, socioeconomic class, gender, age, and mental and physical abilities. For purposes of this chapter I will provide examples only of gender issues, although all of the other issues are represented to some degree in the powwow data. The students, acting as a class or in small groups, sometimes with the aid of and clarification of certain points by community members, are now ready to organize the data they've amassed in relation to specific issues. It is at this point that the students', teacher's, and community's values can be clarified and/or possibly challenged to suggest or to bring about social reconstructionist action. Comparisons between the students' previous perspective(s) and knowledge of the aesthetic/art form and the new sociocultural ways of viewing art, as reflected by the collected data about the related issue(s), should be presented and discussed.

This part of the curriculum project must be overseen with extreme sensitivity. Values and beliefs held dear by many sociocultural groups may be involved. If, for instance, the class or a group within it decided to look at the role of Indian narratives, specifically their influence on gender assignment in the aesthetic production/performance at the powwow, intense sensitivity would have to be shown to the theological/philosophical cultural system from which these gender roles originate. Comparisons could be made to the Judeo-Christian narratives/myths that define the dominant ideology in this area. The repercussions of challenging these value and belief systems as they affect art/aesthetic production must be recognized and discussed by students, teacher(s), and, where possible, members of the community. What might the result be for a young female or a group of young female Chippewa challenging the right of only males to drum? Would the almost certain disenfranchisement of the female(s) from the community be worth the challenge? Could the class think of alternatives or other areas in which to bring about gender equality? Do the students, once presented with the Indian conception(s) of gender roles, even see this situation as a gender issue or point of conflict?

Students, especially when they begin a multicultural program, rarely agree with the teacher's perception(s) of what is important. However, I feel it is extremely important that teachers state their opinions on the issue(s) once the students and community have presented their views. The teacher's opinion should be considered another informed perspective from which to think about the issue(s). If a guest, such as a spiritual leader or a female elder from the community, is invited into the classroom to share his or her insights and perspectives on an issue, such as the one presented above, the students and teacher(s) are cautioned to show respect for that invited opinion. Questions are encouraged, but should always be phrased in a respectful fashion. The classroom should be a forum for thoughtful consideration of all ideas.

Finally, students can be called upon to make reflective decisions, which represent the group as democratically and completely as possible. Compromise should be the encouraged method of resolving disputes and differences of opinion. It must be realized, however, that students may be able to agree only that they disagree. When and if feasible, action should be taken to implement the students' collective decisions. If implementing them at the community level would have alienating and disenfranchising effects, then possibly action can be taken only at the classroom level. For example, if, after much discussion, the students agreed that females should have the right to drum but action at the community level was considered impossible at this point in history, then actions enabling females in other ways and activities in the classroom or school could be suggested and implemented. The class could agree to let female students join in playing on a section of the playground that had been reserved for male students only. Possibly a joint ground mural could be drawn or painted on the blacktop by all students, illustrating their efforts toward gender equity. Further, they might as a group petition the music teacher to recruit female drummers (especially Indian students) for the school band, if none are participating in that position. The students could volunteer to make posters for that end. At the community level, parents and civic organizers could be requested by the students to establish a local drum and bugle corp, in which young females could become involved. Letters could be written to symphony orchestras at the state and national levels to investigate how many, and in what capacity, American Indian females and females in general are employed in their percussion sections. This type of multicultural curriculum activity is always risky. Students may choose to implement democratic action that is in opposition to the teacher's value and belief system(s).

Students who may have developed attitudes concerning their own or their community's powerlessness with regard to the social and political environment in which they live, should be taught to perceive their world (and art world) differently. Their parents, or possibly even former teachers, may have told them that the media and corrupt politicians control these environments and that societies, cultural groups, and institutions, which exist within them, are only pawns of these powers. This kind of thinking produces social and political apathy. In order for students to understand that in a democratic society power resides in the people and is dependent on cooperative political initiative and action, they must be given the opportunity to practice the concept. All subjects in schools, including art, should be taught to fulfill this discovery of democratic ideals.

In addition, when curriculum is conceived of in this way a recognition of the interconnectedness of all subjects is obvious. In the example presented in this chapter, the Indian's visual art could not be seen as separate from their music, dance, politics, geography, societies, and culture; nor could it be understood without considering issues of gender, age, ethnicity, social class, and exceptionality.

The six characteristics that Efland (1990) designated as important attributes toward the development of a postmodern art education — recycling, pluralism, conceptual conflict, eclecticism, democratization, and consideration of the attitudes of all participants and actors — are integrated in this proposed type of multicultural curriculum construction. During investigation of the processes of enculturation, acculturation, and assimilation in regard to sociocultural aesthetic/art forms of the powwow, the *recycling* of images and concepts and *eclecticism* must be considered. The dance that male veterans perform as a consequence or result of a fallen eagle feather during a powwow dance is based on an Indian narrative, which dictates this cultural rite. It is also an opportunity for a spiritual leader to instruct the community and others in proper cultural behavior. A sense of community obligation is taught and renewed through this dance, although the veterans now performing may be veterans from the Vietnam War. Here the narrative is inclusive of the process of enculturation. The use of the P.A. system by the spiritual leader to inform the powwow crowd of what is occurring during the fallen eagle feather retrieval dance, and the use of Indian veterans who have served in the dominant culture's armed services, are examples of acculturated and assimilated cultural features. Eclecticism comes into play through the arrangement of these elements into one cohesive, holistic ritual.

The ethnographic techniques of observation, participation, and interviewing that are encouraged in this form of multicultural curriculum design are employed to discover a *pluralistic* sociocultural perspective. A variety of attitudes held by various participants toward the investigated art forms, in addition to those held by the students and teachers in the classroom, also may be disclosed.

The emphasis on class discussion of issues related to religion, ethnicity, socioeconomic class, gender, age, and mental and physical abilities encourages resolution of *conceptual conflict*. As a matter of fact, this type of exploration demands it.

The final characteristic suggested by Efland is *democratization*. Democratization is fulfilled as both process and concept in the advocated curriculum design. Democratization is practiced as process when all members of the class participate in curriculum construction and reflection on sociocultural issues and then make decisions and implement action based on this reflection. Democratization is fulfilled as concept when the curriculum is inclusive of the knowledge and opinions of other, often minority, sociocultural groups and not solely that of the dominant franchised group.

There are drawbacks to implementing curriculum programs that are multicultural and social reconstructionist in nature. Implementing such a program demands substantial curricular revision. Ideally, it also would involve inservice training to make sure the program would be continual. The units or lessons taught in this manner may take longer periods of time to accomplish than using traditional teaching methods. The issues and problems focused on may be considered controversial by the school, administrators, staff, and community members. Some may be disillusioned by how few meaningful actions students are actually able to contribute toward the resolution of problems or social issues (Banks & McGee Banks, 1989). Those who are opposed to teaching using an interdisciplinary curriculum may argue that art should be taught as a separate subject from the rest of the curriculum.

The reasons for establishing a multicultural and social reconstructionist curriculum program far outweigh these drawbacks. In a multicultural and social reconstructionist curriculum the students are empowered to understand the complexity of ways in which various sociocultural groups participate in life in the United States. This curricular program would help to eliminate racial and ethnic isolation and centrism. It allows an opportunity for the inclusion of all disenfranchised groups' perspectives into the school curriculum. A broader view is given of the development of societies and cultures in this country. Disenfranchised groups are empowered to deal with their exploited state. Most important, students are given the chance to improve their skills in critical thinking and analyzing, and are taught to make decisions and to take democratic action. Through this process students may develop their investigative abilities and learn to work in cooperation for political action (Banks & McGee Banks, 1989). Art taught in an interdisciplinary fashion is better able to reflect and create understanding about the social, cultural, and political conditions that it is a part of.

In the construction of multicultural art curriculum it is not always necessary to produce a product as part of each lesson, as has been done in the past. Investigating, studying, and discussing art/aesthetic production in relationship to sociocultural issues are important in themselves. This type of activity can be supplemented with the documentary use of newer media such as photography, film/video, and computer graphics and texts. These art forms permeate the lives of most students in the United States and therefore hold great value for them. Having students make superficial projects such as construction paper headbands, without explaining the spiritual significance of the feather as a symbol in American Indian life, for example, is a stereotypic and harmful activity (Stuhr, 1990).

The cooperative study of an art form/aesthetic production like the powwow, using ethnographic and historical methods, provides an opportunity for all involved to comprehend and discuss critically the significance embodied in issues related to various sociocultural factors. When these methods are used conjunctively, in curriculum design and implementation, they also provide the opportunity to make significant connections with students' lives that are relevant, moral, and cognitively sound. This process, when studying a culture's aesthetic form such as the powwow, is further assisted when the students, teacher(s), and community "construct learning experiences that consist of critically examining the values and beliefs of the dominant ideology and the students' own and those of other cultural groups" (Stuhr, Petrovich-Mwaniki, & Wasson, 1992, pp. 17–18). This form of teaching/learning encourages and allows the students to implement action based on their investigation and study. The effect of this type of multicultural curriculum may be a more skeptical, informed, and active citizenry intent on a more equitable distribution of the power and resources available in the United States.

Acknowledgment. The author wishes to thank "Amoose," Mike Newaga, Mark Newaga, Sandy Lyon, Walt Bresette, Carol Brown, Jenelle Klumb, and the Odanah Powwow Committee for providing information about their specific powwow, reading rough drafts of this chapter, and providing corrective feedback. Additionally, I would like to thank Ann Sullivan, the daughter of Victoria Gokee, for reading on behalf of her mother and for sharing her insights with me. This chapter is dedicated to the memory of Victoria Gokee, who died in the spring of 1991. My appreciation is also extended to the individuals who informally discussed with me their perceptions of the powwows they attended. And finally, I would like to express my gratitude to Roseanne Hefko, Dr. Terry Barrett, and Dr. Doug Blandy for reviewing this chapter and making helpful recommendations.

NOTES

1. The total population on the Odanah Bad River Reservation reported by the Great Lakes Tribal Agency based on the BIA Labor Force Report (December 1990) was 905 individuals (450 male and 455 female).

2. The Milwaukee Indian Summer Festival Organization is run by a board of

directors consisting of 14 members, overseen by a president, vice president, treasurer, and secretary.

3. Teepees were rarely used as a form of traditional housing by the tribes indigenous to the area now called Wisconsin. Wigwams, lodges, or hogans built from various trees, including birch and elm, with cattail and rush matting, were the common types of housing.

REFERENCES

Banks, J. A., & McGee Banks, C. A. (Eds.). (1989). *Multicultural education issues and perspectives*. Boston: Allyn & Bacon.

Barrett, T. (1990). Fewer pinch pots and more talk: Art criticism, schools, and the future. *Canadian Review of Art Education, 17*(2), 91–102.

Blandy, D., & Congdon, K. G. (1988). Community based aesthetics as an exhibition catalyst and a foundation for community involvement in art education. *Studies in Art Education, 29*(4), 243–249.

Chalmers, G. (1981). Art education as ethnology. *Studies in Art Education, 23*(3), 6–4.

Clifford, J. (1988). *The predicament of culture*. Cambridge, MA: Harvard University Press.

Collins, J. (1989). *Uncommon cultures: Popular culture and postmodernism*. New York: Routledge.

Dufrene, P. (1990). Exploring Native American symbolism. *The Journal of Multicultural and Cross-Cultural Research in Art Education, 8*(1), 38–51.

Efland, A. (1990, October). *Visions of progress in twentieth century art education*. Paper presented at Studia Generalia, Norway.

Grant, C., & Sleeter, C. (1989). Race, class, gender, and disability in the classroom. In J. A. Banks & C. A. McGee Banks (Eds.), *Multicultural education: Issues and perspectives* (2nd ed.; pp. 46–65). Boston: Allyn & Bacon.

Grigsby, J. E. (1977). *Art & ethnics*. Dubuque, IA: Wm. C. Brown.

Johnston, R. (1976). *Ojibway heritage*. Toronto: McClelland and Stewart.

Lurie, N. O. (1971). The contemporary Indian scene. In S. Levine & N. O. Lurie (Eds.), *The American Indian today* (pp. 187–208). Deland, FL: Everett/Edwards.

McFee, J. K., & Degge, R. M. (1980). *Art, culture, and environment* (2nd ed.). Dubuque, IA: Kendall/Hunt.

Nash, M. (1989). *The cauldron of ethnicity in the modern world*. Chicago & London: University of Chicago Press.

Neperud, R. W. (1988). Conceptions of art in the service of art and aesthetic education: A critical view. *Arts and Learning Research, 6*(1), 95–106.

Neperud, R., & Stuhr, P. (1987). A critical analysis of cultural maintenance in a changing society. *The Journal of Multicultural and Cross-Cultural Research in Art Education, 5*(1), 117–130.

Parfit, M. (1994). Powwow: A gathering of the tribes. *National Geographic, 185*(6), 88–113.

Spradley, J. P. (1979). *The ethnographic interview.* New York: Holt, Rinehart and Winston.

Spradley, J. P. (1980). *Participant observation.* New York: Holt, Rinehart & Winston.

Stuhr, P. L. (1990). Wisconsin's Native American art. *Spectrum, 2*(1), 9–16.

Stuhr, P. L. (1991). Ethnic/cultural perspectives on environments as they relate to Indian art. *Arts and Learning Research, 9*(1), 42–56.

Stuhr, P., Petrovich-Mwaniki, L., & Wasson, R. (1992). Curriculum guidelines for the multicultural classroom. *Art Education, 45*(1), 16–24.

Wasson, R., Stuhr, P., & Petrovich-Mwaniki, L. (1990). Teaching art in the multicultural classroom: Six position statements. *Studies in Art Education, 31*(4), 234–246.

Wax, M. L. (1971). *Indian Americans.* Englewood Cliffs, NJ: Prentice-Hall.

CHAPTER 10

Texture of Community: An Environmental Design Education

Ronald W. Neperud

Today, it is virtually impossible to read a daily newspaper, view television, or converse without mention of the environment or environmental issues. So pervasive are the problems that confront us in the spaces in which we live and work, locally and globally, that the condition of the environment has become a prominent concern. The physical and social disintegration of cities, the pollution of waterways with sewage and toxic chemicals, the destructive clear-cutting of forests, the degradation of other natural habitats, and the crowding and overpopulation of communities are but a few contemporary environmental problems.

There is renewed interest among art educators in what I call environmental design. In environmental design, *design terms have been replaced by ecology, place, and biodiversity,* which reflect the changes that have occurred in conceptions of environment. The focus has changed from consumption to production and preservation. Justice, equity, ethnicity, class, empowerment, and gender are now legitimate environmental issues. These *sociocultural changes in environmentalism have been joined to multiculturalism* and are increasingly potent forces in American society. The importance for environmental design education is that it need no longer be isolated; with these alliances it can become an increasingly powerful voice in pedagogy.

In this chapter, the view is emphasized that people, and especially children and youth, need to: (1) develop an awareness of the multiple and interconnected dimensions of their environment, (2) be concerned with local and global environmental integrity, and interpret the meaning of design broadly, and (3) act sensitively and responsibly in improving environmental conditions. Through heightened consciousness people should be encouraged to act, individually and collectively, within communities to improve their situation and to recognize the social and ecological costs of failing to do so. The focus is not on humans *and* environments, but rather on humans *in* the environment.

The focus, then, is on developing changed views of environments and of design, and a socially responsible environmental design education. The chapter concludes with a set of propositions and activities for engaging children, youth, and teachers in a community-based environmental design education.

CHANGING VIEWS OF ENVIRONMENT, DESIGN, AND ENVIRONMENTAL EDUCATION

Environmental design education—those attempts to develop awareness and concern of and ameliorative action toward our surroundings—is very complex, involving views not only of environment but also of design and pedagogy. Assumptions that we hold toward these dimensions will be examined briefly preparatory to suggesting a community-based pedagogy.

New Meanings of Environment

Through the ages, environment represented all of the stuff with which humans contended in the game of survival. Now we have stepped back, having developed the constructs allowing for a more conscious approach to regarding our surroundings. Environment has been differentiated along several dimensions; most commonly, we talk about natural and built environments, which involve increasingly significant degrees of human alteration. Scientific/objective views of environment have developed around the natural sciences, forming the basis for much of environmental education in today's classrooms. The term *built environment* has developed as a designation for human creations such as architecture, cityscapes, or industrial design. In a sense, these objective views are part of the environmental problem, for the division between nature and humans has been institutionalized through language. Environment is often regarded as "something out there" over which humans exert control.

Increasingly, though, the human dimension of environments has been suggested. For example, Rapoport (1977) has recognized that

People must inevitably be considered as members of such groups with particular values, beliefs and ways of understanding the world. . . . People's membership in small groups, families, large social groupings and institutions, subcultures and cultures affects their roles, the ways in which they communicate, the relative importance and ways of handling social networks, kinship systems, values and the many other group characteristics of humans. (p. 2)

Rapoport's comments anticipate the changing emphasis on culturally and community defined environments rather than on objective universal definitions.

Mistakenly, commonsense environmental definitions have assumed humans to be in a separate and domineering role over their surroundings rather than interacting on a more reciprocal basis. Gottlieb (1993) recognizes broader multifaceted dimensions of postmodern environmental views as the basis for a contemporary environmental design education,

> We live today in a period of great upheaval, when environmental issues increasingly reflect crucial social and economic choices, and when new opportunities for change are emerging both within the movement and throughout society. Such opportunities for change have turned out to be unexpected, broad in scope, potentially far-reaching, and radical in their implications. They involve questions of technology and production, decision making and empowerment, social organization and cultural values. (p. 308)

This recognition of social and cultural interfaces with environment represents the basis for developing a socially responsible environmental design education. Manzini (1994), like Gottlieb, recognizes environment as an intertwining of social, economic, political, and ethnic dimensions that question the prevailing global model of development and consumption. Manzini calls for "innovative solutions with a high level of radicalness . . . to propose solutions which contain . . . a new way of behaving and viewing the world" (p. 39).

In summary, several changed dimensions have been added to our views. Environments are now regarded as: (1) *interactive* in the sense that they are shaped by humans and in turn influence human behavior; (2) *sharing with multiculturalism the defining variables of race, class, and gender;* (3) experienced *phenomenologically;* (4) *products of human interpretation;* and (5) *reflecting ideological orientations.* The meaning of environment in environmental design needs to be re-examined since the common anthropocentric view fails to recognize the complex interactive human/environmental relationships that characterize the contemporary world. The meanings of design as an integral part of environmental design also need to be examined so that we do not construct activities on false premises.

Changing Meanings of Design

Humans have always designed objects and environments to suit their particular needs; however, environmental design as a conscious discipline or practice developed in more recent times out of design movements associated with the work of architects, urban designers, landscape architects, and other designers who often issued normative formalistic design manifestoes destined to be followed by others. Elegant form was valued, which reflected the innovative use of materials, structural systems, and techniques more than it did the accommodation of social needs.

Among the critics of failed approaches was Paul Rudolph, noted architect and teacher, who as early as 1956 said of structures entered in *Progressive Architecture*'s Design Awards, "Perhaps the most important single aspect of those designs as a group is the apparent lack of interest in the environment in which the building is placed. . . . This continual thinking in terms of individual buildings as gems unrelated to earlier works is disastrous, creating cities whose buildings tend to brutalize rather than refine" (Banham, 1974, p. 57). Even much earlier, Frank Lloyd Wright had recognized and advocated a more organic relationship between built form and nature.

Gradually, it was recognized that human behavior had been neglected in formulating environmental design. Behavioral scientists, such as psychologists, criticized the modernist movement for its limited design criteria, believing that the consideration of human behavior, including the use and perception of environments, would be reflected in more satisfying and functional human habitats. Basic psychological processes such as learning, perception, cognition, and emotion were viewed as important determinants in understanding human interactions within environmental contexts (Proshansky, Ittelson, & Rivlin, 1970). Analysis of environmental psychological literature "shows that the topics subsumed under that label include perception theory, cognition, social and anthropological psychology, the study of social relationships, and the study of culture" (Lang, 1987, p. 21). It was also thought that human behavior could best be understood in the context of how space was used, such as in notions of privacy and *territoriality* (Scheflen, 1976).

Lang (1987) makes an important distinction between the creation and use of information by behavioral scientists. Behavioral scientists build theories based on the description and explanation of phenomena, whereas planners and designers are concerned about the future. "Every act of an architect, landscape architect, or urban designer is an advocacy for one future rather than another" (p. 22). Designers rather than behavioral scientists determine the goals of design and in the process reflect a particular ideological orientation.

The quality of life also has been associated with human behavior in built environments. Experimental and descriptive studies were developed to study this phenomenon. It was assumed that an understanding of human behavior in particular environments was essential to the design process, but the results failed to offer comprehensive and workable solutions to urban and rural environmental problems. Designers who based their work on a very limited model of human nature and behavior didn't understand the relationship between built environment and human behavior, and lacked an adequate theoretical basis of design (Lang, 1987).

Designers' limited understanding of human functioning resulted in additional problems of conceptualizing environmental design. At the 1970 Aspen Design Conference, *Environment by Design,* the French declined to participate, but offered a dissenting statement: "Problems of design and environment only look like objective ones. In fact, they are ideological ones" (Banham, 1974, p. 209). This recognition of an ideological basis of design was an important turning point in the conceptualization of design. Concerned with the importance of ideology in perceiving and valuing environments, I speculated that one's ideological perspective in perceiving environment is related to actions toward our surroundings (Neperud, 1991). Environmental issues, such as land uses, cannot be solved without resolving conflicting ideological differences.

The point that I want to make after these brief surveys is that the meanings of design and environment have shifted, often in ways that parallel modern/postmodern changes in contemporary society. Hierarchical universal meanings created by experts have given way to a recognition of user meanings reflecting an interactive process in creating environments. Empirical psychological research, aimed at predicting environmental preferences and behavior, has not been completely successful in aiding the design process when it has ignored social/cultural variables that figure prominently in defining human/ environmental relationships.

Gottlieb's (1993) analyses of major environmental organizations, such as the National Audubon Society, the Wilderness Society, the Environmental Defense Fund, and others numbered among the mainline "group of Ten," indicate that since the mid–1970s alternative environmental movements formed that are more local, participatory, action-oriented, and critical of expertise and lobbying in deciding environmental policy than were movements in the past. Historically, these movements have their roots in the earlier industrial and urban movements, the new Left, countercultures, underrepresented constituencies, citizen empowered movements, and pollution reduction efforts. The "new environmentalists" have advocated the freedom of neighborhoods from toxicity and other pollutants, the exercise of environmental choices, and the overall quality of living conditions that have been correlated to race, class, gender, and other social and economic variables. Issues of empowerment, equity, and choice are as much environmental as they are multicultural.

In effect, contemporary environmental designers can no longer take comfort in simply planning the "well designed" building or cityscape without attention to the many human issues that define the environment. Manzini (1994) suggests that the designer create form opportunities for "new types of behavior and new lifestyles in keeping with a new notion of social quality" (p. 43). *Humans have, indeed, been joined to environmental concerns and are not outside looking in,* and are beginning to demonstrate the effectiveness of community-based environmental movements.

Environmental Design in Art Education

It was the earlier views of environment, design, and environmental design, heavily weighted toward modernist perspectives, that provided the foundation for the expansion of art education to include environmental design education. Initially, art educators were intrigued with the idea that a universal approach to design and aesthetics applied to environments would somehow trickle down and alleviate environmental problems. It was assumed by art educators that the additional focus on environmental concerns would result in change. It came as a shock to discover that artists and art educators were little more concerned about their environments than anyone else, except in relation to the making of art objects. This view has changed substantially in recent years with the growing interest among eco-artists who have manipulated natural materials, forces, and processes to comment directly on environmental matters (Gablik, 1991).

Within the history of art education, environmental design education is of relatively recent origin, tracing its roots back a mere several decades. My own involvement goes back to the 1960s when I attended a conference sponsored by the Community Arts Study Program, University of Oregon, directed by June King McFee (1969). Inspired by the design literature to which I was introduced at this conference, I proposed that the qualities of human activities, as differentiated by social, ethnic, and cultural variables, be the focus of environmental aesthetics (Neperud, 1973). McFee and Degge, in their book *Art, Culture, and Environment* (1977), introduced environmental design as a legitimate concern for art educators.

Art educators drew from several disciplines ranging from architecture and city planning to anthropology and psychology. The contents of a symposium on environmental design held at a National Art Education Association Conference in St. Louis were later published as an issue of *Art Education* (Neperud, 1978). It was disappointing to me that art teachers had not assumed an active role as visual critics of their environments.

My perspective of design and environment was further developed in observations of urban design in the United Kingdom, particularly during visits with the late Russell Thomson (1978), art/environmental design educator and activist, in the Glasgow area. Situated at what had been a center of the

Industrial Revolution, this area experienced earlier many of the environmental problems that industrial nations continue to experience today. The used and discarded buildings, slag heaps, abandoned mines, polluted areas, and wasted human potentials were reminders of the problems that were to be experienced later by other industrializing areas. Not far from this area are the Scottish *new towns,* such as Cumbernauld, completely new communities designed to alleviate crowded and blighted urban areas devastated by industrial excesses.

The earlier forms of environmental design in art education paralleled the prevailing conceptions of environment and design. Recent studies in art education have demonstrated a renewed interest reflecting changes in environmentalism based on ecology and issues of ideology, and empowerment. For example, jan jagodzinski (1990) postulates a "green aesthetics," set within the postmodern condition, that is *"an aesthetic ecosophy of deep ecology"* (p. 2). jagodzinski believes that changes in the use of land, agriculture, and housing are to be found within the context of a green aesthetics that is strongly allied to ecofeminism. In a similar vein, Blandy and Hoffman (1993) argue that the environmental crisis can be remedied through a holistic world view "by enlarging the idea of community to include a bioregional perspective. The result is an art education of place" (p. 28).

An example of art education that recognizes an ecological and multidisciplinary approach has been the work of Barbosa (1991) in Brazil. She advocates that "art educators should join with other specialists — sociologists, ecologists, scientists, geographers, as well as architects, urban planners, communications specialists, social psychologists, and anthropologists — in the search for the equilibrium between preservation and development that leads to a better quality of life and a better environment" (p. 60). Barbosa's educational efforts with the poor children of Sao Paulo have successfully combined art and ecology in the preservation of nature and humans in nature. These are but a few of the major changes in recent years that have had a profound bearing on how we view environmental design education theory and the practices necessary to make them an integral part of contemporary pedagogy. To be effective, I believe that educational programs must be teacher initiated with strong student participation set within local communities. How can art education respond to the problems centered on social, gender, and racial inequities as revealed through recent critical studies?

Types of Environmental Design Education

A survey of three prevailing types of environmental design education provides some indication of problems inherent in existing pedagogical approaches.

Many elementary, and some secondary, programs have included some form of *environmental studies* in the curriculum. Usually, the focus is on the natural sciences; it may include an ecological orientation, but from an apolitical perspective that does not involve students in taking a particular stance with regard to preservation or other processes. This approach, just as the common value-free view of science, keeps environmental issues "clean and neat" so as not to offend anyone by the introduction of social, economic, political, or other significant issues. Topics such as ecological sensitivity, recycling, endangered species, and other similar topics are important, but if significant contextual issues are not addressed, ecological concerns result in little more than attractive art products.

Good design focuses primarily on objects, architecture, graphic design, industrial design, and urban and landscape architecture; it assumes that application of an objective form of evaluation and aesthetics can differentiate the "quality" of objects. The function of education is to prepare students to make aesthetic and good design judgments, usually through a study of formal design elements and structures. Many art educators still assume that the sensitive application of design principles to the environment is sufficient to improve their surroundings. *Good design, like science, is not apolitical; it merely is assumed to be so.*

Ecological studies assume that all natural systems in the world, such as biological and physiological, are interconnected. The term *deep ecology* was first used in the early 1970s by the Norwegian philosopher Arne Naess. Naess sought to distinguish between a radical, biocentric view of ecosystems — one that recognized the need to bring humans into harmony with the natural environment — and a shallow, anthropocentric view that placed humans at the center of the human–environment relationship (Gottlieb, 1993). Recent developments in art education environmentalism fit the description of deep ecology; however, most art education is still dominated by anthropocentric views that allow too comfortable a distance from the degradation of local and distant environments.

Art education, with its strong focus on aesthetics and design, remains the central and logical field for an environmental design education. The changed concepts of environment and design, and the emerging roles of teachers, have provided the foundations for environmental design education that actively seeks to involve teachers and students in transformative environmental activities through an engagement with community.

THE RE-EMERGENCE OF COMMUNITY

Community seldom has been mentioned in art education literature, especially in discipline-centered approaches. But as social considerations have entered the critique of schooling, it is much more frequently a consideration. Hicks

(1990) uses a reference to community that goes beyond geographic and demographic considerations in claiming, "We can only empower a student relative to particular communities of power. The process of empowerment involves a realignment of the individual from one community to another, or a relocation of that individual within a particular community" (p. 43). Her view is based on group membership, which is an important consideration in defining communities, as has been recognized by the "new environmentalists." It is quite likely that most students are members of several, often overlapping communities, a fact that argues against the application of simplistic environmental design curricula.

It is assumed that membership in a community or communities can contribute to empowered actions, and that such actions within some form of social organization are desirable in achieving democratic goals. Bowers (1987) recognizes that the added burden placed on schools by their assumption of socializing roles normally fulfilled by other institutions will be increased, "if teachers, as well as others, do not address the educational aspects of restoring a sense of community. . . . Education that contributes to the restoration of community will involve looking at the nature of teaching and the curriculum through a different set of conceptual lenses" (p. 141). Bowers suggests using the traditional curriculum in ways that strengthen bonding and participatory processes, while incorporating the relevant culture of the community into the curriculum. He does recognize the difficulties in this enterprise, as, for example, in the differences between the explanation of the work process in school and that encountered in work. "The symbolic knowledge — the words and concepts necessary for thinking about the nature and purpose of work — often oversimplifies the complexities of the work process and obscures the political issues requiring negotiation" (Bowers, 1987, p. 145).

Shannon (1992) relates the notion of community to a practical process of educational and community renewal through design, development, and maintenance of community. Education is in *"the context of community"* (p. 2). "The concept of Education-Based Community Development (EBCD) is founded on the profound interdependence of learning and life, of education and society" (p. 3). There is a vital link between education and daily living in which education is not confined to schools alone, but involves a reintegrative effort between the entire community and schools.

> Alienated youth and adults become community resources instead of community problems. Lifelong, shared, and cooperative learning become a part of every citizen's life, young and old, student and retiree, lay and professional. Lives are changed by working with, serving, teaching, and learning from others in multicultural and intergenerational contexts. (p. 3)

Kids shouldn't have to leave school to get into the real community. Academic studies and authentic community work need to be linked more significantly than is currently the case. Education-based community development is one such approach through which environmental design education becomes situated within the texture of community.

Deconstructed modernist beliefs have recentered curriculum construction between teachers and students (May, 1989) and led to multicultural changes within education (Banks & Banks, 1993). Art and aesthetics have been recentered on meanings within the life of all people. These same changes in attitude recognize that an environmental design education must engage students, teachers, and others outside schools in a form of community-focused education.

While community-focused pedagogy is receiving renewed attention, one needs to return to the social reconstructionists of an earlier era to realize the full meaning of such attempts. Space does not permit an extensive examination of social reconstructionism, which emerged in the 1920s and continued through the depression years, but the major tenets of reconstructionist thought are examined as a basis for development of a vital environmentalism. Theodore Brameld, through his numerous papers, discussions, and, later, *Toward a Reconstructed Philosophy of Education* (1956), was a dominant force in reconstructionism. Chambliss (1988) indicates that Brameld was concerned that all dimensions of culture be reconstructed, not just the social dimension.

Advocates were viewed by many conservatives as a bit naive at best, and as an un-American influence on our educational system at worst (Stanley, 1985). Although reconstructionism had little apparent lasting effect on our educational system as a whole, more recent social educators have found a congruence among the issues addressed by reconstructionists, such as ideology, indoctrination, and relativism, and the changes prompted by postmodern thought (Cherryholmes, 1988; Giroux, 1981; Stanley, 1981). As can be seen from this brief examination of reconstructionism, some of its major tenets provide a means of connecting an active environmental design education to the lives of children and youth.

The reconstructionists accepted many of Dewey's views, particularly reflective inquiry, but argued that more was required for social education. Reconstructionists argued that if education was to result in social changes, it could not remain neutral.

1. The very nature of education involves a certain amount of imposition of values. *Education is not a neutral enterprise.* The bias inherent in education serves some groups, but not others. This leads to the issue of whose values are being served in education.
2. *Education serves the interests of certain dominant groups, but not others.*

Critical analysis reveals the dominant groups that are being served and perpetuated.

3. *Schools need to play a role in ameliorating social conditions by reconstructing our institutions and culture.*

Education must insist on those values that lead to democracy and social and economic justice, a position that is heard more frequently than in the past among some art educators and environmental design educators.

The past two decades have seen advances in the critical examination of education and schooling as situated in a sociopolitical context (Apple, 1982, 1988). Several traditions have developed that reveal the socializing role of schooling and the meaning of the *hidden curriculum*. Among these positions, the social phenomenological approach — the new sociology — holds that meaning is constructed interactively. According to Giroux and Penna (1979), "the organization, distribution, and evaluation of knowledge are not absolute and objective; instead, they are socio-historical constructs forged by active human beings creating rather than simply existing in the world" (p. 24), a view in keeping with an active environmentalist position.

It is such a transformative environmental design education, developed on a sense of community, multicultural, and reconstructionist principles, that must become a legitimate part of social and art education content. Areas that are central to the redress of social problems, including environmental problems, through a reconstructionist approach include: (1) human/environmental relationships, (2) how humans differing by race, class, and gender are represented in environmental matters, (3) the hidden agendas of dominance and power embedded in visual and environmental phenomena that must be addressed by citizen empowerment, and (4) views of creative and aesthetic behavior that include not only the specificity, but the context, of objects, wherein lies the texture of community.

What I mean by the *texture of community* is that social and environmental problems are revealed not through abstract generalizations, but through the specificity of particular community contexts. The phenomenon of existence lies within the context of everyday life constituting our "eye upon the world," which through our educated consciousness allows access to the deep ecology that defines a broad connected context. Without attention to the particulars of spaces within which we live and work, ecological matters have little connection to our daily being. jagodzinski's (1990) texture is situated within the lived experience of the home and community in his view of a "green aesthetic."

Texture is the conversation with "things" to enable one to know them intimately. . . . Texture is our personal communication with Nature's dialogue: it is the experience of craft which intimately binds our consciousness with Gaea's (the Earth's) material consciousness . . . . One cannot get closer to the Earth than through the touch of the hand. (p. 8)

This suggests that knowing the environment begins with the familiar, the close at hand, providing a base from which to move toward more distant spaces, measured from one's body, in a knowing, understanding manner. Textures mean that there is a differentiation among things resulting not in a rejection, but in a dynamic tension and dialectic between and among things. The old is not discarded, but repaired and preserved, which in environmental terms results not in never-ending material consumption, but in use, repair, and preservation.

The environment is measured from that which can be touched to the more distant in Norberg-Schulz's (1971) existential space. Space is measured by directional orientations such as the vertical and horizontal, above and below, and near and far. The ideas of both jagodzinski and Norberg-Schulz support an examination and an environmental knowing that begin with the body and move outward to more distant spaces — objects, rooms, house, neighborhood, communities, and regions. Thus, the green aesthetic and existential space support an ordering of environmental orientations as a broad direction for environmental design studies.

Environmental design education must not only develop new awareness and understanding among children and youth, but also continue to engage them, long after they have left formal schooling, in an education based on social responsibility. In cooperative efforts among teachers and community members, questions such as these need be addressed.

1. What is meant by *environment*?
2. How have local environments been formed, including analyses of power, ideology, and economic and political forces that lie beneath the surface of one's surroundings?
3. How have material and technological conventions contributed to the formation and shaping of local environments?
4. How are the poor, the rich, farmers, artists, businesspeople, and particular ethnic groups presented in visual material, recognizing that culture is embedded in environmental representations?
5. How do people create, shape, and make things "special" in their environments?

Art education, and environmental design education in particular, needs to build upon a reconstructive education. There have been recent attempts in art education to profit from these revelations, but much remains to be done (see

Freedman, 1994, for an issue of *Studies in Art Education* that focuses on reconstructionism in art education).

What I have suggested is that an art education, including a focus on environmental design education, founded upon reconstructionist principles and critical studies, can move us in the direction of alleviating social inequities. I agree with Kohl (1980) that we should not be naive enough to think that a new social order can be built solely through schools; however, I agree that "schools will be an essential part of a new order that is built through the cooperative effort of all of us: teachers, miners, factory-workers, professionals — all the people who believe in the social and moral imperative of struggling toward a new order" (p. 60). Together community members will become a revitalized dimension in environmental design education, as suggested by Shannon (1992).

Giroux (1983) agrees with the questions that Kohl raises, but suggests that while radical theorists have helped unravel the relations between schools and the dominant society, they have either succumbed to pessimism or have failed to establish a dialect between agency and structure. Giroux believes that

> Struggles within the schools have to be understood and linked to alliances and social formations which can affect policy decisions relating to the control and content of schooling . . . excluded majorities who inhabit the neighborhoods, towns, and cities in which schools are located . . . working-class people, minorities of color, and women actively involved in the shaping of school policies and experiences. Rather than being the object of school policy, these groups must become the subject of such policy making. (pp. 237–238)

Giroux has pointed to important connections between schools and community that are essential to making an environmental design work — that is, a cooperative engagement of students, teachers, and community members.

Issues to be addressed include student and teacher roles essential to achieving a new texture of community. Giroux (1983) points to several things that teachers can do in the struggle toward the ideological and cultural conditions necessary for a transformation of society through engaged citizenship in the public sphere. He sees the need to reformulate the dialectic between the sociocultural realm of society and the state. In effect, formal schooling is state dominated, whereas education occurs outside schools. Teachers can play a number of roles in these struggles: (1) developing an understanding of political and economic interests outside of schools that affect the processes of schooling through policy statements, decisions on how resources are distributed, and awareness of tax matters; (2) actively engaging minorities, working-class people, and women in the shaping of school policies and experiences, thus broadening the opportunities for community support of teachers; (3)

bringing the concrete back into radical pedagogy by taking seriously the "specific needs, problems, and concerns of everyday life" (p. 238); (4) producing experiences, beyond the classroom, that deal with concerns that promote dialogue and democratic forms of communication "to work with adults around issues directly related to their lives, their cultural capital" (p. 239); and (5) developing alliances with other teachers within schools to prevent isolation, which allows for hierarchical decision making and authoritarian control. These suggest some ways that community can be achieved as the context supporting a new environmental design education.

A COMMUNITY-BASED ENVIRONMENTAL DESIGN EDUCATION

To realize the roles that Giroux suggests, it is apparent that art teachers must be actively engaged in creating their own curriculum materials and teaching activities, hopefully through a real dialogue with their students as well as with other teachers. If an environmental design education is to be developed around the texture of community, that is, particular places and students, teachers must recognize their own and students' environments and avoid pre-packaged curricular materials contradictory to their own situations. What, then, are the more specific goals of an environmental design education?

An environmental design education based on the texture of community should allow students to

1. Develop an interactive view of *environment* as reciprocally affecting and being affected by them.
2. Understand the ecological nature of environment in which all things are related and affected by overlapping processes, resulting in a valuing of biodiversity.
3. Realize that their classrooms and schools are their environments which they should have some voice in shaping and maintaining.
4. Develop a feeling of empowerment with respect to the environments of which they are a part, and in the communities of which they are members: issues of land use, preservation, input in design solutions.
5. Understand the ideological meanings of environments and work toward those positions that respect class, gender, and ethnic differences, realizing the euphemism of *balance* as a solution to contending issues.
6. Become sensitive to their own interpretation and valuing of environments as a legitimate form of evaluation.
7. Discuss, weigh, and adjudge issues of private/proprietary ownership versus public use and control of environments.
8. Develop a socially situated and responsible view of aesthetics as opposed

only to formalistic considerations, and understand the interaction of environmental specificity and social dimensions.

9. Develop an awareness of and concern for environmental issues ranging from within one's communities to more distant ecological issues.
10. In evaluating and making decisions about environmental actions, give attention to aesthetic, qualitative versus only economic values.
11. Realize that all environmental concerns, issues, and problems are contextually situated.
12. Understand that all environmental matters are historically situated.
13. Become involved in developing creative, imaginative solutions to environmental problems, both in an ideational and material sense.
14. Develop a sense of empowerment to recognize, improve, and reconstruct neglected environments through individual and communal actions.

If these goals seem heavily weighted toward qualitative, socially aware, public versus private ownership, and multicultural sensitivity, it is intentional. It may be recalled that a socially reconstructive education in not neutral, but rather recognizes and holds to particular values. So-called "balanced" approaches invariably condemn socially responsible values so that desired proprietary views, representing the balance, are little if at all changed. As critical theorists have pointed out, no educational force is ideologically neutral. I have outlined some goals for socially responsible environmental design education. It also should be recognized that teachers, together with their students in particular community settings, are the final arbiters of goals, emphases, and activities. *The curriculum resides not in curriculum guides or expert specifications, but in the texture of each community.*

In these discussions, teachers have not been designated as art, elementary, or social studies teachers, for teachers at any level or subject designation can have an effect through the texture of community. Ideally, a cohort of teachers in a school might address environmental issues most effectively, each with his or her own strengths and concerns. At the middle school, junior high, or high school level, the art teacher might be the leader, calling upon social studies, history, biology, and other teachers to provide support and assistance. At the elementary school, any teacher with strong environmental interests could be the organizer, working cooperatively with her or his cohorts. It is also important that each group, or teacher if working alone, develop contacts within each community to make environmental efforts not only a schooling effort, but a true educational experience for students and other community members. Community leaders could be drawn from the design professions, such as architects, landscape designers, and planners, as well as from economic, social, and political arenas.

In spite of the risks that have been noted in outlining curricular approaches that might contradict the texture of particular communities, in the section that follows several selected propositions, along with some educational activities, are suggested. These are designed to be more suggestive than prescriptive, for in the final analysis each teacher must particularize her or his approaches in sympathy with local community textures. Thus, they may be further elaborated, simplified, and changed to develop the major thrust of each. The view of student/teacher-constructed knowledge supported under the texture of community means that both should contribute to the development of educational activities.

SELECTED ENVIRONMENTAL PROPOSITIONS

Propositions about environments are offered as means of orienting perception of and behavior toward facilitating human–environmental interactions. Rapoport (1977, 1982) has situated investigations of environmental meanings within a cognitive framework in which the perceptual process is central. Norman (1988) refers to schema theory, frame theory, semantic networks, or propositional encoding. Using a similar approach, Neperud (1988) developed a propositional view of aesthetic experiencing, in which "individuals are motivated to make sense of their environments. This interaction of individual and environment revolves around the generation and testing of propositions" (p. 288). Visual/verbal propositions in memory are tested against one's environmental focus and may be altered in the process, thus accommodating new information. Emotion is ever present in the process, coloring the interactions, or even precluding further perceptual processing if affective reactions to the environment are extremely strong. This propositional/schema approach provides access to information from environments through perception, in which children and youth use visual/verbal propositions to acquire meanings through continuing explorations and interactions with their environments.

Environments Are Experiential

This means that students need to develop a detailed sensory awareness of environments. Individuals interact existentially (Norberg-Schulz, 1971) and phenomenologically (Bachelard, 1964) with their surroundings. Children experience their surroundings directly through play and creative, manipulative behavior in the course of which they touch, smell, and listen. Noted developmentalists, such as Piaget and Vygotsky, have recognized the manipulation of concrete phenomena as essential to children's development of meaning. Children aged 3, or even younger, may profit from their interactions with surroundings in a way that leads to their understanding that environments

respond to their actions. Propositions serve as the interactive mediators between individual and experience; words and visuals serve to direct experiencing. However, overly strong insistence on verbal/cognitive propositions can
limit rather than expand experiencing. Thus, for example, insistence on the
observation of formal qualities, such as texture and color, can restrict explor-
atory tendencies leading to new experiential discoveries.

The cultural variability of environmental propositions also must be recognized so that there will not be a tendency to generalize propositions across
ethnic and social groups. Having recognized these cautions, direct sensory/
phenomenological experiencing of one's surroundings can enhance attention
to nonverbal propositions that figure so importantly in affective responses
to environment. This means that students need to be provided numerous
experiences that will enhance sensory awareness. Hiss (1990) urges an experiential role in guiding the development that is certain to occur in the next
quarter century; he suggests that individuals need to determine and make
known the kind of experiences they want in their surroundings. This is certainly a role that students can discuss and evaluate in their own environments.

Environments Have Meaning Through Direct Experiencing

Children's environmental awareness is developed through a variety of experiences, concepts, and propositions acquired through several methods. An
individual interacts environmentally with various levels ranging from objects,
living space, home, and the several communities of which he or she may be a
member to geographic considerations. Concepts of place, community, and
ecology have been added to our talk about environments. Children experience environments through perceptual and creative processes, and through
interpretation and reflection in their search for meaning. Just as spatial types
are not linear, these processes are differentially emphasized as circumstances
prevail; for example, evaluation may precede other processes, may be intertwined with them, or may be a final judgment of environmental preference
or worth.

Several techniques can be used to increase environmental awareness, including drawing, surveying, and mapping (Neperud, 1977). Unless attention
is somehow focused on qualities of surroundings, a child simply may name a
space and its functions without attending to dimensions actually experienced.
Experiencing the phenomena of environments involves all of the senses—
sight, hearing, smell, taste, feeling, and movement as one performs daily tasks.
The object is to become conscious of qualities rather than merely attending
to verbal functional categories. A technique focused on visual qualities of a
familiar space is to have someone stand in the middle of the classroom with
eyes closed and ask, "Tell us what you can remember about the room without

A pictorial map by a first grader depicting home in relationship to major places in a small community

looking. Then, describe the floor. Of what material is it made?" Next, have someone walk around the room; then ask, "When you walk on it how does it feel and sound? What does this tell you about the floor and wall surfaces?" Similar activities may be repeated with rooms less familiar to students.

Another approach is to change familiar surroundings incrementally, such as by addition of color or texture panels, and ask someone, "Close your eyes; describe the surface of the room as you remember it." The amount of change needed to produce awareness should be observed. Repetition of this process will begin to sharpen students' awareness of and attention to immediate surroundings. These approaches are only suggestive of the many possibilities that innovative teachers can create to heighten environmental awareness.

A series of auditory activities will help develop more acute awareness of the many sounds that surround us. The teacher can record sounds from everyday environments — airplanes landing and taking off, street noises at different times of the day, playgrounds, city center, rural areas, farm noises, wave sounds, running water, and animals and birds in different settings. Then the teacher can ask, "What made these sounds, and where were the sounds made?"

These activities, as well as those involving taste, smell, and combined sensations, can direct attention to varied qualities as at least a partial basis for evaluation of environments. One can grow so accustomed to traffic and other city sounds, or so inattentive to the subtleties of a rural landscape, that one has a diminished capacity to evaluate and make judgments.

Environmental Meanings Are Context Specific

Environments have meaning for humans within particular contextual circumstances such as rooms, houses, places, communities, regions, and ecosystems. How can awareness of this extended view of environment be developed? This probably can be accomplished best in terms of an individual's everyday activities, such as home life, going back and forth to school, shopping, and recreation, among other individual/environmental interactions.

The aim is to help children develop a consciousness of interactions with several levels of surroundings, including objects, rooms and other intimate surroundings, their home, the neighborhood, community (schools and other activity centers), parts of a city they may have frequented, and regions visited. What kinds of experiences do they have with these? How can identity of these objects and places be established? The many objects that surround individuals serve a variety of purposes ranging from functional to associational ones, such as mementoes that remind one of past experiences. In considering the relationship of things to people, Csikszentmihalyi & Rochberg-Halton (1981) consider objects, furnishings, and the things that people collect to be expressions of themselves since these are the objects over which they have some control.

Consequently, the methods of study may vary depending on uses of the object. The teacher might have a student select a favorite object that he or she has saved for a long time. "Why is it important to you? How do you feel about it? Tell us about the circumstances surrounding how you obtained it, or why it is important to you? Or, in a sequence of drawings depict your answers to these questions."

One way of developing awareness of commonly used spaces is to draw a room, such as a bedroom, from memory. The teacher might ask someone, "Make a drawing of your bedroom. Put into it everything that you can remember, including the things that you use." Or, "if you could change your room, house, or living space, draw what you would like." These studies could be expanded to larger communities and regions. This indicates what students value about their surroundings and why. Findings from such activities, when contrasted among student groups, will indicate the importance of context. In addition, information would be provided about the cultural variability to which Rapoport (1982) has referred.

Environments Are Culturally Variable

Environmental design based on objective approaches has assumed that "good design" is universally applicable across cultures and societies. Architectural styles such as modernism were assumed to be most functional, whether applied to apartments or offices; sometimes they were applicable, but usually they were not. Environments that people create or toward which they gravitate differ among groups by race, class, ethnic difference, and so on. Some choices apparently are made on geographic features; some years ago while tracing ancestral roots in Norway I was amazed by the similarity of Norwegian landscapes to those areas in the United States chosen by immigrants from Norway. Scheflen (1976) and other behavioral scientists have indicated differing spatial use of apartments and other facilities by ethnic grouping.

When discussing or teaching about environments, one cannot assume universal characteristics, but must attempt to determine how individuals differ in using and creating spaces, so as not to do injustice to the very nature of the texture of community and multiculturalism. Activities can range from comparative studies of differing cultures and ethnic groups to simple observational reporting in different areas of a city or countryside.

People Need to Have an Effect on Their Environments

People plant gardens, landscape their surroundings, rearrange and decorate their living spaces, and engage in other activities in order to have an effect on their surroundings. In fact, destructive and constructive behaviors represent different points of a continuum from asocial to social behavior rather than mutually exclusive categories. Graffiti and murals created to celebrate ethnic identity and history represent differing points on a continuum of the need to have an effect. Recently, Dissanayake (1988), art historian and ethologist, has pointed to this need to have an effect and to make things special.

From an educational perspective, teachers not only can study cultural differences, especially in local communities, but also need to engage students in creating spaces, including their classrooms; planning for anticipated community changes; and actually renovating and changing neglected neighborhood spaces.

People Need to Develop Evaluative Criteria

It has been demonstrated that affect is present throughout the perceptual and experiential process to the extent that emotion may even preclude further

Having an effect on one's environment through gardening

analysis (Neperud, 1988). Rapoport (1982) also concludes, "It can therefore be shown that people react to environments globally and affectively before they analyze them and evaluate them in more specific terms. Thus the whole concept of environmental quality is clearly an aspect of this — people like certain urban areas, or housing forms, because of what they mean." Citing examples of classrooms, student dormitories, wilderness areas, housing, and other examples, Rapoport continues, "In all these cases the initial affective and global response governs the direction that subsequent interactions with environment will take" (p. 14).

Thus, individuals do evaluate their surroundings, much as they do the visual arts, probably based on criteria subtly acquired through the ongoing educational processes associated with family life, life on the street, and ethnic, class, and gender associations. Or, as suggested in the *biophilia hypothesis*, through the evolutionary process humans have acquired a genetically based emotional need for interaction with nature and landscapes (Kellert & Wilson, 1993; Wilson, 1984). This information means that additional evaluative processes and criteria are not automatically acquired, but need to be developed. However, evaluative criteria applicable to various environments must recognize sociocultural differences, precluding the applicability of universal design-

Florence: Most cities reflect development over a long period

based evaluative criteria. Students can be encouraged to evaluate their own communities in ways leading to the discussion and analysis of criteria, thus avoiding top-down, critics' evaluative approaches.

In one such effort, I organized a panel of architects and landscape architects and invited townspeople of a small western city to a planning session. Everyone was given 15 minutes to design a particular building and a park space, using paper and pencil. The resulting sketch plans, in effect, reflected each person's evaluative criteria for particular environments. This approach engaged individuals in reflecting about and sketching the qualities desired of each space and provided useful environmental materials for further discussion and analysis.

People Need to Understand How Environments Are Formed

It is relatively simple to understand how carpenters and other construction workers build a house. It is much more complex to understand the social, economic, political, and psychological forces, as well as the design and planning arts, that form the basis for building that single house. Why do styles of houses change? Why do some residences have more space around them than others (why row houses in inner cities as contrasted to suburban houses with large lawns)? By contrasting types of housing, students can begin to discern the interrelationships of economic, social, and political contextual factors in affecting environments. The local communities should be a basis for studying, using descriptive and analytic methods, how environments are formed.

At another level, the evolution of a city over several centuries may reflect many styles of architecture and patterns of development. By surveying and contrasting different sections of a city, one can begin to trace the history of a place and then begin to ask questions about the differences: "Why does an old section of a city develop over several centuries, whereas contemporary residential developments and shopping malls may spring up, virtually over-night, on what was formerly a farm?" These contrasts provide a basis for ana-lyzing social, economic, and political forces that shape environments. The resulting environmental forms can be evaluated critically for their relation-ships to the quality of human existence. By developing propositions about the shaping of local environments, whether of recent or ancient origins, stu-dents begin to realize that their surroundings are created through complex interactions of forces. Likewise, they realize that there are no simple roads to improvement. An environment carries traces from earlier periods relating to how people lived and valued their communities; such information provides a perspective for valuing one's surroundings.

CONCLUSIONS

Environmental design education is not firmly established as a part of the pub-lic school curriculum, but it should be as a means of planning for an increas-ingly diverse and interrelated world. In elementary education, a physical and biological science approach to environmental education exists as a form of shallow ecology. At the secondary level, art teachers sometimes extend art curricula to include some architectural studies, but it is usually from an histor-ical or traditional design perspective. This is not to say that some art teachers aren't concerned with a more comprehensive ecological approach to design and environment, but most traditionally educated art educators with a heavy preparation of studio art and art history are simply not prepared to develop an environmental design program without resorting to universal design and aesthetic values. This has implications for teacher education, for unless future teachers truly experience and understand what contemporary environmen-talism is all about, the addition of another course won't do the job.

The meaning of environment has changed dramatically in recent decades. The integrity of ecology, place, community, and biodiversity have been added to "good design" as measures of environmental design. Social responsibility, justice, equity, ethnicity, class, empowerment, and gender are now legitimate environmental issues. These changes in environmentalism, now joined to multiculturalism, become increasingly potent forces in American society.

The earlier forms of environmental design education developed by college and university art educators during the 1970s paralleled the prevailing conceptions of environmental design, heavily weighted toward universal absolutist design and aesthetic manifestoes, or behavioral psychology. Neither approach dealt with the interface between human behavior, environments, and designers' practices. A new environmental design education is developing that promises to address the problems of livability of the spaces we create and have inherited.

The greatest source of energy in realizing improvements is the *motivated human energy* of our children and youth. They have real interests and concerns about the environment, for it is they who are inheriting what we leave them. Their enthusiasm and idealism represent an untapped force for change, when situated within the new environmentalism and multiculturalism. These potentials can be realized through the texture of community in which environmentalism becomes an active force within students' lived experiences set in local communities. In this way, community issues of housing, preservation, development, open places, and where waste dumps are located become the focus through which environmental propositions and values are developed and tested.

Not only art educators, but all teachers with vision, need to work with students in constructing understanding and knowledge of local environments. Environmental propositions need to be developed and constructed that can be tested and redeveloped in the give-and-take of local communities. These approaches raise some central pedagogical issues. I believe that an environmental design education focused on the texture of community will prepare students to practice a citizenry alive to the reality of their own situations, not just to the abstractions disseminated by others. Teachers are not, and must not be, pessimists. Working cooperatively with other teachers and with community residents, teachers and students can be a powerful constructive force in achieving positive changes in environmental education.

Acknowledgment. The author wishes to thank Joanne Guilfoil and Michael J. Shannon for reviewing this chapter and making helpful recommendations.

REFERENCES

Apple, M. (1982). *Education and power.* Boston: Ark Paperbacks.
Apple, M. (1988). *Teachers & texts: A political economy of class & gender relations in education.* New York: Routledge.

Bachelard, G. (1964). *The poetics of space.* (M. Jolas, Trans.). New York: Orion Press.

Banham, R. (1974). (Ed.). *The Aspen papers.* New York: Praeger.

Banks, J., & Banks, C. (1993). *Multicultural education: Issues and perspectives* (2nd ed.). Boston: Allyn & Bacon.

Barbosa, A. (1991, Fall). Art education and environment. *Journal of Multicultural and Cross-Cultural Research in Art Education, 9,* 59–64.

Blandy, D., & Hoffman, E. (1993). Toward an art education of place. *Studies in Art Education, 35*(1), 22–33.

Bowers, C. (1987). *Elements of a post-liberal theory of education.* New York: Teachers College Press.

Brameld, T. (1956). *Toward a reconstructed philosophy of education.* New York: Holt, Rinehart & Winston.

Chambliss, J. (1988). Reconstruction remembered: Theodore Brameld, 1904–1987. *Educational Theory, 38*(3), 379–388.

Cherryholmes, C. H. (1988). *Power and criticism: Poststructural investigations in education.* New York: Teachers College Press.

Csikszentmihalyi, M., & Rochberg-Halton, E. (1981). *The meaning of things, domestic symbols and the self.* Cambridge: Cambridge University Press.

Dissanayake, E. (1988). *What is art for?* Seattle: University of Washington Press.

Freedman, K. (Ed.). (1994). *Studies in Art Education, 35*(3).

Gablik, S. (1991). *The reenchantment of art.* New York: Thames & Hudson.

Giroux, H., & Penna, A. (1979). Social education in the classroom: The dynamics of the hidden curriculum. *Theory and Research in Social Education, 7*(1), 21–42.

Giroux, H. (1981). *Ideology, culture, & the process of schooling.* Philadelphia: Temple University Press.

Giroux, H. (1983). *Theory and resistance in education: A pedagogy for the opposition.* South Hadley, MA: Bergin & Garvey.

Gottlieb, R. (1993). *Forcing the spring: The transformation of the American environmental movement.* Washington, DC: Island Press.

Hicks, L. (1990). A feminist analysis of empowerment and community in art education. *Studies in Art Education, 32*(1), 36–46.

Hiss, T. (1990). *The experience of place.* New York: Knopf.

jagodzinski, j. j. (1990). *The poetics of green esthetics: Situating "green criticism" in the postmodern condition.* Unpublished position statement.

Kellert, S., & Wilson, E. (Eds.). (1993). *The biophilia hypothesis.* Washington, DC: Island Press.

Kohl, H. (1980). Can the schools build a new social order? *Journal of Education, 16*(3), 57–66.

Lang, J. (1987). *Creating architectural theory.* New York: Van Nostrand Reinhold.

Manzini, E. (1994, Spring). Design, environment, and social quality: From existence minimum to quality maximum. *Design Issues, 10,* 37–43.

May, W. (1989). Teachers, teaching, and the workplace: Omissions in curriculum reform. *Studies in Art Education, 30*(3), 142–156.

McFee, J. (1969). *Community arts study program* (Final Report Project No. 6-3054). Washington, DC: U.S. Department of Health, Education and Welfare.

McFee, J. K., & Degge, R. M. (1977). *Art, culture, and environment: A catalyst for teaching*. Belmont, CA: Wadsworth.

Neperud, R. (1973). Art education: Towards an environmental aesthetic. *Art Education, 26*(3), 7–10.

Neperud, R. (1977). The development of children's graphic representations of the large-scale environment. *The Journal of Environmental Education, 8*(4), 57–65.

Neperud, R. (1978). The what and why of environmental design education. *Art Education, 31*(4), 4–7.

Neperud, R. (1988). A propositional view of aesthetic experiencing for research and teaching in art education. In F. Farley & R. Neperud (Eds.), *The foundations of aesthetics, art, and art education* (pp. 273–319). New York: Praeger.

Neperud, R. (1991). A propositional view of environmental experiencing. *Arts and Learning Research, 9*(1), 27–41.

Norberg-Schulz, C. (1971). *Existence, space and architecture*. New York: Praeger.

Norman, D. A. (1988). *The psychology of everyday things*. New York: Basic Books.

Proshansky, H., Ittelson, W., & Rivlin, L. (Eds.). (1970). *Environmental psychology: Man and his physical setting*. New York: Holt, Rinehart & Winston.

Rapoport, A. (1977). *Human aspects of urban form*. New York: Pergamon Press.

Rapoport, A. (1982). *The meaning of the built environment*. Tucson: University of Arizona Press.

Scheflen, A. (1976). *Human territories: How we behave in space-time*. Englewood Cliffs, NJ: Prentice-Hall.

Shannon, M. J. (1992). *Education-based community development* (Position statement). Englewood, NJ: Center for Design Studies.

Stanley, W. (1981). The radical reconstructionist rationale for social education. *Theory and Research in Social Education, 8*(4), 55–79.

Stanley, W. (1985, May). Social reconstructionism for today's social education. *Social Education*, pp. 384–389.

Thomson, R. (1978). The art teacher and environmental education: A Scottish viewpoint. *Art Education, 31*(4), 4–7.

Wilson, E. (1984). *Biophilia*. Cambridge, MA: Harvard University Press.

About the Contributors

ARTHUR EFLAND is Professor of Art Education at the Ohio State University. He authored the elementary and secondary guidelines in art education for Ohio, winning an award of excellence from the National Art Education Association in 1982. He has published regularly in *Studies in Art Education, Visual Arts Research,* and the *Journal of Aesthetic Education.* He is author of *A History of Art Education: Intellectual and Social Currents in Teaching the Visual Arts* (Teachers College Press, 1990) and is currently working on a publication for the National Art Education Association on postmodernism as a curriculum challenge. He has been appointed a Distinguished Fellow of the NAEA.

KERRY FREEDMAN is Associate Professor of Art Education and Curriculum & Instruction at the University of Minnesota. Professor Freedman holds a Ph.D. in Curriculum & Instruction with a major in Art Education and minors in Art and Psychology from the University of Wisconsin-Madison. She has published several chapters in books and articles in journals such as *Studies in Art Education, Journal of Curriculum Studies, Visual Arts Research,* and *Journal of Research on Computing in Education.* Her research focuses on the history and sociology of art education and includes work concerning the influences of mass culture, social science, and technology on art knowledge and teaching. She is currently co-authoring a book about postmodernism and art education.

MAXINE GREENE is Professor Emerita at Teachers College, Columbia University, where she has been on the faculty since 1965, holding the William F. Russell Chair in the Foundations of Education since 1975. Her courses have dealt with the philosophy and history of education, social philosophy, aesthetic education, ethics, literature, and phenomenology and existentialism. She has also taught at Montclair State College, New York University, and Brooklyn College and has lectured widely at universities and educational associations. She is the author of many journal articles and chapters as well as *Existential Encounters for Teachers* (Random House, 1967), *The Public School and the Private Vision* (Random House, 1965), *Teacher as Stranger* (Wadsworth, 1973; winner of the 1974 Education Book of the Year from Delta Gamma Kappa), *Landscapes of Learning* (Teachers College Press, 1978), and *The Dialectic of Freedom* (Teachers College Press, 1988).

KAREN HAMBLEN is Professor of Art Education in the Department of Curriculum, and Instruction at Louisiana State University. She has been the recipient of the Outstanding Higher Educator in California Award, the Mary Rouse Award, Manuel Barkan Award, and June King McFee Award. She was the Director of the Southeast Regional Higher Education Division of the National Art Education Association and the Senior Editor of *Studies in Education*. She is currently the Vice Chair of the Art Committee of the National Board for Professional Teaching Standards and a member of the Steering Committee of the National Research Agenda in Art Education. She has served as consultant, writer, and evaluator for art museums, teacher institutes, school districts, art councils, state departments of education, and the U.S. Department of Education. She has publications in art education, art policy, anthropology and sociology research journals.

DON KRUG is Assistant Professor of Art Education at the Ohio State University. He received his B.S. in Art Education, M.A. in Art Education, and Ph.D. in Curriculum & Instruction with an Art Education major and an Art minor from the University of Wisconsin-Madison. He has published in the *Journal of Multicultural and Cross-cultural Research in Art Education*. He taught in the public schools for more than 10 years and is a designer and a painter. His research interests center on social, cultural, and political issues in art education, including critical curricular theory and practice, communication, multicultural studies, and environmental restoration.

WANDA MAY is Associate Professor of Curriculum in the Department of Teacher Education at Michigan State University. She is Senior Researcher for the Arts in the Center for the Learning and Teaching of Elementary School Subjects, in the Institute for Research on Teaching at Michigan State. Her work has appeared in *Studies in Art Education, Curriculum Inquiry, Journal of Curriculum and Supervision, Journal of Teacher Education*, technical reports, and book chapters. She is a former elementary art and music teacher in the Metropolitan Public Schools, Nashville, TN, where she provided leadership in curriculum development and in-service activities in the visual arts. As an accomplished artist, she has exhibited in regional and one-woman shows and received awards in juried competition.

JUNE KING MCFEE is Professor Emerita of Art Education at the University of Oregon. She holds an Ed.D. from Stanford and an Honorary D.Ed. from Eastern Michigan University. Professor McFee developed doctoral programs at Stanford, Arizona State, and the University of Oregon. An early editor of *Studies in Art Education,* she is author of *Preparation for Art* (2nd ed., Wadsworth, 1970) and (with Rogena Degge) *Art, Culture, and Environment: A Catalyst for Teaching* (Kendall/Hunt, 1980), textbooks in Arabic and Japanese translations, and numerous articles and chapters in anthologies and handbooks. Her research includes cultural and cross-cultural impacts on art and education; psycho-social dimensions of learning and creating art; perception, creativity, and cognitive style; and environmental design. Her National Art Education Association awards include: Distinguished Fellow, Distinguished Service, Studies Lecture, and Women's Caucus McFee Award.

RONALD W. NEPERUD is Professor of Art and of Curriculum & Instruction at the University of Wisconsin-Madison. He holds B.A. and M.A. degrees from Willamette University, Salem, OR, and a D.Ed. from the University of Oregon, with graduate work from the University of Washington. He has contributed numerous articles to *Studies in Art Education, Art Education, Arts and Learning Research, Visual Arts Research, Social Theory Caucus, Journal of Multicultural and Cross-cultural Research in Art Education,* and *Leonardo.* He is Senior Editor of the *Journal of Multicultural and Cross-cultural Research in Art Education* (on whose Editorial Advisory Board he has also served) and Book Review Editor of *Studies.* He is co-editor (with Frank Farley) and contributor to *The Foundations of Aesthetics, Art, and Art Education* (Praeger, 1990). His major research interests have included the perception of art among groups differing in education and ethnicity; the art and aesthetics of non-academically educated artists, and environmental design and education. He is a Distinguished Fellow of the NAEA. A practicing painter and printmaker, his work is included in several museums and has been shown in numerous exhibitions.

PATRICIA L. STUHR is Associate Professor of Art Education at Ohio State University. She received a B.S. in Art Education from the University of Wisconsin-Stevens Point, an M.S.T. in Art Education from the University of Wisconsin-Oshkosh, and a Ph.D. in Curriculum & Instruction with an Art Education major and minors in Anthropology and Painting from the University of Wisconsin-Madison. She has published numerous papers in such journals as *Studies in Art Education, Journal of Multicultural and Cross-cultural Research in Art Education, Art Education, Arts and Learning Research,* and *Social Caucus Theory.* Her major research interests include the anthropological investigation of contemporary Wisconsin Indian artists and art, cultural maintenance and change. This research has influenced her approach to implementing sociocultural and environmental elements within the art education curriculum, work for which she has received several grants and awards.

JANET WOLFF's work is in cultural studies and the sociology of art. Her books include *The Social Production of Art, Aesthetics and the Sociology of Art* (St. Martin's, 1981) and *Feminine Sentences: Essays on Women and Culture* (Allen & Unwin, 1983). She taught for several years at the University of Leeds, where she was Reader in the Sociology of Culture and founding Director of the Center for Cultural Studies. She has had numerous appointments as Visiting Professor in Canada and the United States. Currently, she is Professor of Art History and Director of the Graduate Program in Comparative Arts at the University of Rochester.

Index